THE FINAL DAYS

The Last, Desperate Abuses of Power
by the Clinton White House

Barbara Olson

Since 1947
**REGNERY
PUBLISHING, INC.**
An Eagle Publishing Company • Washington, DC

Library of Congress Cataloging-in-Publication Data
Olson, Barbara, 1955–2001
    The final days : the last, desperate abuses of power by the Clinton White House
    / Barbara Olson.
        p. cm.
    Includes bibliographical references and index.
    ISBN 0-89526-167-7 (acid-free paper)
        1. Clinton, Bill, 1946– 2. Clinton, Hillary Rodham. 3. Clinton, Bill, 1946–
    —Ethics. 4. Clinton, Hillary Rodham—Ethics. 5. Presidents—United States—
    Biography. 6. Presidents' spouses—United States—biography. 7. United States—
    Politics and government—1993–2001. 8. Political corruption—United States—
    History—20th century. I. Title.

E886.2 .O47 2001
973.929'092—dc21

                                                                    2001048327

Published in the United States by
Regnery Publishing, Inc.
An Eagle Publishing Company
One Massachusetts Avenue, NW
Washington, DC 20001

Visit us at www.regnery.com

Distributed to the trade by
National Book Network
4720-A Boston Way
Lanham, MD 20706

Printed on acid-free paper
Manufactured in the United States of America

10 9 8 7 6 5 4 3

Books are available in quantity for promotional or premium use. Write to Director of Special Sales, Regnery Publishing, Inc., One Massachusetts Avenue, NW, Washington, DC 20001, for information on discounts and terms or call (202) 216-0600.

A Note from the Publisher

Barbara Olson was killed on September 11, 2001, when the airplane she had just boarded for Los Angeles was hijacked by terrorists and crashed into the Pentagon.

She had finished this book, and we had completed the editorial and prepublication work on it the week before she died. The book had been sent to the printer but the presses had not started rolling. Advance orders were huge, and every sign indicated it would be a bestseller, as was her previous book, *Hell to Pay*. On the Thursday before she died, Barbara came to our offices for a long meeting to plan the promotional effort for the book, which was to include the many interviews, talk shows, lectures, and other media events that were Barbara's hallmark.

Needless to say, her death presented a difficult dilemma to us. Should we cancel the book, or should we proceed? Would people be interested in the topic after the terrorist attack? Would it be unseemly to proceed with the book under the circumstances? Would Barbara have wanted it to be published without her?

After agonizing over the decision—and after lengthy conversations with Barbara's family, friends, and colleagues—we decided that the proper thing to do was to proceed.

Though invariably charming and gracious, Barbara was both passionate and courageous. She held strong opinions, and nobody who was in the same room with her ever had any doubt about what she believed. She did not apologize for what she thought or said, and she always spoke her mind articulately and clearly. We imagined what she might have said about the situation the world found itself in after the attacks, and we knew that she would have, as always, voiced her strong opinions. We firmly believe that the last thing she would have wanted would be for us to withdraw the book rather than let her have her final say.

Barbara Olson was a champion of freedom. And she was a champion of the rule of law—of the need to maintain a free and civil society by means of a well-defined body of law that protects the individual from government tyranny. That is why she was sufficiently appalled by the behavior of the Clintons in their final days in office to write a book about it, and that is why she believed so strongly in the book you are about to read.

The Final Days is vintage Barbara Olson—a frank and hard-hitting book. As we pondered the decision whether or not to proceed with it with her friends and her family, we decided that we could think of nobody for whom a book like this one would be a more fitting statement, after being murdered by terrorists, than Barbara Olson.

Alfred S. Regnery
President and Publisher
Regnery Publishing, Inc.

To my best friend, Ted

Contents

1 | The Final Frenzy: Finishing Touches on the Legend   1

2 | Clemency for Cop Killers   11

3 | A Vietnam Memorial   25

4 | Hillary Moves Onto Center Stage   35

5 | Bill and Hill Join The Donald   51

6 | Movers and Takers   61

7 | "Stroke of the Pen, Law of the Land"   77

8 | Sex, Lies, Audiotape, and DNA   97

9 | So Much Forgiveness, So Little Time   113

10 | If I Were a Rich Man   127

11 | Empty the Prisons   143

12 | Bill and Hillary "Explain" the Pardons   169

13 | The Toll Bridge to the Twenty-First Century   193

14 | A Bang, Not a Whimper   209

Notes   217

Index   227

The Final Frenzy: Finishing Touches on the Legend | 1

On January 17, 2001, Air Force One lifted off from Washington bound for Little Rock, Arkansas. It was the last ride as president on the magnificent Boeing 747 for William Jefferson Clinton, the forty-second president of the United States, who had become used to its style, a stratosphere as rarefied as the White House itself. Beyond any of the trappings and benefits of the office, this state-of-the-art aircraft is the ultimate in presidential perks.

In addition to all the sophisticated communications gear, here are all the comforts of both home and office. The president, known as "the Big Guy" to White House staffers ("the Big He" to interns), has his own spacious one-bedroom apartment in the plane's front section, with full bath and king-size bed. For his entourage, hot meals and drinks are served around the clock. You can lounge on posh couches and snack on fresh fruit, or watch television or first-run movies from the well-stocked library. Nothing is more special than Air Force One.

Though he wasn't on board for this trip, former intimate Clinton adviser George Stephanopoulos, once a frequent flier, observed that Bill Clinton was in his element here. On Air Force One, Stephanopoulos remarked, "Clinton patrolled the halls like the captain of a cruise ship."[1] On this final trip the comparison was no less appropriate but required elaboration.

The president, after all, is the captain of the ship of state. The citizens are the passengers, and for eight years Bill Clinton had taken them on a relatively safe and prosperous, if tumultuous, ride. His tenure had coincided with a period of prosperity practically unequalled in American history. Unemployment was lower than it had been in a decade, the stock market had skyrocketed—at least until the last six months—and the high-tech industry had generated more jobs than it could fill. American currency was strong and stable. Inflation was under control. Most people had forgotten the "misery index," the combination of high inflation and interest rates that had plagued the presidency of Jimmy Carter, the nation's last Democratic president.

The nation was also at peace. The Cold War had ended before Bill Clinton took the helm, and his presidency had experienced nothing that could be called a major international crisis. Turmoil in the Balkans and Middle East was nothing new. Iraq required attention but no massive deployment of Americans. There had been devastating, but fortunately isolated, terrorist attacks in Africa and in Oklahoma City. But the North Koreans had not invaded South Korea, nor had they lobbed one of their missiles in our direction. Communist China did not invade Taiwan. Libya remained quiet.

Wars of insurgency still raged in many countries near and far, but the sixties' slogan "no more Vietnams" had become a fulfilled prophecy. In the new century, the United States stood alone as the only legitimate superpower, with powerful allies in Europe and elsewhere. Objections to American dominance may have been heard in some portions of the world, but Pax Americana had made the nineties the most peaceful decade in recent memory.

How much credit to accord William Jefferson Clinton for the peace and prosperity was, of course, a matter of considerable debate. But even his critics acknowledged that his actions and policies had not caused major economic or military disruptions. And no one could deny that Clinton had maintained remarkably high popularity ratings despite seemingly perpetual scandals and personal crises that were almost exclusively of his own making.

On this, his last Air Force One flight, it would have been understandable for POTUS, the president of the United States, to bask in a sense of accomplishment. But the mood was different. As the last grains of sand trickled through the hourglass of his administration, Bill Clinton, the second president to be impeached, was thinking about the miles to go before he slept, the many tasks that remained undone. Was there anything left he could do to pad his legacy? Great deeds to diminish memories of that irritating Monica scandal? Pardons, for example—the ultimate in unchecked and unrestrainable presidential prerogatives?

In 1794 George Washington pardoned two leaders of the Whiskey Rebellion, Pennsylvanians who had risen up against the federal excise tax. After the war of 1812 James Madison pardoned the pirate Jean Lafitte. Andrew Johnson in 1865 issued amnesty for ex-Confederates willing to take an oath of loyalty to the United States. After Filipino nationalists had lost a guerrilla war against American control of the Philippines, Theodore Roosevelt in 1902 issued amnesty for followers of their leader, Emilio Aguinaldo. In 1974, Gerald Ford pardoned Richard Nixon for crimes he may have committed in office. Jimmy Carter pardoned Vietnam War draft evaders and deserters. Indeed, had Clinton been less successful in escaping the draft by devious means, and had he carried out his threat not to serve in the military, he might have been the beneficiary of Jimmy Carter's 1977 blanket pardons to those who went to Canada rather than put on their nation's uniform. George Bush created a huge stir when in 1992 he pardoned Caspar Weinberger, former secretary of defense, and several others tarred by the Iran-contra scandal involving the sale of weapons to Iran and aid for anticommunist rebels in Nicaragua.

Previous presidents had exercised the pardon power relatively evenly throughout their respective terms in office—with the usual bulge during the Christmas season. But Bill Clinton had granted few pardons during his early years as president. He now intended to make up for lost time. The journalists on board Air Force One received a hint of what was to come.

On the way to Arkansas, the president strode into the press section and said, with a laugh, "You got anybody you want to pardon?"[2] Any candidates that might have surfaced from that peculiar, yet uniquely Clintonesque, invitation would, as it turned out, have had to stand in a very long queue.

"I've got 400 to 500 requests for commutations and pardons," Clinton had said three days earlier, on January 15, when the Clintons closed the deal on their new house in Washington, in response to a suggestion by one of the real estate people to relax and enjoy his last few days in office.[3] Relaxation was not then on Bill Clinton's radar screen. Aside from the fact that Bill Clinton's idea of relaxation was likely to induce fierce countermeasures from a spouse who was on the alert for that sort of thing, the soon-to-be ex-president had turned his attention to clemency as one of the last remaining opportunities to set new presidential records. And there was an ample supply of crooks, drug dealers, and other sleazy characters, in and out of prison, on which his beneficence would not be wasted.

Air Force One landed in Little Rock, where Bill Clinton had once held forth as governor. In a speech before the Arkansas legislature, he indulged in some characteristic public hand-wringing over his last-minute presidential duties.

"We're still getting applications in the mail," Mr. Clinton glee-fully confided to the perplexed legislators. "It's crazy."[4] Clinton basked in the applause from the home folks. Afterward several Arkansan cronies and other supplicants took the president aside and added more candidates to the pardon list. Then it was back to Air Force One for the return flight to the White House and an orgy of emotional presidential excess.

For days Clinton had been putting in a schedule worthy of Stakhanov, the legendary worker of Soviet propaganda, laboring nearly around the clock, bidding repeated emotional and self-indulgent goodbyes to staff, attending ceremony after ceremony whenever he was asked. Between tearful and self-congratulatory farewells and affectionate hugging, he wolfed down food, giving onlookers a chance to verify the observation of one former classmate who said that "anyone who thinks this guy never inhaled never saw him around a pizza."[5]

On January 18, FLOTUS, the first lady of the United States, Hillary Rodham Clinton, showed up at a West Wing ceremony in the Indian Treaty Room to celebrate the administration's accomplishments in health care, ignoring the fact that it had been her most profound and memorable public failure. Bill Clinton duly put in an appearance, which took him away from the task of preparing for his farewell address. Later that night, he gave it over national television.

He spoke of fiscal responsibility, American global leadership, and the need to treat all Americans with dignity and fairness. Doing something of a George Washington, he concluded:

My days in this office are nearly through, but my days of service, I hope, are not. In the years ahead I will never hold a position higher nor a covenant more sacred than that of

President of the United States. But there is no title I will wear more proudly than that of citizen. Thank you. God bless you, and God bless America.

But there remained much to do, and the president seemed determined to do it all personally. A black-and-white *Newsweek* photo shows him, backdropped conveniently by a painting of George Washington, head in hands and tilted to one side as though it might roll off without support. The photo gives the impression of a weary warrior in the final moments of battle. In fact, Clinton was far from finished—he was determined to make every remaining moment count.

Although not particularly athletic, William Jefferson Clinton had approached the presidency as a perpetual one-person Olympics. He assaulted and relished every presidential task: head of state, reserved for a monarch in other countries; head of the executive branch; commander-in-chief of the armed forces; chief law enforcement officer; as well as America's chief mourner, present at nearly every domestic crisis or disaster, constantly on television, living his presidential life in public. Bill Clinton knew every aspect of the president's vast constitutional powers. He had been committed to using them all to the fullest.

White House aides told reporters that Clinton was determined to leave a legacy that incoming Republicans would have a hard time erasing (how true that turned out to be). Clinton himself told reporters that his final days as president, as long as he could stay awake, would be equivalent to four more years in office. Perhaps thinking of Genesis and how God had rested on the seventh day after creating the heavens and the earth and populating the planet, the Baptist president decided *he* was not going to waste *his* final days.

Bill Clinton tried his best. He set aside eight new national monuments and signed new executive orders like a rock star at an autograph session. On a last-minute spree, he launched enough new pages of federal regulations to fill a law library, dealing with everything from snowmobiles in national parks, to air conditioning, to the very definition of human existence. He also nominated nine new federal judges and packed every available board and commission with his pals, supporters, and contributors.

But the president's most irreversible, almost God-like power is the authority granted to him under Article II, Section 2, of the United States Constitution, "to grant Reprieves and Pardons for Offenses Against the United States. . . ."

The power is absolute—even a serial killer could be pardoned—and utterly unreviewable. It cannot be rescinded by the next president. The president may grant a pardon before a trial, after a trial, or without a trial. Once granted, a pardon can never be taken away. In the final days of the Clinton administration, the word had gone forth that the president was revving up for one final convulsive orgy of presidential excess. The White House was to be turned into a palace of favors, with a memorable mélange of characters coming and going at all hours. Think of a suburban swap meet combined with an open house at a bail bondsman's office.

Some of those seeking a slice of the president's beneficence were familiar to the press and public. The Reverend Jesse Jackson, pastoral counsel to Bill Clinton, while simultaneously embroiled in a paternity and financial scandal, was applying his familiar leverage on behalf of a number of candidates. So were former presidents Gerald Ford and Jimmy Carter, and Lady Bird Johnson, widow of former president Lyndon Johnson. Even historian Arthur Schlesinger had a clemency candidate for Clinton, as did rock star Don Henley.[6]

According to Secret Service records, Denise Rich was a regular visitor at the White House, especially during the final days. Rich, a woman in her late fifties, bejeweled, coiffed, studiously made up, working hard at looking younger than her chronological age, is the author of the song "Frankie," recorded by Sister Sledge, and "Free Yourself," from the movie *To Wong Foo, Thanks For Everything! Julie Newmar*. She runs a record label called DV8 Records and was nominated for a Grammy for a gospel number recorded by Tramaine Hawkins, with a prophetic title: "I Don't Wanna Be Misunderstood."

"I love tailoring a song for an artist's needs," says Denise, "getting out of myself and into somebody else's mind and giving them what they want. I really enjoy that."[7] Among her motives for her many visits to Bill Clinton was to fill the needs of someone who could not be present at the White House—or even in the United States. He was euphemistically described to pardon attorneys at the Justice Department as "living abroad." In fact, Denise's ex-husband, Marc Rich, was one of America's most notorious fugitives.

Denise carried herself with the assured air of someone who belonged in the Clinton White House. So did Beth Dozoretz, a Democratic Party fundraiser whose smile radiated dollar signs. Dozoretz was a familiar and dependable aide to the Clintons. As it turned out, she too was dedicated to the cause of the exiled Marc Rich.

But not all the White House guests looked like they belonged in the White House, even if they were actually staying there at the time. Hugh Rodham, a rumpled, sprawling man, is the brother of Hillary Rodham Clinton. He and his brother-in-law president formed a symbiotic relationship, perhaps because both were at heart undisciplined men of large appetites who loved cigars, food, golf, and male camaraderie. Rodham stalked the family palace like a Sumo wrestler between bouts, consuming food and drink and chatting with all comers. He and his brother, Tony, had accompanied Bill and Hillary on their honeymoon to Acapulco in 1975. More recently, Hugh had been bringing various questionable enterprises before his brother-in-law. He was, after all, family. Aides could not keep either Rodham away even if they wanted to.

Another seeker of presidential favors who claimed a similar advantage was Clinton's half brother, Roger, a wanna-be musician who, after a tour of North Korea, was quoted as saying that the level of performance of North Korean artists was "higher than that of any country in the world."[8] Roger Clinton was a convicted drug dealer whose notoriety for drunken antics ratified his Secret Service name of "Headache."

The White House had planned to announce President Clinton's last batch of pardons on Friday, January 19, the day before the inauguration. But the announcement kept getting pushed back. Many at the White House wanted to party, and many of them did, but there was also work to do. That pardon list had to be vetted and finalized, and it was unclear who would make the final decisions, and what they would be.

For example, should the president pardon Susan McDougal, yet another of Clinton's alleged ex-girlfriends, convicted of bank fraud as a result of the investigation of the Clintons' financial dealings in Arkansas? McDougal had spent ten months in jail for refusing to answer grand jury questions about what the president knew and when he knew it.

The president and his aides huddled in the Oval Office discussing the cases Friday night until 9 P.M., when they recessed for one last social event. That night, the Clintons hosted their last White House wingding, an engagement party for political consultant Erik Mullen and Kelly Craighead, a longtime aide to the first lady. The pardon announcement would have to wait until the last breathless moments of the Clinton presidency.

While obsessed with granting last-minute pardons, the president had not forgotten a predicament of his own. He needed to finalize a deal with independent counsel Robert Ray to avoid prosecution for false testimony in the Paula Jones case. It proved one of the tougher tasks, and it rankled. The litigation of the unshakable Paula Jones had led to the despised Kenneth Starr–Monica Lewinsky investigation and the deposition in which the president was questioned about the meaning of sex and his relationship with that troublesome White House intern. That case, which had harassed and humiliated him, was very much on his mind as he turned to the pardons.

On that very last day, hours before he handed over the keys to the White House, Bill Clinton issued a torrent of 140 pardons and thirty-six sentence commutations. Said one television commentator, "Not since the opening of the gates of the Bastille have so many criminals been liberated on a single day."[9]

As the details trickled out, the pardons and commutations produced consternation, outrage, and disbelief. But it took time because of the incredible cast of weird characters, and the seemingly infinite variety of subplots, sidebars, curiosities, and potential criminal misconduct. A single day's hearings on key Clinton pardons yielded more than 60,000 words. And those who knew the most refused to testify.

Ironically, the pardons helped to distract the public, for a while at least, from the full story of the last days of the Clinton White House. The president left office trailing an immense wake of bizarre, excessive, shameless, and self-indulgent actions. The president was so intent on leaving a legacy, he seemed to have forgotten everything he had learned during the preceding eight years about how he would be remembered and what he would be remembered for. All of his superhuman flaws, his energy, and his appetites betrayed him during those last few weeks. It was as if the strange outcome of the presidential election had so shocked and upset him that he lost his senses, his political compass, and any ability to listen to his more level-headed advisers.

The story of these last few weeks is ultimately traceable to, and the culmination of, the president's life and history. In fact, it is the perfect metaphor for Bill Clinton, the man and the president.

Clemency for Cop Killers | 2

From the beginning, it had been clear that the Clinton presidency was unique in one key respect. It was America's first joint presidency, a phenomenon foretold by candidate Clinton's "two-for-one" campaign rhetoric and welcomed by feminists, the prestige press, the liberal punditry, and, of course, co-president Hillary Rodham Clinton.

Hillary's first act of her co-presidency was to set up an office in the West Wing of the White House, the first First Lady ever to do so. Hillary knew that her husband would never have been elected without her complicity in keeping a lid on some of his missteps, and she was resolute in her determination to share in the fruits of that victory. Even to sympathetic journalists, her early moves revealed clearly her intention to exercise, and exercise aggressively, the power of the presidency.

Hillary was promptly placed in charge of the Clinton administration's most ambitious signature project, health care reform. She developed and championed a plan that would nationalize one-seventh of the national economy. As George Stephanopoulos described it, Hillary "had established a wholly owned subsidiary within the White House, with its own staff, its own schedule, and its own war room, called the Intensive Care Unit."[1]

It was as though Ronald Reagan had in 1981 placed his wife Nancy in charge of reforming the Social Security system, or if our first President Bush had charged Barbara with oversight of military reforms. Such moves would have provoked shrieks of outrage. Indeed, in the past even a hint of first lady involvement in presidential policy, or even personnel, had been greeted with nearly unanimous hand-wringing and media angst. Yet Hillary's assumption of leadership over the restructuring of a major segment of the American economy was met with wide approval, particularly among liberal opinion-makers. Measures that would have affected everyone in America were developed in virtual secrecy, with Hillary's panel of nongovernmental, handpicked experts working behind closed doors, cloaked in anonymity. There were remarkably few protests.

Hillary was transformed into a luminous "Saint Hillary," with her own cult of adoring acolytes. She put out a book, *It Takes a Village*, to offer a twentieth-century socialized view as to how to raise children. But her true political profile remained largely hidden. Even those close to her never got very close.

Hillary's intensely aggressive nature is only vaguely sensed by those who know just her public persona—carefully coiffed and robed in regal blue or feminine pink, or matronly pants suits, depending on the occasion. But some have been able to look beneath the surface. Biographer Roger Morris wrote in the bestselling 1996 book *Partners in Power* that Hillary and Bill's "mutual strong point" was "a single-minded dedication to their own inextricable advance." His initial judgment had only been confirmed by 2001 when he wrote that Bill's "indomitable wife . . . will be a force on the American scene."[2]

I discovered firsthand Hillary's fierce persona, as chief investigative counsel for the congressional committee that investigated Travelgate and Filegate, and later when I researched and wrote *Hell to Pay*, a book about Hillary's political life. Hillary is a cool, battle-hardened operator. It is more than a little ironic that Hillary was a staffer on the House Judiciary Committee that prepared articles of impeachment against President Richard Nixon, because she's very much like the public's image of Nixon: ambitious, cold, ruthless, and willing to evade, stonewall, or even lie when it serves her purpose.

Indeed, Hillary is an accomplished expert on political search-and-destroy missions. "We have to destroy her," Hillary said in 1991 about Gennifer Flowers, her husband's longtime mistress. Flowers was thereafter savaged by a smear campaign that painted her as a tabloid hustler. The Arkansas state troopers who answered questions about the affair were themselves portrayed as sex-obsessed liars.[3] Quite a stretch given that part of their job was helping to score women for Governor Clinton and to keep the little woman from finding out what was going on.

Roger Clinton, the president's irrepressible half brother, was initially puzzled because Hillary was different from the dance-hall types that Bill usually found attractive. He was quick to learn that Hillary is "the kind of person you want working with you and not against you."[4] Paula Jones also discovered firsthand that the Clinton smear team, which also involved Hillary, played nasty when she found herself the target of a campaign portraying her as a practitioner of serial fellatio.

Hillary is a woman determined to gain the power necessary to bring her ideas to fruition. And those ideas, at their core, are old-line leftist notions that most Americans have long abandoned—if they ever held them at all.

While many members of Hillary's generation have had second thoughts about their left-wing radicalism, Hillary moved the other way, from a middle-class brand of Republicanism steadily leftward. As I explained in my political biography of Hillary, *Hell to Pay*, she was shaped by liberation theology, a Marxist variation of the Christian faith, radical feminism, and the outer reaches of the political Left. In 1972, she interned for former Communist Party lawyer Robert Treuhaft, husband of prominent communist writer Jessica Mitford. Both were Stalinists and rigidly pro-Soviet, and as such shunned by the leadership of the New Left and regarded with suspicion even by supporters of the Black Panther movement.

Hillary Clinton has never repudiated her involvement with these extremists or explained her opinion of their beliefs. She hasn't had to. Few journalists seemed motivated to ask the questions. These days, Republicans have to justify their membership in a benign debating group such as the Federalist Society. But Hillary has *never* had to answer even soft questions about her lengthy flirtation with leftist radicals.

In our political culture, the incantation of "McCarthyism" serves as a kind of permanent restraining order on legitimate inquiries about the political past of people on the Left. Bill Clinton actually got away with calling President George H. W. Bush a McCarthyite when Bush raised questions about Bill Clinton's political past.[5] For Hillary, any such question is simply characterized by her as confirmation of the vast right-wing conspiracy she sees on every street corner.

So Hillary has been relatively free to operate. My research found Hillary involved, in one form or another, in virtually every White House scandal—even if just masterminding the defense and counterattacks as in the Lewinsky affair. In fact, Hillary was the consistent, stable, and reliable guiding organizational hand for the entire Clinton presidency.

As early as 1992, signs were announcing: "Hillary, Mrs. President." During the following eight years, the long-term question was whether "Mrs. President" would actually someday take the oath of office entitling her under the Constitution actually to hold that title. Many of those who studied her career, as I did, concluded that that was precisely where her ambition was planning to take her as early as the 1992 presidential campaign. The only questions were how she would use her husband's presidency to realize that goal, and how he would help her get there. The answer, surprisingly enough, was to come from the State of New York.

Pardons for Terrorists Send a Signal

The venerable Daniel Patrick Moynihan, New York's senior senator, a national Democratic icon, was drifting toward his emeritus years. In our political culture, seats long occupied by a member of one political party tend to become regarded as the private property of that party. Hillary Clinton set her sights on the Moynihan Senate seat. Never mind that Hillary grew up in Illinois, attended law school in Connecticut, and had lived for years in Arkansas and in a government home in Washington, D.C. Never mind that she had the same degree of political affiliation with New York as Minnesota governor Jesse Ventura—that is to say, none.

The relevant facts as far as Hillary was concerned were that New York was a big and powerful state which traditionally voted overwhelmingly Democratic; it was a vital international, financial, and media center. And it had an upcoming open Democratic Senate seat in 2000—just what Hillary needed and felt that she deserved.

Hillary had done a lot of heavy lifting for her husband, much of it, such as the various bimbo eruptions, that required her to hold her nose. She'd sustained repeated public mortification and personal humiliation. She'd had to cover for her husband and lie. As Bill's second term played out, it was sauce for the gander time, time for him to play a supporting role.

His first return on her investment would be curiously predictive of the future. There are more than two million Puerto Ricans in the

United States, many in New York. As a group, Puerto Ricans tend to vote Democratic. Puerto Rico's links with the United States date from the Spanish-American War, but Puerto Rico has repeatedly voted to maintain its commonwealth status with the United States, from which its people derive enormous benefits. During—and after—the Clinton administration, Puerto Ricans protested U.S. navy bombing on the nearby island of Vieques, but most Puerto Ricans still wanted to maintain their American connections. Most, but not all.

Some want to sever those connections by evolution and ballots. Others prefer to do so by revolution and bullets—and also by bombs. These were the people Bill Clinton chose to help in order to boost his wife's Senate campaign. The evidence that his actions were political was overwhelming and clear from the start.

In August of 1999, Bill Clinton exercised his presidential clemency power in favor of a group of Puerto Rican terrorists euphemistically referred to as "separatists," in the same sense that Timothy McVeigh is a "separatist." The action caught nearly everyone by surprise—there seemed little legitimate reason for his action, and the terrorists had not even formally petitioned to have their sentences commuted.

Most of the Puerto Rican recipients of the president's unexpected grace were members of the FALN, the *Fuerzas Armadas de Liberacion Nacional* (Armed Forces of National Liberation), a Marxist group responsible for a reign of terror that included 130 bombing attacks in the United States from 1974 to 1983. Chicago, New York, and Washington were prime FALN targets, with attacks against the New York office of the FBI, military recruiting centers, and the Chicago campaign headquarters of Jimmy Carter. All told, the terrorism racked up six deaths and scores of wounded. The victims included the husband of Diana Berger of Cherry Hill, New Jersey, six months pregnant with her first child when her husband fell victim to an FALN bomb.

Joseph and Thomas Connor, nine and eleven, lost their father in the same bomb attack. Other attacks left police officers maimed and blind.

In one of the cases, U.S. attorney Jeremy D. Margolis urged the maximum sentence because the motive was "purely one of terror." The defendants threatened the lives of federal judge Thomas R. McMillen and other courtroom officials. The judge said he would have imposed the death penalty had the law allowed it.[6]

Naturally, these killers had their supporters. A lawyer for the FALN compared them to anti-apartheid hero Nelson Mandela of South Africa. Jose Serrano, a Democratic New York congressman of Puerto Rican background, actually characterized them as political prisoners. Serrano was one of those who signed a December 9, 1994, open letter to President Clinton in the *New York Times* demanding the release of fifteen Puerto Rican prisoners. But the facts were hard to conceal: Carlos Romero-Barcelo, Puerto Rico's nonvoting delegate in the U.S. House of Representatives and a former governor of the island, wrote to Clinton asking the president to keep the FALN members behind bars.

"These are people who acted in cold blood with the purpose of imposing their will," Romero-Barcelo said. "These are the worst crimes in a democracy. If they said they are sorry for what they've done, if they accepted their guilt, then maybe my thoughts would be different. But they refuse to say that. How can we responsibly set them free? What if they kill somebody else? What do we say, 'Too bad'?"[7]

Prudence, morality, common sense, and custom suggest that executive clemency should be reserved for the repentant and reformed. The FALN's Adolfo Matos made it clear that he and his colleagues were not ashamed of what they had done, saw no need to ask forgiveness, and fully intended to continue their personal war against the United States and innocent bystanders.

The Justice Department, FBI Director Louis Freeh, and the U.S. attorneys offices in Illinois and Connecticut all opposed the release of the FALN terrorists. The Justice Department explicitly made its opposition known in a 1996 recommendation to the White House. This was weighty opposition indeed, on issues related to national security, to which any president would normally have given great deference. The Justice Department, said former U.S. attorney Joseph DiGenova, "strikingly disapproved of [the president's actions], adamantly disapproved of them, insistently disapproved of them." The FBI's assistant director of national security, Neil Gallagher, said that the people turned loose by Clinton "are criminals, and they are terrorists, and they represent a threat to the United States."[8]

But the combined and fierce opposition of law enforcement and national security officials carried no weight at all with the one person who mattered, Bill Clinton, president of the United States. In September of 1999, fourteen of the sixteen FALN members accepted Clinton's clemency offer. Eleven of those were released from prison, two had fines wiped out, and one had his sentence reduced to five years.

President Clinton had not bothered to consult with relatives of the victims of FALN terrorism. In fact, the survivors of those murdered and those whose lives had otherwise been destroyed by the terrorists were not even informed that their attackers were being released. Deputy Attorney General Eric Holder, who would be a key factor in the subsequent pardons, conceded that the nation owed much greater consideration to the victims. And Holder's boss, Janet Reno, explicitly acknowledged that groups aligned with the FALN still posed a threat to national security.

Indeed, the president himself could easily have been one of their targets. In 1950, Griselio Torresola and Oscar Collazo of the Puerto Rican Nationalist Party attempted to gun down President Harry Truman when he was living in the Blair House across Pennsylvania

Avenue while the White House was being repaired. Torresola and a guard were killed in the attack. Collazo was sentenced to death but Truman, not wanting to create a martyr, commuted the sentence to life.

White House spokesman Jim Kennedy said that President Clinton made his decision to release the FALN terrorists after careful consideration of all the facts. The White House tried to claim that the late John Cardinal O'Connor backed clemency for the FALN terrorists, an assertion subsequently denied by the archbishop of New York.

One fact that Clinton surely had considered was the by-then emerging senatorial campaign of his wife. The lively *New York Post* quipped that it knew the president had granted the pardon to help his wife because he said he hadn't.

Frank Pastorella, who had been blinded by an FALN bomb, said, "This is really, truly pandering to the Hispanic community."[9]

Former U.S. attorney DiGenova remarked, "Let me just say, categorically, the Puerto Rican terrorists were pardoned because they were a political benefit to the president's wife. Make no mistake about it. There is no justification for those pardons."[10]

Hillary's first response to her husband's extraordinary actions was to plead complete innocence. She proclaimed to an incredulous public that she was not sufficiently familiar with the FALN to offer an opinion on whether clemency should have been granted and claimed no advance knowledge of the president's intentions. But she indicated that, in retrospect, she supported what her husband had done. Hillary quickly learned how far her instincts had drifted from mainstream American opinion.

Her stance drew fire from police groups and local politicians who were mindful of the Oklahoma City bombing, the attacks on American embassies in Africa, and new threats from the Macheteros, another Puerto Rican terrorist group, over U.S. navy activity on the island of Vieques. Hillary quickly reversed course and stated her opposition to the pardons, trying to recover ground by seeming to be independent from her husband. This was classic Clinton. The Puerto Ricans knew that they had been the beneficiaries of Hillary's political ambitions. But Hillary was able to claim to opponents of the clemency that she not only had not been responsible but that she would have opposed the actions.

The president's use of his constitutional power to free the FALN terrorists apparently showed him that he could use the pardon power for personal and political ends, ignore the Department of Justice, and get away with it. All he had to do was to say that a pardon had nothing to do with politics, that his actions were based strictly on the facts and merits of the case, and claim that the sentence commutation served the interests of justice. Indeed, in the FALN case the president actually told the American people that the terrorists "were not convicted of crimes involving the killing or maiming of any individual." The audacity of the president's lie was matched only by the staggering ease with which he got away with it.

In the mind of Bill Clinton, political considerations outweigh even life-and-death matters of great concern to his own law-enforcement officials, not to mention the nation. As many in his own cabinet had repeatedly stated, terrorism, both foreign and domestic, was the nation's primary security anxiety. Since the end of the Cold War, Soviet aggression had been replaced by a number of particularly venomous threats, from Timothy McVeigh to Osama Bin Laden.

Margaret Love, a former pardon attorney with the Justice Department, said the number of situations in recent decades in which a pardon was granted without a prior Justice Department investigation and recommendation from the attorney general "could be counted on the fingers of one hand." Love saw in the FALN clemency the president's willingness to let White House staff usurp the role of the Justice Department.

"The thing that seems to me personally the most significant about those cases, particularly in retrospect," Love said, "was that he [Clinton] did not rely on the Justice Department. He did his own investigation in the White House. That was a foreshadowing of what happened later. I think it was a big mistake not to rely on the Department of Justice."[11]

"We should have seen a big red flashing light because of the FALN cases," Love said.[12]

The FALN incident was the first time the president used his pardon power to grant clemency to terrorists. He would return to this theme again at the end of his presidency.

Clemency for Communist Bomb Throwers

Susan Rosenberg was a member of the Weather Underground, one of the most violent of the left-wing militias that disrupted the nation from the 1960s through the 1980s. The Weather Underground was part of an interlocking directorate that included the May 19th Communist Organization (May 19 is the birthday of both Ho Chi Minh and Malcolm X), the Black Liberation Army, the Red Guerrilla Resistance, and others, together known as "The Family." One of their objectives was to establish the "Republic of New Afrika" in the American South, a vision that was part of the Communist Party policy that did not view blacks or Jews as genuine Americans.

Rosenberg was born on Manhattan's upper west side. Emanuel Rosenberg, her dentist father, was sufficiently wealthy to send her to the Walden School and Barnard College. After college she worked in a drug counseling program run by the Black Panthers and the Young Lords, a Puerto Rican revolutionary gang. (Note the coincidence, not only with young Hillary's work for the Black Panthers and similar groups, but her education at exclusive enclaves like Wellesley and Yale.) Rosenberg received further political education as a member of a youth work brigade in Cuba but did most of her serious political work stateside, where The Family launched a string of robberies and bombings in Bonnie-and-Clyde style.

"I rob banks with black people," said Rosenberg, alias "Elizabeth" and "Barbara Grodin."[13]

In October of 1981, Rosenberg's gang held up a Brink's truck in Nanuet, New York, killing guard Peter Paige and two police officers, Edward O'Grady and Waverly Brown, the first black officer on the local force. Rosenberg drove the getaway car and managed to escape.

The Family also bombed the United States Capitol. The November 7, 1983, blast ripped through a conference room near the Senate chamber and the offices of then–minority leader Robert C. Byrd. The bombers said in a communiqué that "we purposely aimed our attack at the institutions of imperialist rule rather than at individual members of the ruling class and government. We did not choose to kill any of them this time. But their lives are not sacred."[14]

The Family's other targets included the Naval War College at Fort McNair, the Washington Navy Yard's computer center and its officers club, the FBI office in Staten Island, New York, the Israeli Aircraft Industries Building in New York, the South African consulate in New York, and the Patrolmen's Benevolent Association in New York.

Rosenberg was also involved in the escape from prison of Joanne Chesimard, sentenced to life for killing a New Jersey trooper. In 1984, police caught Rosenberg at a warehouse in Cherry Hill, New Jersey, where she was unloading 640 pounds of explosives—what she called "combat materiel." That amount of explosive is literally a weapon of mass destruction, enough to create a holocaust of Oklahoma City proportions. She also possessed fourteen firearms, including an Uzi submachine gun, and fake identification.

During her trial, Rosenberg wore a shirt reading "Support New African Freedom Fighters," and "What Is a Nation Without an Army?" She claimed she was not a criminal but a revolutionary guerrilla and repeatedly harangued the court about Central America and the Middle East. She was sentenced to fifty-eight years, the maximum. In light of that sentence, prosecutors decided not to pursue murder charges stemming from the Brink's attack.

Following her sentencing she proclaimed, "Long live armed struggle. By taking up armed action to attack South Africa, the United States military, the war profiteers, and the police, we begin to enact proletarian internationalism." She continued to sign her letters "Venceremos." Legal appeals for reduction of her sentence were rejected.

Rosenberg became a celebrity of the far Left, with prominent leftists such as Noam Chomsky and William Kunstler lobbying for her release. When she became eligible for parole, Clinton's appointee as U.S. attorney for the Southern District of New York, Mary Jo White, warned the parole board that the damage Rosenberg had caused outweighed any ambiguously phrased change of heart about violence. But Rosenberg managed to get the usual favorable leftist publicity, including what amounted to a puff piece on *60 Minutes* and support from Jerrold Nadler, a New York congressman and ardent Clinton defender. Rosenberg petitioned for clemency. She finally got it, from Bill Clinton, on his last day in office.

The outgoing president went the second mile and also commuted the sentence of Rosenberg's comrade Linda Sue Evans. She had been convicted in the plot to bomb the United States Capitol in 1983. Evans also served a five-year sentence for two other federal convictions.

Those outraged by the president's commutations included Charles Schumer, senator from New York and a gun-control advocate, and New York City mayor Rudolph Giuliani, who had prosecuted the Brink's attack as an assistant U.S. attorney. Relatives of the victims were also outraged but lacked any recourse. The Weather comrades, including the more famous Bernadine Dohrn and Kathy Boudin, were already the beneficiaries of an ongoing campaign of historical revisionism that painted them as, at worst, misguided idealists. Now they were enjoying freedom, courtesy of President Clinton.

Clinton's actions left many wondering just what merits he had seen in these last terrorist pardons. The answer perhaps lies in the degree to which Bill Clinton was shaped by the events of the 1960s. His first political crisis, in fact, was how to avoid the draft, to avoid service in Vietnam. More than thirty years later, as his second term wound down, Bill Clinton would finally make it to Vietnam.

A Vietnam Memorial | 3

"Clinton's favorite remedy for personal and political malaise was to hit the road," recalls George Stephanopoulos.[1] In fact, Clinton loved being on the road and making use of Air Force One whether he was melancholy or euphoric, angry or pleased, up or down. Clinton needs people and will go wherever he can find them.

Bill Clinton made 133 visits to foreign nations, more than any other president, and spent a total of 229 days in those countries, nearly one full working year. Clinton took more foreign trips than presidents Dwight Eisenhower, John F. Kennedy, Lyndon Johnson, and Richard Nixon combined.

In 1998, when the crisis over his affair with Monica Lewinsky led to his impeachment by the House of Representatives, Clinton went abroad for forty-five days, nearly twice his average in previous years. The 1998 trips included eleven days of visits to six African nations and ten days in China. The total cost of these excursions to the taxpayer was estimated at half a billion dollars.[2] There is no evidence that the cost of this therapy/recreation troubled—or was even noticed by—Bill Clinton.

The chief executive travels on Air Force One, with his usual entourage, in superdeluxe ultra-first-class style, with journalists in tow, happy on an exotic assignment. When the president arrives, he is greeted with the pomp of officialdom. If the host government is capable, it can choreograph the appearances of cheering masses. The American president is hailed as a great leader and often joins the host in lofty statements about trade, disarmament, or world peace. Journalists can make new friends, and it usually makes for good copy back home, unless of course, like George Bush, the president vomits on his host. That is not considered presidential. In that respect at least, Bill Clinton was always presidential.

Clinton arranged a curious, but apparently strategic, trip late in his presidency while he was absorbed in thinking about his place in history. He was undoubtedly influenced by some of the more memorable travels of his predecessors.

Richard Nixon, for example, visited Communist China in 1972—a grand move on the global chessboard that, in the long view, provides a partial counterweight to Watergate and his resignation in disgrace. But a Bill Clinton visit to China would hardly have had much dramatic political significance. Besides, he had already done that to get his mind off Monica.

The best Clinton could do in Nixon-to-China style was North Korea, which invaded South Korea in 1950 at Stalin's request and remains a Stalinist state after all these years. Since the democratization of Albania, North Korea easily qualifies as the dreariest dictatorship on earth. Here as nowhere else, the principles of Marxism-Leninism show the consequences of one-party rule, a megalomaniacal "great leader," misery, poverty, and a dispirited and starving population. Like so many despotisms before it, North

Korea held itself together with a massive police force and a huge commitment to a muscle-bound military.

North Korea deploys a massive conventional army, long-range missiles, and the occasional bloody act of international terrorism. President Clinton was fortunate that, on his watch, the Stalinists in North Korea had not decided to invade South Korea or launch a missile at some other target. So why *not* reward their restraint with a visit by the president of the United States?

After a North Korean visit by Secretary of State Madeleine Albright, Bill Clinton tried to arrange a trip to Pyongyang, where Kim Jong Il, the son of Kim Il Sung, who had launched the 1950 invasion, had recently taken power. But the visit never came off, perhaps because conditions in that country were so bad that they would have been hard to paper over for visiting journalists.

That left Vietnam, where so many Americans had died, and which Bill Clinton had been so reluctant to visit thirty years earlier. The problem was, there was no diplomatic reason to go there. The regime was not, as in the past, threatening or invading its neighbors or sponsoring terrorism in the style of Iraq or Libya. No crisis required Clinton's attention, and no new trade deal was in the offing and not likely to be, for good reason.

Vietnam is still a Soviet-style dictatorship and, like the Eastern Bloc before it, produces virtually nothing that Americans want or need. Nike's Vietnamese operation, for example, makes goods only for the Asian and European markets. The regime stands in stark contrast to other nations in Southeast Asia, economic powerhouses because of their free-market economies. No Vietnamese politician stands out as someone who, with encouragement from the United States, would promote multiparty democracy, free elections, and economic liberty.

So, since the reasons for the Vietnam trip were not political or diplomatic, they had to be personal. Bill Clinton's squalid personal history with regard to Vietnam may provide the key.

On September 2, 1992, Bill Clinton told the *Los Angeles Times* that "it was just a fluke" that he had not been drafted. "I certainly had no leverage to get special treatment from the draft board." In fact, as everyone in America except Bill Clinton still remembers, the facts were quite the reverse. In 1968, the looming draft was young Bill Clinton's first political crisis, and he handled it in the same way he would respond to future crises: a crafty combination of lying, evasion, and using others.

One college graduate in ten would go to Vietnam during the war, with only a few of those seeing combat, but young Americans with a high-school education or less were far more likely to be called up for service and see combat duty. That was particularly true in Clinton's home state of Arkansas, with one of the lowest income levels in the nation.

For Bill Clinton, intervention by his Uncle Raymond and others enabled him to leave the country without a formal deferment, and eventually to avoid the draft altogether, despite his 1-A draft status. Clinton dodged the draft by joining an ROTC program and then abandoned the ROTC after drawing a high number in the draft lottery. He escaped the draft and missed a trip to Vietnam. But it was no fluke.

Those without similar connections and agility became part of an intensely unpopular effort to contain the expansion of communism around the world. America ultimately withdrew from Vietnam, due in large part to an antiwar movement that Bill Clinton actively supported.

The 58,220 Americans who died fighting communism in Vietnam are commemorated on a black granite wall not far from the White House. Those who survived and returned were often shunned, vilified, and caricatured in movies as psychotics, ready to explode at any moment.

The draft Bill Clinton avoided no longer existed when he finally became the commander-in-chief of the men and women in and out of uniform whom we count on to defend our country. Of all his presidential duties, this suited Bill Clinton the least, and he was never able to shake his image of someone who would never be accepted by those in his command.

"Clinton's military salute [was hard] to fix," recalled George Stephanopoulos. "Sheepish at first, he seemed to be working out his internal conflicts every time he tentatively raised his hand. The tops of his finger would furtively touch his slightly bowed head, as if he were being caught at something he wasn't supposed to do."[3]

Some even noticed that when Clinton was president, marine guards failed to execute a right face to stand facing his back as he walked away. The marines somehow relearned this maneuver on January 20, 2001, when the new commander-in-chief, President George W. Bush, took office.

During his eight years as president of the United States, Bill Clinton expressed no public recognition that American efforts to prevent the North Vietnamese regime from conquering the South had been part of a cause aimed at stopping communist domination of the world. He was also notably quiet about the sacrifices made by the young men and women of his age who had served when called.

Thus, his trip to Vietnam, the first by an American president since Richard Nixon in 1969, was an opportunity for Clinton to reveal whether he now viewed his own actions or the actions of his country in a different light. But that was not to be.

In Ho Chi Minh City, formerly Saigon, crowds cheered Clinton's motorcade, and when he strolled down a street near his hotel so many jostled around him that Secret Service agents had to set up a makeshift rope line. The president shook the hands of dock workers and extolled the benefits of trade.

"Today we have a shared interest in your well-being and your prosperity," he said. "We have a stake in your future and we wish to be your partners. We wish you success."[4]

In Hanoi, on the first leg of the trip, Clinton met with Communist Party boss Le Kha Phieu, the country's senior leader, and with President Tran Duc Luong, to whom he promised more assistance in dealing with damage that the Vietnamese attributed to the military use of the defoliant Agent Orange. For their part, Vietnam's elite treated the president to a piece of old-fashioned propaganda theater, a ceremony detailing the many land mines and 300,000 tons of unexploded bombs that allegedly remain buried in that country and which still cause casualties. The proceedings included appearances by four maimed children, including an eleven-year-old boy whose left hand was blown off by a bomb. Presumably warned by his advance team about this bit of exploitation, Clinton was a willing participant.

At Tien Chau, a village seventeen miles northwest of Hanoi, the President of the United States watched as Vietnamese workers searched for remnants of Lieutenant Colonel Lawrence Evert, an American shot down in 1967 and never seen again. Accompanying President Clinton were George C. Duggins, president of Vietnam Veterans of America, and the pilot's two sons, Daniel and David Evert of Chandler, Arizona. Escorted down a long bamboo and plywood bridge to the excavation site, the Americans watched as fifty workers in conical hats and purple smocks scooped mud into buckets, passing it through a sieve in the search for clues.

As he watched, the lachrymal president bit his lower lip and teared up. Perhaps the tears were genuine. Perhaps the president was experiencing the same kind of sentiment that affects those who visit the Vietnam Memorial, whatever their views about the war during the 1960s. Or maybe he was thinking of Mike Thomas, his boyhood friend and classmate, who perished in the conflict. Whatever the case, the president promised more cooperation on the MIA issue. The

United States still lists 1,498 servicemen as missing, and during the Clinton presidency the remains of 283 servicemen were found. At Hanoi airport, Clinton attended a ceremony to send home, in aluminum caskets covered with American flags, three sets of remains recovered earlier that year.

Beyond these rites and the presidential tears, the president's views on Vietnam and American military action there were revealing: "When we look back on it, the most important thing is that a lot of brave people fought and died in the North Vietnamese army, the Viet Cong, and the South Vietnamese army and the United States army.... And the best thing we can do to honor the sacrifice and service of those who believed on both sides that what they were doing was right, is to find a way to build a different future."[5]

The key phrase is "on both sides." An attempt to draw a moral equivalence between those fighting against a Stalinist state and those fighting to impose a Stalinist state. Yes, it is always good to mourn the deaths of ordinary soldiers. But it is shocking to suggest a moral equivalence between freedom and tyranny, democracy and totalitarianism, capitalism and communism. That is something that President Clinton never seemed to understand.

It is unimaginable that Franklin Roosevelt, Harry Truman, John Kennedy, or Dwight Eisenhower would have attempted to draw a moral equivalence between the forces of the Allies and those of Hitler. Harry Truman would surely have seen no moral equivalence between the forces in North Korea and those battling their aggression. And President Reagan was savaged by the press when he attempted to express a modicum of sympathy for the families of German soldiers resting in an army cemetery. But Clinton escaped any condemnation for his insensitivity to the Americans who died in Vietnam fighting world communism.

The president had a chance to redeem himself and set the record straight at Hanoi University on November 17. Here was Bill Clinton's chance to state his version of Reagan's "Mr. Gorbachev, tear down this wall," or to emulate his idol, John Kennedy, when he declared solidarity with the oppressed Berliners.

But the Clinton speech included no ringing defense of political and economic liberties. Indeed, President Clinton took pains to say that the United States had no desire to impose such values on the people of Vietnam. Liberty and human rights, he said, would have to be woven into "the Vietnamese national identity." Le Kha Phieu and his comrades were doubtless pleased; they, at least, had found the trip useful. Above all, there had been no attempt by Bill Clinton to meet with Vietnamese political opposition, most of whose leaders remain in prison.

It is not outside the realm of possibility that the Vietnam trip was Bill Clinton's way of flipping half a peace sign at his detractors, especially those who dared to point out his draft-dodging exploits in the early days of his first presidential campaign. Bill Clinton is a man who not only enjoys winning but who needs to gloat over his victories. Or, perhaps he thought that it was better to see Vietnam during his presidency than not at all and to keep observers mystified about the motive. But it is a safe bet that neither his skillful avoidance of the Vietnam conflict nor his eleventh-hour presidential visit will do much to burnish the Clinton legacy.

Hillary Rodham Clinton joined her husband in Vietnam. In fact, she arrived before he did, flying in from Israel, where she attended the funeral of Leah Rabin. In Hanoi, Hillary drew crowds when she went shopping and visited a gallery.

"It's our great pleasure to see her here because we've heard a lot about her, we've read a lot about her," said Tran Hien Lan, an English literature teacher whose father's paintings hung in the gallery Hillary visited. "She is one of the most well-known women in the world. She is a very talented woman."[6] She was also the newly elected senator from the state of New York, a representation—at least up to that point—without taxation.

A new—and profoundly disturbing—aspect of that talent was about to emerge.

Hillary Moves Onto Center Stage | 4

FLOTUS Becomes Senator

In 1946, Harold Ickes, former interior secretary for Franklin Delano Roosevelt, urged Eleanor Roosevelt to run for the Senate in New York. Though enormously popular, she declined the challenge. More than half a century later, one of Bill Clinton's fiercest and most partisan aides, Harold Ickes Jr., resurrected his father's concept and urged First Lady Hillary Clinton to give New York one more opportunity to convert a first lady into a senator. But first, in accordance with Washington custom, a trial balloon had to be launched. Tim Russert of the immensely important NBC show *Meet the Press* agreed to provide the venue. Just prior to the January 3, 1999, interview segment of the program, Senator Robert Torricelli of New Jersey, head of the Democratic Senate Campaign Committee, hinted to Russert that he believed Hillary Rodham Clinton would run for the United States Senate, specifically the seat from New York being vacated by the retirement of Daniel Patrick Moynihan.

Russert dutifully asked guest Gail Sheehy, author of *Hillary's Choice*, whether such a move would surprise her. Sheehy said it would not surprise her at all. David Maraniss, author of the best-selling, Pulitzer Prize–winning Bill Clinton biography, *First in His Class*, said it would not surprise him either. Nor did it surprise this author, who was familiar with how Hillary, eyes blazing, had told journalist John Robert Starr that "I want to run something."[1] I never did think that a little thing like never having lived in New York would deter Hillary. Nothing like a U.S. Senate seat to satisfy the urge "to run something."

Democratic insiders had long suspected that Hillary would want to start at the top once her "First Ladyship" tenure was over. At first, I thought it might be the World Bank, where her college roommate and friend Jan Piercy already held a top-level position. But the Moynihan vacancy was fruit that was too ripe not to pick, so she opted for the role declined by her hero Eleanor Roosevelt, with whom, she confided to an interviewer, Hillary had established psychic communications.

The first person she called after the *Meet the Press* teaser was Ickes, who had been the boyfriend of Hillary's friend Susan Thomases. Ickes's relationship with Bill Clinton went back to 1970 when they both worked on Project Pursestrings, an effort to cut off funding to the Vietnamese war effort. By the late 1990s, the hard-nosed Ickes was a thirty-year veteran in the rough and tumble of New York politics, which surely helped Bill Clinton carry the state by wide margins in 1992 and 1996.

"If you don't want to do this," he told Hillary, "don't mouse around with it."[2] But she did want to do it, and, consistent with her character, she didn't mouse around with it. For the first time, a sitting first lady would seek public office, and not just any office. By July 1999 she had hit the campaign trail for real.

Hillary's initial opponent for the "Battle of New York" was New York mayor Rudolph Giuliani. He withdrew in the face of highly visible domestic turmoil and the prospect of debilitating treatment for prostate cancer. Representative Rick Lazio, young and long on ambition but short on experience, and certainly not in Giuliani's league, took over. It would be the most expensive Senate race in history, a tick under $50 million overall.

In order to establish at least a façade of New York connections, Hillary bought a house in Chappaqua and donned a New York Yankees' cap, proclaiming herself a lifelong Yankees' fan. The Yankees' cap was a bit laughable since Hillary did not seem to know the difference between Yogi Berra and Yogi Bear, Mickey Mantle and Mickey Mouse, or Joe Torre and Mel Torme. And Giuliani, her first opponent, was a real Yankee fan with a whole office full of Yankee memorabilia. But such obvious canards do not fluster Hillary. You either believed what she was saying, or you were part of a conspiracy.

The Chappaqua house was also a stretch. Prior to deciding to run for the Senate, Hillary had no connection with that neighborhood. And only the most credulous supporters ever believed she would ultimately make a home there. But she needed a New York address, and a place on which to pay taxes, at least after the election if not before.

The Senate campaign had its rough moments. During the campaign, a book emerged, *State of a Union: Inside the Complex Marriage of Bill and Hillary Clinton* by Jerry Oppenheimer, with the explosive charge that, after her husband was defeated in an early congressional race in Arkansas, Hillary had called campaign worker Paul Fray a "fucking Jew bastard." The book also cited state trooper Larry Patterson, who claimed that the Clintons in anger would call each other "Jew bastard" and "Jew motherfucker." Fray paid a passing, backhanded tribute to Bill Clinton, saying, "There's not a son of a bitch alive in this country that can raise money like he can. I'll venture to say he'll go down in history as the finest man, as it relates to conning somebody out of dollars."[3] But, he said, the "Jew bastard" incident was true.

Hillary denied it. "It did not happen," she said. "I have never said anything like that. Ever. Ever."

Bill Clinton called journalist Michael Kelly and the *New York Daily News* to say, "In twenty-nine years my wife has never ever uttered an ethnic or racial slur against anybody, ever. She's so straight on this she squeaks."[4] He did not deny the other language.

Hillary also faced a problem with Jewish voters for kissing Suha Arafat, the wife of Yasir Arafat, moments after the lovely and charming first lady of the Palestine Liberation Army charged Israelis with using poison gas on Palestinians. The first lady of the United States explained that she hadn't understood the translation of Madam Arafat's remarks. When the actual—and quite clear—translation was made public and that excuse evaporated, she retreated to a mushier explanation, and then silence. The opposition made much of the incident, but the fury subsided when a photograph surfaced with candidate Lazio shaking hands with Yasir Arafat. Not exactly a kiss, but at least a chance to claim some form of moral equivalence—a standard Clinton tactic, as we have so often seen.

Hillary campaigned like a trouper. (Not to be compared with her husband's utilization of Arkansas troopers.) One of her stops was the New Square Hasidic community in Rockland County, north of New York City, where she met with the chief rabbi. Her energy and drive prompted writer Michael Tomasky, who wrote a book about the senatorial race, to call her the Energizer bunny.

Hollywood connections served her well. Linda Bloodworth-Thomason produced a promotional video that was stunningly effective, although staggeringly banal in parts. The boilerplate phrase "for more than thirty years I've been an advocate in behalf of children and families" began appearing in every speech, without, no one seemed to mention, any reference to what she had accomplished in these three decades beyond a fatuous book entitled *It Takes a Village*, which won her, of all things, a Grammy Award for her vocal rendition of her ghostwritten book.

When the dust settled on election day 2000, Hillary won 55-43, carrying 53 percent of the Jewish vote, 73 percent of the city vote, and 47 percent of the vote upstate, where she had not been expected to do well.

With a lot of help from her friends and husband, Hillary Rodham Clinton had parlayed her position as FLOTUS into a senatorial seat. A few days after being sworn in, Hillary Rodham Clinton was appointed to three Senate committees, including the powerful Senate Health, Education, Labor, and Pensions Committee, with jurisdiction over health care, an issue on which she enjoyed previous experience—that is, in the sense that a driver with several accidents is considered by an automobile insurer to be an experienced driver. She was also appointed to the Environment and Public Works Committee and the Budget Committee, which deals with an array of important fiscal issues.

That would amount to a substantial burden, but by Christmas the new senator took on another task. A number of books had been written about Hillary Clinton. Now she wanted her turn, and everybody wanted a piece of the action.

"Very, Very Gargantuan"

In early December 2000, so many publishers descended on the White House that they began running into each other at Washington's Reagan National Airport. In the Diplomacy Room of the White House, Hillary auditioned them, as they inquired just how much she planned to disclose.

Hillary told them she wanted to write an "honest" and "dignified" book, modeled on the memoir of Katharine Graham, the former publisher of the *Washington Post*, who knew a tiny bit more about writing than Hillary Clinton, and whose autobiography had won a Pulitzer Prize. Hillary Clinton's became the subject of a heated auction, with all major publishers taking part. The rights were expected to go as high as $5 million,[5] but those prognostications failed to anticipate the market for a piece of Hillary Rodham Clinton.

On December 15, Simon and Schuster, which had published *It Takes a Village*, prevailed upon her to accept an advance of $8 million for her book about her White House years. The amount of the advance was truly breathtaking. The pope had done slightly better, getting $8.5 million, a record for a nonfiction book. The pope, of course, was a little older and had a few more accomplishments. But then the pope has never been before a grand jury. In any event, Hillary's $8 million was by far the largest such advance offered to any government official.

Mrs. Clinton did not run the book advance by the Senate ethics panel before accepting it. The Clintons do not ask permission. They have found that it is much easier to act first and explain later. Especially when their contemplated actions come with so much baggage.

The $8 million flowed from a corporate conglomerate that had business before the Senate, the body to which Hillary Rodman Clinton had just been elected. Simon and Schuster is owned by Viacom, a media conglomerate controlling Paramount Pictures, CBS Television, MTV, the UPN television network, and Blockbuster video stores. The entertainment giant has substantial interest in what happens in Washington ranging from television station licensing to potential federal regulation of broadcast violence. Viacom was at the time also battling a federal regulation that prevents any one company from owning broadcast stations that reach more than 35 percent of U.S. households. It employs highly paid lobbyists, such as former senator and Ronald Reagan friend Paul Laxalt, and Tony Podesta, brother of Bill Clinton's former chief of staff John Podesta.

Several watchdog organizations saw in Hillary's $8 million book deal a quintessential example of influence peddling. Because of conflict of interest concerns such as these, members of the House cannot accept advances for books, only royalties. Senators, on the other hand, may accept a book advance that is "usual and customary." Hillary's monster deal did not strike some public interest ethics groups as either usual or customary.

"An $8 million advance is not a usual or customary contractual term. It's very, very gargantuan," said Gary Ruskin, director of the Congressional Accountability Project, not known as a Hillary critic.[6] Indeed, Ruskin, who also runs an entertainment watchdog group called Commercial Alert, had earlier in the year praised the first lady for her proposals targeted at advertising to children of preschool age.

The Congressional Accountability Project asked Hillary to submit the book deal to the Ethics Committee for review, noting that Senator John McCain of Arizona had made the same suggestion in a letter to the new senator. "Given Viacom's extensive efforts to affect the outcome of numerous matters pending before the Senate and federal government, if you accept the $8 million book advance from Simon & Schuster, you may violate Senate Rules regarding conflicts of interest," which state that "no Member, officer, or employee shall engage in any outside business or professional activity or employment for compensation which is inconsistent or in conflict with the conscientious performance of official duties."

The letter concluded, "The sheer size of your $8 million book advance raises questions about whether you and Senate processes may be affected by large cash payments from a major media conglomerate. This book contract, with its uniquely lavish advance for an elected official, may be, in fact, a way for that corporation to place money into your pockets, perhaps to curry favor with you."

Jake Siewert, White House press secretary, responded that the first lady was not bound by any Senate rules since she had not yet taken office. Hillary thus found herself in a convenient spot. The rules governing the receipt of gifts, ethics, and outside employment which covered White House employees did not apply to her. She wasn't a White House employee—merely a "first lady." For these purposes at least, she was not a co-president. And technically, she was not yet a senator. She may have been a new resident of New York, but she also resided in the land of no ethics.

Though the president had not yet inked a similar package—though he would in August 2001, reporting an even more gargantuan $10 million—he was "pleased" by Hillary's $8 million advance. "I think, obviously, everyone wants their spouse to do as well as possible, and the president is no exception to that rule," Siewert said.[7] The president, who is represented by the same Washington attorney for book deals, the respected Robert Barnett, knew that he could look forward to a book advance that would be at least as great as Hillary's, especially if he would just promise to air out some of his secrets.

The reason members of the House may no longer accept advances, only royalties, is because of the immense eruption in the media when former Speaker Newt Gingrich made a book deal somewhat akin to Hillary's as he was about to become Speaker of the House of Representatives in the groundbreaking takeover of the House by the Republicans in 1994. Gingrich had accepted an advance of $4.5 million from the publisher HarperCollins owned by Rupert Murdoch. Democrats howled in protest, loudest among them Charles Rangel, David Bonior, and John Lewis, with the *New York Times* and the *Washington Post* leading a savage media attack. Bill and Hillary each expressed concern, without explaining precisely why. Of course, they did not need to. Gingrich finally gave in and surrendered the $4.5 million, settling instead for an advance of one dollar.

The House changed its rules and decided to prohibit author advances, but the Senate declined to follow suit. Gingrich duly wrote his book, *To Renew America*, which landed on the *New York Times* bestseller list.

When Hillary scored her $8 million advance, the response from the Democrats was silence, and the media behaved as if a cloud of valium had settled over the nation's editorial suites. "They're not disturbed when Mrs. Clinton gets $8 million" said Bill O'Reilly of Fox television's *The O'Reilly Factor*. "So are we talking rank hypocrisy here?"

"Look," responded Gingrich, "I think that this $8 million will go right next to the cattle futures money and right next to the Whitewater money. And the fact is that the Clintons have learned over the years, [to] ignore the press, ignore their critics, do what you're going to do, and win." Of course, it is easy to ignore the press when it is friendly and in a collective coma.

The former Speaker also said: "You notice on her side, people who attacked me now say nothing about her. And on our side, because Republicans do believe in free enterprise and because a lot of Republicans were really angry when the Democrats unfairly attacked me, you're not getting the kind of just pure partisan reaction. So Hillary in a sense gets a free ride."[8]

That was true. Wary of picking a fight with New York's senator-elect, congressional Republicans were ducking the potential controversy. "I'm not going to start off being critical of her," said then–Senate majority leader Trent Lott, who had previously warned that Hillary Clinton had better get used to being one of one hundred coequals in the Senate, where she would get "no special treatment."

"I think what the Democrats did to Newt in the House was unfair," said then–Senate assistant majority leader Don Nickles. "I know we won't duplicate that action in the Senate."[9]

Republicans were also frightfully concerned not to do or say anything that would make the public feel sorry—yet again—for Hillary. She seems to grow wings when she is perceived as a victim, a role in which she thrives and which she obviously cherishes. Her eyes literally glowed during the Lewinsky months and her ratings with the public glistened proportionately. When poor Rick Lazio dared to move physically close to her during the first senatorial campaign debate, Hillary's campaign apparatchiks gleefully pounced on Lazio's "bullying tactics"—so much for tough New York–style campaigning—and his standing in the polls never recovered.

Republicans were not about to open Hillary's Senate career with another victimhood popularity spike. Even conservative commentators were restrained. One prominent conservative couldn't get beyond "unseemliness," whatever that means. "I think these are questions of seemliness rather than the law," said Tucker Carlson of CNN and the *Weekly Standard*. "When you're negotiating an $8 million deal you probably would hire a lawyer to make certain that it's not illegal before you embark on it. But I don't think that's the point. The point is for eight years the question has been, you know, to what degree should we ask Mrs. Clinton questions about her private life when she does interviews? And the consensus has always been, gosh, it's somewhat uncomfortable about asking the first lady of the United States about her marriage, et cetera, and here she is making, you know, this profit on her private life, and there's something—I think whatever the legal question turns out to be—[there's] something unseemly about that."[10]

CNN commentator and *Time* columnist Margaret Carlson, one of Hillary's most slavish apologists, seemed to think that the only rule Hillary had bumped was the obligation to remain "interesting," a new standard for lowered thresholds. "Well, it takes a senator to get $8 million. I think there's a combination. I mean, she's even more interesting now because she's the first First Lady to become a senator. But as much as seemliness, I object on grounds of impending boredom. She is the most private person, especially everything that's swirled around her, and she's protected it by this zone of privacy and everything that the prurient public is interested in, I think we know for free in the Starr report."[11]

Of course, the White House had the best explanation. Gingrich couldn't possibly have been worth the advance his agent negotiated, but Hillary was star quality: "There was also some question about whether his story was really worth $4.5 million," said Clinton spokesperson Jake Siewert, "whereas no one doubts that Mrs. Clinton's story is worth any amount of money."[12]

Will her story be worth the advance? I actually believe that it could be. If, that is, Hillary is willing to open up. Not, however, if her ghost writers are going to produce another banality like *It Takes a Village*.

To earn her $8 million advance, Hillary might begin by explaining her right-to-left political odyssey. Of particular interest would be her views on liberation theology, a Soviet propaganda concept now abandoned by all but a few aging seminarians who still see Che Guevara as a latter-day Jesus Christ. It would also be refreshing to hear Hillary explain her views on Robert Treuhaft, the Communist husband of self-proclaimed Stalinist Jessica Mitford. What insights did this creaky old communist bring to Hillary's life? Did he or wife Jessica ever say anything with which Hillary disagreed? If so, what, and why? Here is a chance for Hillary to set the record straight and demonstrate whether she is capable of anything approaching independent thought.

The most momentous events of our time, the demise of communism, the collapse of the Eastern Bloc, the demolition of the Berlin Wall, the end of the Cold War, have drawn virtually no comment from the supposed big-thinking Hillary. What did she think of it all? Did she believe, like Deputy Secretary of State Strobe Talbott in the Clinton administration State Department, that the doves had been right all along?

Domestic events also cry out for sunlight. Tommy Robinson, director of public safety during the first Clinton term as governor of

Arkansas, said that Hillary was the real governor for ten years. "She is one very professionally tough bitch," he said. "She did not want screwups of any kind. She was all business."[13] Was this really the case or more right-wing conspiracy rhetoric? And in 1991, did she really, as some have testified, tell a state trooper, in front of the governor's mansion, "Where is the goddamn fucking flag? I want the goddamn fucking flag up every fucking morning at fucking sunrise."[14]

I would also love to hear a real explanation of the cattle futures bonanza. Not that we will get one; certainly not a true account. But as one observer put it, finding the Dead Sea Scrolls in front of the Arkansas Governor's Mansion was as likely a development as Hillary's famous futures trade. With unlimited space, she can now give the full version and perhaps help others to parlay $1,000 into $100,000. Maybe she could explain how that kind of fandango squares with the anticapitalist, anticorporate outlook she expounded during her radical days and used to criticize Reagan-era Republicans. She and Bill repeatedly and self-righteously characterized those years as times of unalloyed greed and rapacity. Where did cattle futures trading fit in that picture?

Or Hillary can provide a firsthand account of what it was like on the personal airplane of Dan Lasater, the hamburger magnate and cocaine dealer her husband conveniently pardoned when he was governor. Patsy Thomasson's duties for Lasater, before she moved on to the Clinton White House, could also be explained, along with the story underlying the flap about why most of the people initially brought into the White House by the Clintons had trouble with security clearances.

The big stories, of course, are the realities behind the eight drama-packed Clinton years in the White House. Now that would be worth the $8 million book advance.

One such drama, as you might recall, occurred in 1993 when Hillary's close friend Vincent Foster was found dead in a Virginia park, the highest ranking official of the executive branch to die under suspicious circumstances since John F. Kennedy. What was Hillary's relationship with Foster? Had it changed once she got to the White House? Those who had previously occupied Foster's position did not have access to National Security Agency files. What was Vincent Foster doing with NSA material?

What really happened in Foster's office after his death and his files went missing? Who made all those telephone calls to Arkansas that night, and what for? What did Hillary's chief of staff, Maggie Williams, do in Foster's office that night? What was Patsy Thomasson really looking for in Vince Foster's desk that night? Why in the world did friends of Hillary vacuum Foster's office and hold the Justice Department investigators at bay?

The three key figures those first few days after Foster's sudden death were counsel to the president Bernie Nussbaum, Hillary's mentor from their days together on the House Judiciary Committee's Richard Nixon impeachment inquiry; Hillary chief of staff Maggie Williams; and Hillary's closest friend, Susan Thomases. Hillary, please explain what these people were up to, why they didn't want a Justice Department investigation, and to whom they were reporting. Now there would be some news worth a good piece of the $8 million.

The world would surely also love to hear a forthright explanation of Hillary's role in the firing of the White House Travel Office employees early in the Clintons' first term, the action that became known as Travelgate. She responded to this author under oath that she had "no role" in the firings and repeated that story to Ken Starr's investigators. But the facts were overwhelmingly to the contrary. Starr's successor, Robert Ray, issued a report stating that he did not feel that he could mount a successful prosecution but made it plain that he did not believe Hillary's version, contradicted as it was by so many witnesses and contemporaneous documents.

And what about Filegate, in which a former nightclub bouncer named Craig Livingston managed to procure massive numbers of sensitive FBI files on key Republicans? Maybe this was, as Bill Clinton explained, a simple bureaucratic snafu. But who hired Livingston to head the sensitive White House office in charge of security? And why? And what about the infamous White House database that combined official White House lists with Democratic Party fundraising data? Was this Hillary's idea as so many have suggested?

Conspiracy theories are always of interest. In her forthcoming book, Hillary can offer further elucidation and updates on the vast right-wing conspiracy, so ubiquitous and Machiavellian that it engineered virtually all the criticism of herself and her husband, not to mention Bill's Oval Office happy times with Monica Lewinsky. Readers will surely be interested to learn how it was that this vast, all-powerful conspiracy became powerless to prevent her from becoming a senator from New York.

The various "bimbo eruptions," from Paula Jones through Monica Lewinsky, also remain of interest. Hillary's description of what really went on in the White House during these exciting sagas would itself be worth the price of the book. She told the *New York Times* that she would tell the Lewinsky story. But will she?

After more than twenty-five years of marriage, Hillary surely knows Bill Clinton better than anyone else. David Maraniss, Roger Morris, Dick Morris, R. Emmett Tyrrell and others have tried to unlock the mysteries of the forty-second president. Now the former FLOTUS will have her turn. She can explain, for example, whether, as George Stephanopoulos described, she would feed Bill lemon slices dipped in honey, and he would call to her in baby talk, "Hee-a-ree, Hee-a-ary."[15]

Hillary Rodham Clinton has indicated that her book will be two years in the writing. With that schedule, let us hope she will give her ghostwriter something to tell us beyond gobs of tedious detail about the health care system, the treatment of women in Africa, and dreary ceremonial visits by and to foreign heads of state (although some further light on the Suha Arafat encounter would be illuminating). At a minimum, I hope that this book will prompt Hillary to tell her version of those halcyon days in December 2000 and January 2001 as she and her husband prepared to leave office and dispensed and received so many favors.

Bill and Hill Join The Donald | 5

Now that Hillary was to be a senator from New York, now that she had a fat $8 million advance from a New York publisher, and now that Bill was to vacate Washington and launch a lecture business from Manhattan, these new New Yorkers needed big time New York real estate. The way they went about it, they must have taken lessons from New York's leading real estate baron, Donald Trump, known to his public—and his ex-wives—as "The Donald."

Real estate was something of a new thing for Mr. and Mrs. Clinton. Most Americans have had an opportunity to buy or rent a place to live. But the Clintons had had two decades of free public housing, not to mention drivers, shoppers, chefs, nannies, bodyguards, and miscellaneous gofers. Not much preparation for the real world. Perhaps that excuses their extravagances, both with their own and the public's money, when they plunged into the real estate market while planning for their extraordinarily splashy exit from the

White House. And maybe The Donald told them that it never pays to own modest real estate.

The Chappaqua house was first. Of course, Hillary did not want to live in Chappaqua, but Manhattan was the wrong signal for a senatorial candidate, so a suburban county it had to be. But the price was more than they could afford, so why not take a free loan guarantee from their favorite benefactor, Terry McAuliffe, fundraiser extraordinaire, later rewarded with chairmanship of the Democratic National Committee? The loan guarantee, however, had to be rescinded when that was just a little too much for even the liberal New York press. But spending too much was an instinct that would return with the purchase of the Clinton Washington home and again, with a vengeance, when taxpayer money was the funding source for their New York office spaces.

The posh offices Hillary Rodham Clinton snapped up on the upper east side of Manhattan will cost taxpayers in excess of $514,148 per year, $90,000 more than the Senate's next highest digs, the San Francisco offices of California Democratic senator Dianne Feinstein. The tab is more than double the amount paid by Hillary's fellow Democrat and New York senator, Charles Schumer, whose offices are in the same neighborhood. Senator Schumer pays $209,532 a year. Of course, he makes do with 3,900 square feet, while Hillary needs 7,900 square feet, more than twice the space. He is a senator. She is a superstar.

Hillary's office is three blocks from the United Nations and one block from the famed Waldorf-Astoria Hotel. No one should have been surprised that when it came to selecting her office, Hillary pushed the envelope to its absolute limit and squeezed every available dime from the American taxpayers.

The General Services Administration sets a maximum of $91.14 per square foot on such space. That alone seems generous; it is the equivalent of renting a fairly sizable 3,000-square-foot house for

$23,000 per month. But the Clintons weren't going to leave any portion of that subsidy on the table. The new senator's quarters on the 26th floor of a fifty-story Third Avenue building owned by the Teachers Insurance Annuity Association of America came in at approximately $91 per square foot. The seventeen-year-old building, covered in peach-colored Finnish granite, offers a terraced 154-seat auditorium with television facilities, plus two conference rooms in Hillary's suite.

There were plenty of lower-priced alternatives. In fact, staffers for her husband, who had been singed by criticism over his selection of high-end space in Carnegie Towers, discussed later in this chapter, warned Hillary's staff that, based on their experience, opting for the pricier location wouldn't look good.[1] With characteristic arrogance, Hillary went ahead anyway, ignoring criticism and showcasing her vast sense of entitlement. She undoubtedly believed both that she deserved it and that it was appropriate given her status not only as a senator but as a celebrity.

"She's like royalty. She's the ex-president's wife. She lived in the White House for eight years, for crying out loud," said Mitch Arkin of the Cushman and Wakefield real estate firm.[2] Hillary's staff and defenders portrayed the selection as a cost-cutting measure, arguing that they actually *saved* taxpayers money by not renewing the lease on the offices of former senator Daniel Patrick Moynihan, which were overdue for a rent increase and would have jumped to $625,000 per year. She could also have rented Trump Towers from The Donald. Think of how much she saved taxpayers by not doing that!

There were, of course, contrary voices. But they were relatively muted: "To spend lavishly on her office sends a small but noticeable signal that perhaps she has less respect for the taxpayer than she ought to," said Gary Ruskin of the Government Accountability Project. "Taxpayers, I think, would smile if the senator had an office with a bit less glitz, but cost us all less."[3] Mr. Ruskin must be new in town. When had the Clintons demonstrated any respect for taxpayers? To use a phrase from another context, but which applies to them in a variety of contexts, the Clintons are net-takers.

Congressional committees and Clinton watchers, however, were too busy with other issues, particularly pardons, to press the matter at the time. Meanwhile, Bill Clinton had his own office issues. Clinton aficionados will not be shocked to learn that while Hillary was becoming the highest-costing senator, Bill was becoming the most expensive ex-president.

Harlem Nocturn

In the parlance of New York real estate, few buildings offer "trophy status." One of them is the ultra-exclusive Carnegie Hall Towers in Manhattan, right next to the famous Russian Tea Room. Some 10,000 square feet was available on the ninth floor of the Towers at $58 per square foot, a good rate for the area. Clinton turned it down on the ostensible grounds that it was more space than he needed and would pose security problems.

But he liked the building. He deserved to be in New York—who would want an office in Arkansas? And he deserved a trophy building. But he wanted the entire 56th floor—all 8,300 square feet—with breathtaking views of Central Park, to be sure, but a prime-time rent of $98 per square foot. The asking price had risen from the $90–$95 range because of Clinton's interest in the property.

Clinton first informed the General Services Administration (GSA), which oversees office expenditures, that his lease would cost $650,000 per year, more than double his previous estimate for post-presidential office space. The figure soon inflated to more than $800,000, with the possibility that preparation costs could bring the figure to $830,000.[4] Even the lower amount was nearly triple what American taxpayers have shelled out for any former president. Ronald Reagan's now vacated office space in Los Angeles, the next most expensive, had cost $285,000.

Clinton spokesman Jake Siewert came up with a Clintonesque denial, saying that the rent for Clinton's palatial digs would not be $800,000, but a mere $789,000. (Depends upon the meaning of $800,000, of course.) But $789,000 is close enough, as they say, for government work. Representative Ernest Istook of Oklahoma said he had seen the figures, and the rent was $811,000 per year. Even at a lower figure, he saw the rent as excessive. "If you're still asking taxpayers to pay half a million a year...it's exorbitant." He urged the public "to look at the specifics of this lease."[5]

New York Democrats fired back, and, according to some, Clinton loyalists even planned a "war room" media operation to defend their former boss. But before the Clinton partisans had taken to their battle stations, Clinton showed that he still had the ability to dodge and weave and seek out a path of least resistance. First he tried, without considering a host of legal complications, to suggest that his Library Foundation would pay $300,000 per year toward the rent. When that did not fly, he came up with a public relations stroke of genius—or hypocrisy—depending on your point of view.

"I want to go to Harlem," Clinton told his chief of staff Karen Tramontano.[6]

On February 12, 2001, Bill Clinton announced that he was dropping his bid for the 56th floor of the Carnegie Hall Tower and would instead set up his postpresidency shop in the capital of black America. Tramontano called Harlem representative Charles Rangel, one of Clinton's steadfast defenders, to facilitate the move.

The site in question was the top floor, the fourteenth, at 55 West 125th Street. The building had been recently renovated and also housed a navy recruiting site, Harlem Legal Services for battered women, and an office of the Internal Revenue Service, an agency that had developed an appetite for auditing opponents of President Clinton during the nineties. Rent was expected to be in the range of $300,000, still higher than the next most expensive ex-president's office. Clinton wanted to tamp down the controversy but not to the extent of spending less of the taxpayers' money than any of his fellow ex-presidents.

The building featured a private shower and views of Central Park and the Triborough Bridge. Clinton showed up to visit in an SUV, accompanied by a convoy packed with postpresidential security. Crowds spilled into the streets.

"I love it," he said. "I feel at home here. This *is* home."[7]

That was true in one sense. African-Americans were by far Clinton's most loyal supporters. His occasional golfing foray at racially restricted country clubs had done little to discourage that following, cultivated so carefully at black churches and ostentatious soulful meditations with the Reverend Jesse Jackson.

Karen Tumulty of *Time* magazine noted the irony that the inspiration to make the Harlem move came to Clinton while he was playing golf at a Florida country club that has been accused of discriminating against blacks and Jews. But it was "a ploy so transparent it actually worked, bringing happy headlines to the tabloids and a cheering crowd onto Malcolm X Boulevard."[8] The move not only quashed criticism over the original choice of Carnegie Hall Tower. It revived a bizarre canard that had started midway through Bill Clinton's second term, that William Jefferson Clinton was the nation's first "black" president.

Novelist and Nobel laureate Toni Morrison came up with the "first black president" concept because, in her view, Clinton displayed "almost every trope of blackness." These included being raised in a single-parent household, poverty, playing the saxophone, and liking junk food, especially from McDonald's. There was more— some not so flattering to the group Clinton was being anointed to represent. The president was being persecuted, Morrison continued, for his "unpoliced sexuality," and he was "metaphorically seized and body-searched." All this—dysfunction, victimhood, irresponsibility, sexuality—gave Bill Clinton genuine blackness, she proposed.

In the *Village Voice*, Tom Carson quipped that perhaps "that's what got Monica hot: the whole Mandingo thing."[9] But it ultimately was no laughing matter. Toni Morrison's regurgitation of some of the worst stereotypes of blacks had to rankle individuals who had worked hard throughout their lives to rise above the concept that their race was their identity and that their identity had to be seen through, and only through, that prism—people such as Condoleezza Rice, Colin Powell, Clarence Thomas, Walter Williams, and Thomas Sowell. Conservative blacks perhaps considered it beneath a response while liberal blacks who knew better held their fire because Clinton had been such a dependable political ally.

But when the "black" Clinton emerged to barnstorm Harlem, it was too much for Jabari Asim, the liberal editor of the *Washington Post Book World* and author of *Not Guilty: Twelve Black Men on Life, Law, and Justice*. "It is time to put this putrid idea to rest, bury it deep in the compost pile where it belongs," Asim wrote. "Let me make this perfectly clear: Clinton is not black. He does not 'talk' black, whatever on earth that means. He does not 'walk' black either. I'm sure I'm not the only black man in America who finds such woefully distorted logic insulting and distasteful. Surely others can't help but see the painful irony of Clinton being celebrated as a hero in a legendary community where giants once walked the streets. Harlem helped nurture the talents of men like W. E. B. DuBois, Paul Robeson, Langston Hughes and James Weldon Johnson, and when we carelessly tolerate the connection of Bill Clinton to their storied legacy we sully the names of immortals."

Asim speculated that although Clinton had perhaps once been mistaken for a shoplifter, mugger, drug courier, or carjacker, "one thing he certainly has not done is pursue his livelihood as most

African-American men have done, with grace, dedication and integrity, far beyond the spotlight." In conclusion: "Mr. President, I've worked with black men. I've known black men. Some black men have been friends of mine. And you, sir, are no black man."[10]

Asim's stinging denunciation of the silly and insulting mantle that Clinton had wrapped around himself should have exposed Clinton's gambit for what it was. Like the young child pointing out to a mesmerized public that the emperor was parading through the street without clothing. In fact, Bill Clinton had promoted an even worse variation, that authentic blackness is political—the creed that if you are black, you must be a liberal and you must embrace certain political shibboleths, such as racial discrimination disguised as "affirmative action," the tyranny of the public school system for young black students, and tolerance for the ravages of black-against-black inner city crime.

In this worldview, liberal-left politics, above all uncritical support for the welfare state and lowered standards, constitutes authentic blackness. Support for personal responsibility, limited government, and free markets are denounced as heresy, Uncle Tomism, and racism. Liberals such as Lani Guinier and Vernon Jordan are thus more authentically black, in this distorted view, than Clarence Thomas and Thomas Sowell.

That concept of political blackness, like Toni Morrison's, will outlast the two terms of Bill Clinton. But both definitions of blackness are rooted in stereotypes. It is unfortunate that President Clinton would perpetuate the damage they do by embracing both. By parity of "reasoning," one might also claim, insultingly, that Clinton was the first woman president, based upon his "I feel your pain" style, blatant emotional displays, lip biting, tears, excessive displays of contrived empathy, and so forth. But, how demeaning to women!

In his office move to Harlem episode, Bill Clinton once again displayed his insatiable need for approval and his capacity for self-glorification. He also manifested his infinite capacity to believe his own propaganda and public relations spin, and to do so against all common sense.

After a postpresidency appearance early in 2000 to raise money for earthquake victims in India with rapper M. C. Hammer ("U Can't Touch This") in San Jose, Clinton headed south to Los Angeles where he appeared at the NAACP Image Awards in Universal City to receive an award, presented by NAACP boss and former Democratic representative Kweisi Mfume.

"What really matters is our common humanity," Clinton said. "When we forget it, we suffer. When we remember it, we prosper." Seated beside the former president was comedian Chris Tucker, who joked that many think of him as the first African-American president. "That's why I went to Harlem," responded Clinton. "Because I think I am the first black president."[11]

The quip, evidently made with a straight face, not only displayed the president's usual cognitive dissonance, but it also replicated the classic Clinton modus operandi of brazenly tailoring his remarks precisely for the specific audience at hand. This was situational rhetoric at its very finest, with the former president at his opportunistic pinnacle.

No one has bothered to raise the point that former Atlanta mayor Maynard Jackson, an African-American, had sought to become leader of the Democratic National Committee, only to be brushed aside in favor of Clinton's choice, Terry McAuliffe, who had raised money for both Hillary and Bill Clinton and their $150-million presidential library, and offered more than $1 million in securities as collateral for the Clintons' house in New York.

"When Clinton vacated the Oval Office, he basically left as his forwarding address the Democratic National Committee," wrote Karen Tumulty in *Time*. "In his final weeks as president, he helped arrange for his good friend and chief fundraiser Terry McAuliffe to take over as party chairman; perhaps he wanted the vehicle to be well oiled and shiny should someone else in the family decide to take it out for a spin."[12]

Movers and Takers | 6

Craving Luxury

Contrary to the Lincolnesque myths created by their Hollywood friends, neither Hillary Rodham nor Bill Clinton rose from log cabins or poor circumstances to become America's most luminous couple. Both came from solidly middle-class families of sufficient means to enable them to attend privileged—and expensive—private educational institutions such as Wellesley, Georgetown, and Yale. Try sending your children to these places without ample resources, very good connections, or both. While in college, Hillary bestowed special favors on well-to-do friends and yearned for a yellow Jaguar XKE sports car, the quintessential badge of the materialistic lifestyle she and many of her generation were contemporaneously purporting to repudiate.[1]

Both Clintons are lawyers, a profession whose members are generally able to buy food, clothing, shelter, and comfort for themselves. Hillary is a veteran of what was once the leading law firm in

Arkansas. Overcoming the handicap of being married to the state's governor, source of all manner of legal business, Hillary was made a partner, earning more than $100,000 per annum, plus additional income from serving on various boards and corporate directorships. This is a very decent living, especially in a low-income state like Arkansas—and especially with a taxpayer-provided home, meals, child care, and other benefits.

None of this prevented Hillary from combining rhetoric about the poor with a taste for personal indulgence. In 1989, Hillary spent $10,000 on a new wardrobe, including $2,400 for one cashmere jacket.[2] And in 1991 her income shot up into the $200,000 range, a handsome figure anywhere in the country.

"Hillary craved luxury," says Dick Morris, the Clintons' former strategist. "From the first days of Bill's career (when she made a cool $100,000 from insider trading in cattle futures) to her Whitewater investment and her profiting from state business at the Rose Law Firm, she chafed at the constraints of politics."

In an early sign of things to come, Morris recalls that in 1985 she proposed building a swimming pool at the Governor's Mansion. How to pay for it? Gifts from friends, of course. "Why should my daughter not have a pool just because my husband is governor?" Hillary asked as if her husband's position was some form of unwanted curse. Morris cautioned that the pool might be perceived as a luxury, misunderstood by poorer people, and a blow to the Clinton image in the minds of the voters. Morris warned, "Next time you fly into Little Rock, count how many pools you see."[3] Hillary solved that problem. The pool project was deferred until after the election.

The Clintons are members of the mandarin class—public officials, accustomed to influence, respect, and privilege. People listen to them. People flatter them. And people do things for them, like feeding them, paying their bills, and giving them gifts. The Clintons may not even realize how much they have come to regard as an entitlement public financing and ubiquitous sycophancy. They can thus disparage the wealthy and rail against the "decade of greed" without any sense of shame at never really having had to pay bills, meet a mortgage, or fix a roof. The perquisites and comforts of eight years in the White House further insulated them from the harsher economic realities of life. Bill and Hillary gave every indication of believing that this form of life was their due: they were doing good things; therefore, they ought to be treated well—very well.

For more than twenty years the Clintons have enjoyed the very best in food, entertainment, housing, child care, housecleaning, transportation, security, and staff, virtually all of it at the expense of others: ordinary taxpaying Americans. In eight years, you can become used to a staff of 450, a personal Boeing 747, the right to have several blocks of city streets cleared of parked cars to accommodate your choice of restaurants or a place to jog.

Gradually, the sense of nobility became a part of their political persona. "Slowly we learned that maintaining a slightly regal aura in office is as effective as the populist touch during a campaign," explained White House adviser George Stephanopoulos. "Americans want their president to be bigger than life."[4] As Maureen Dowd of the *New York Times* put it, Hillary Rodham Clinton is "a populist with a sweet tooth for the perquisites of arriviste life."[5]

Hillary was not in a mood to walk away from her cherished lifestyle simply because the Twenty-second Amendment forced her husband from office on January 20, 2001. She took the trouble to register with luxury retailers, as though she were about to become an impoverished new bride. This sent clear signals to donors as to the kinds of items they needed to buy if they expected to stay in Hillary's good graces. No first lady had ever been quite so crass. To put it in economic terms, the supply side was strong but so was the demand. John Podesta, Clinton's chief of staff, conceded to Tim

Russert on *Meet the Press* that friends of Mrs. Clinton solicited others, saying, "Would you please buy this silverware, these gifts for Mrs. Clinton for her new houses?"[6]

The supply side was particularly robust among Hollywood's A-list Democrats, the Clintons' most reliable supporters, who have never understood why the first couple's occasional lying, cheating, and obstruction of justice should be a matter of concern to the voting public, the press, or ordinary folks. One wonders, of course, what these wealthy people really think of the Clintons, who always seem to have their hands out—like a needy and unwelcome nephew. But if they harbor such sentiments, they did not show them.

The China Syndrome

"We're putting together a little gift for Hillary," said one Hollywood political activist in a phone call to Steven Spielberg. "We're in," responded the director of, among many films, *Schindler's List, Jaws,* and *Close Encounters of the Third Kind.* Mr. Spielberg had experienced a close encounter with Hillary Rodham Clinton, who sat with the blockbuster director when he was awarded an honorary knighthood at the British Embassy in Washington.[7]

Spielberg and his wife, Kate Capshaw, gave china to the Clintons worth $4,920, a "little" gift by Hollywood standards. Had Mary Steenburgen and Ted Danson of Los Angeles compared notes with entertainer Spielberg, they might have added a butter plate or something to their own gift. Their china was worth only $4,787. Seems a shame to underbid the Spielbergs for a lousy $133. Actor Jack Nicholson contributed a golf driver worth $350. Sylvester Stallone gave a $300 pair of boxing gloves. It was not known if the actor was trying to evoke his series of *Rocky* movies or to send the Clintons a message.

Two of the most eager benefactors were Ron and Beth Dozoretz. The daughter of a Worcester dentist, Beth was earning a six-figure salary at age thirty-one as president of Clyde's Sportswear, a women's clothier. In 1989, after three divorces, she married Ronald Dozoretz, a former navy psychiatrist, a former Reaganite, erstwhile senatorial candidate, and vice chairman of the Virginia Democratic Party. Ronald Dozoretz also oversees FHC Health Systems, Inc., a billion-dollar mental-health-care business. He took Beth to the 1992 Democratic National Convention in New York, where Beth had something akin to a seizure on beholding the spectacle of Hillary Rodham Clinton, followed by another when she heard the words of Bill.

"All of a sudden this beautiful woman comes walking by, and it was Hillary. Almost involuntarily, I jumped out of my seat and yelled, 'You're fabulous!'" Hillary thanked her. "Then Bill gave his speech and I'm jumping out of my chair."[8]

The couple moved to Washington, where they bought the home of Senator John Warner for $2 million, but, before moving in, found and purchased a preferable mansion for $4 million that had belonged to Michael and Arianna Huffington. Soon the couple became part of the Clintons' inner circle, spending nights at the White House, golfing, partying, and joining the Clintons at Camp David and Martha's Vineyard.

The Dozoretzes named Bill Clinton the godfather of their daughter, Melanne Rose. After the ceremony, Rabbi Jeffrey Wohlberg remarked, "I don't know whether in the back of their minds is the idea that, God forbid, anything happens to them, he [Clinton] would take over the moral education of the child."[9] Godparents are expected to do different things these days. Character building is not necessarily part of the plan.

Beth Dozoretz served as the chief fundraiser for the Democratic National Committee in 1999. She hosted a fundraiser at her Washington mansion that raised $1 million. In May of 2000, Dozoretz herself pledged to raise $1 million for the Clinton Library. The Democratic power couple of Washington, D.C., gave as their contribution to the Clinton welcome wagon, a dining table, server, and golf club worth a total of $7,000.

Songwriter Denise Rich of New York City, the ex-wife of the famed tax cheat and fugitive Marc Rich, gave two coffee tables and two chairs worth $7,375. Ms. Rich explained later to *Vanity Fair*, "*Everybody* gave furniture. There was a list going around from the decorator."[10] As Margaret Carlson of *Time* magazine observed, the Rich gifts raised the question of a quid pro quo, since Bill Clinton bestowed upon her ex-husband a presidential pardon that was utterly without rational justification.

The rest of the gifts somehow suggested a care package for a couple who already had too much. Highlights include:

- Ely Callaway, Carlsbad, California, $499, golf driver
- Iris Cantor, New York, $4,992, china
- Robin Carnahan and Nina Ganci, St. Louis, Missouri $340, two sweaters
- Glen Eden Carpets, Calhoun, Georgia, $6,282, two carpets
- Dale Chihuly, Seattle, $22,000, glass sculpture
- Colette D'Etremont, New Brunswick, Canada, $300, flatware
- Dennis Doucette, Coral Gables, Florida, $310, golf bag, clothing, book
- Martin Patrick Evans, Chicago, $5,000, rug
- Lee Flicks, Cincinnati, $3,650, kitchen table and four chairs
- Lynn Forester, New York City, $1,353, cashmere sweater
- Paul Goldenberg, La Habra, California, $2,993, television and DVD player
- Barbara Allen, Belfast, Northern Ireland, $650, a watercolor of the Clinton ancestral homestead (one can only

imagine how much this piece of art would fetch on the open market)

➤ Georgetown Alumni, class of 1968, $38,000, Dale Chihuly basket set

➤ Arthur Athis, Los Angeles, $2,400, dining chairs

➤ Dendez Badarch, Ulan Bator, Mongolia, $1,300, drawings of Mongolian landscapes

➤ Robert Berks, Orient, New York, $2,500, bust of Harry Truman

➤ Bruce Bernson, Santa Barbara, California, $300, golf putter

➤ Mr. and Mrs. Bill Brandt, Winnetka, Illinois, $5,000, china

➤ Ken Burns, Walpole, New Hampshire, $800, photograph of Duke Ellington

➤ Myra Greenspun, Green Valley, Nevada, $1,588, flatware

➤ Vinad Gupta, Omaha, $450, leather jacket

➤ Richard C. Helmstetter, Carlsbad, California, $525, golf driver and balls

➤ Hal Hunnicutt, Conway, Arkansas, $360, golf irons

➤ Ghada Irani, Los Angeles, California, $4,944, flatware

➤ Jill and Ken Iscol, Pound Ridge, New York, $2,110, china and jacket

➤ Mr. and Mrs. Walter Kaye, New York City, $9,683, cigar travel humidor, china cabinet, and copy of President Lincoln's Cooper Union speech

➤ David Kilgarriff, North Yorkshire, England, $300, golf driver

➤ Steve Leutkehans, Morton Grove, Illinois, $650 golf driver

➤ David Martinous, Little Rock, Arkansas, $1,000, needlepoint rug

➤ Steve Mittman, New York, $19,900, two sofas, easy chair, and ottoman

➤ Katsuhiro Miura, Japan, $500, golf driver

➤ Jan Munro, Sarasota, Florida, $650, painting of New York City

➤ Brad Noe, High Point, North Carolina, $2,843, sofa

➤ Margaret O'Leary, San Francisco, $595 pantsuit and sweater

➤ Mr. and Mrs. Joe Panko, Concord, North Carolina, $300, three putters

➤ Mr. and Mrs. Paolo Papini, Florence, Italy, $425, Italian leather box

➤ Mr. and Mrs. Morris Pynoos, Beverly Hills, California, $5,767, cashmere shawl and flatware

➤ Brian Ready, Chappaqua, New York, $300, painting of Buddy, the Clinton's dog

➤ David Rowland, Springfield, Illinois, $500, check signed by President Harry Truman in 1934 (no word yet on whether Hillary has cashed the check)

➤ Stuart Shiller, Hialeah, Florida, $1,170 lamps

➤ Mr. and Mrs. Vo Viet Thanh, Ho Chi Minh City Vietnam, $350, framed tapestry

➤ Joan Tumpson, Miami, Florida, $3,000, painting

➤ Edith Wasserman, Beverly Hills, California, $4,967, flatware

➤ Mr. and Mrs. Allen Whiting, West Tisbury, Massachusetts, $300, painting "Oyster Pond"

➤ James Lee Witt, Alexandria, Virginia, $450, cowboy boots

➤ Mr. and Mrs. Bud Yorkin, Los Angeles, $500, antique book on President Washington

It is not hard to figure out from this catalogue who was preparing the Christmas list for Santa Claus. Mrs. Clinton pulled in over

$50,000 worth of china and flatware. Not much in that for the family member whose culinary taste runs to burgers and pizza. But only about $4,000 worth of golf stuff. One must presume that Bill was lining up for other forms of gifts. Hard to put a precise value on the favors he is known to seek.

And what in the world could Mr. and Mrs. Kaye have been thinking? The Kayes had done enough damage, getting Monica Lewinsky the job as a White House intern. And how could Mr. Kaye possibly have sent a travel cigar humidor to the new Clinton household? What kind of a sense of humor does Mr. Kaye have? Surely that little item was not on Hillary's department store registration.

The spectacle of a woman, who had just received an $8 million advance for a book she hadn't yet written and who was about to become a United States senator, soliciting china, furniture, pant suits, and cashmere sweaters, as if she were about to go on missionary duty in Africa, was too much for the public to take. And all the gifts had to be wrapped up, so to speak, before January 3, when Senate gift rules would have limited her to $100 per year, per donor. Tough to get china for that price even at Costco Warehouse prices.

And the former president stood to make about $100,000 per speech once freed from his White House duties. The public seemed to think that maybe, at that rate, he could swing, as they say, for his own golf clubs.

The Clintons finally announced that they would pay for half the gifts. No one explained exactly how that compromise was arrived at. Nevertheless, in the eyes of many, the Clintons had debased themselves for gifts that they could easily have afforded.

Michael Tomasky of *New York Magazine* had traveled with Hillary for months and written *Hillary's Turn: Inside Her Improbable, Victorious Senate Campaign*. He was not surprised by the gifts. "I watched her go from a lousy politician to a pretty good one," Tomasky said. "But then she went back to her old habits. If I got an $8 million advance, I'd buy my own dishes."[11] Pant suits, too, one would think.

As for old habits, friends and foes alike had probably forgotten that Hillary had once claimed a tax deduction for contributing her husband's and daughter's used underwear to what must have been a truly desperate charity. Even Leona Helmsley never thought of that. The spectacle of the first couple trolling for things they could easily afford, in the wake of an $8 million advance and assured huge speaking fees for the former president, left even typically fawning journalists such as Margaret Carlson wondering about the quid pro quo angle. "There may be no connection between the disgraceful pardon Clinton gave Marc Rich and the coffee table Denise Rich gave the Clintons," Carlson wrote. "But I'd never be comfortable putting my feet up on it."[12] (Mrs. Carlson thus in one breath inadvertently revealed something about her own modest ethical standards and her manners.)

The term-ending gift frenzy sparked some observers familiar with the Clintons' habits to look into the possibility that other gifts had not been disclosed. The first couple is required to file an annual disclosure form, listing all gifts. These papers disclose many items for Bill Clinton, such as, in 1995, two saxophones worth a total of $4,500, nearly $3,000 worth of golf clubs, a $900 gavel made of wood from the USS *Constitution*, a watch worth $375, and even a $350 cartoon from Hollywood mogul Steven Spielberg.

In 1997, the president disclosed, among other gifts, $360 for four ties and golf attire worth $625. Walter Kaye, Monica Lewinsky's benefactor, gave Chelsea $1,027 of stock in the Coca-Cola company. (Mr. Kaye should have limited his gifts to stocks.) Buddy, the Clinton's Labrador retriever, even got $750.

Neither year, curiously enough, listed anything for Hillary Clinton. How could this be? It seems unlikely that Hillary suddenly became a gift magnet in 2000. But then, perhaps she just doesn't like disclosure forms.

On a state visit the king of Morocco gave Hillary five dresses, including a gold lace dress she was seen wearing. None of the dresses appear on the disclosure forms. Neither does a selection of handbags from designer Judith Lieber, including one with a beaded image of the Clintons' cat, Socks, and another with a beaded rose. The bags were worth more than $10,000.

Other items missing from disclosure include gifts Hillary and Chelsea received on a trip to India and an eagle pin courtesy of Phyllis George Brown.[13]

Hillary lashed out at the reports of these undisclosed gifts, calling them "false," and lamenting that nobody had bothered to call her about the story. A Clinton spokesman explained that she received one of the Lieber bags before arriving at the White House. The gold lace dress worn during the royal visit was given to the National Archives, she said, and the other four were returned to the Moroccan Embassy. "I can only say that all the gifts were appropriately dealt with, and if you have specific questions about any of them, my staff can give you all the details," said Hillary.[14]

Hillary's staff, we came to learn during eight White House years, are not known for being either forthcoming or particularly truthful. They are known for their loyalty to Mrs. Clinton. Absent such loyalty, as I showed in my earlier book, there would be "hell to pay." Those pesky questions about the gifts, their size, their source, and the timing went unanswered.

But the landslide of personal gifts was far from the only curiosity of the Clinton's final days as first couple. Other first families had received gifts upon leaving the White House. But there was no precedent for taking the contents of the White House with them.

Looting the White House

While still in office, Bill and Hillary shipped seventy museum pieces, donated to the White House by prominent American artists, to the Clinton Presidential Library in Little Rock. The items were part of a White House Americans Craft Collection and featured a Dale Chihuly glass piece. The National Archives confirmed that the art pieces had been shipped to an Arkansas warehouse, and White House curator Betty Monkman said the decision to move them was made by "Mrs. Clinton herself."[15]

In January 2000, the Clintons began shipping furniture to their $1.7 million Chappaqua home, despite concerns raised by White House chief usher Gary Walters about whether they were entitled to remove the items. Walters rightly believed they were government property, donated as part of a $396,000 White House redecoration project in 1993.

The Clintons' interior decorator, Kaki Hockersmith, had been soliciting gifts for that project even before the 1993 inauguration, assuring donors that the furnishings were for the executive mansion rather than the Clintons personally. Hockersmith also told the late White House counsel Vincent Foster (found shot in Fort Marcy Park in July of that year) that the furnishings she was soliciting for the redecoration project were meant for the White House collection, not the Clintons personally. Foster sent a March 24, 1993, memo requiring that the gifts be accepted with formal acknowledgments, thereby making them government property.

As January 20, 2001, approached, the Clintons had two big houses to furnish, neither of which was—for once—the taxpayers' responsibility. This was a new experience for the Clintons. It had been a long time since they had had to buy chairs and sofas. Hillary solved the problem—as usual—by having her subordinates deal with recalcitrant White House employees charged with following the rules. Eric Hothem, an aide to Hillary Clinton, told chief White House usher Gary Walters that the items were "the Clintons' personal property." That was the same line White House associate counsel Meredith Cabe used, asserting that each item was given a special finish "to match the design decor selected by the Clintons for individual rooms in their personal space in the Residence."

Not being a lawyer, Walters felt intimidated by Ms. Cabe but later regretted not standing up to the pressure. "I shoulder the blame for not saying, 'Hey, wait a minute.'"[16]

The Clintons reportedly returned "the four items," along with a vague reference to "other furnishings" returned which had been designated official White House property by the National Park Service.[17] In one report, the Clintons returned "a truckload of couches, lamps and other furnishings taken from the White House."[18] Unfortunately, no one knows for sure how much the Clintons got away with. That information has been withheld despite numerous attempts for disclosure. All everyone knows is that they tried.

Some saw entertainment value in the attempt to loot the White House. An e-mail circulated showing Hillary opening a dark overcoat to reveal a collection of pilfered silverware. In Woody Allen's movie *Sleeper,* a man cryogenically frozen wakes up far in the future to find that all records have been wiped out. He is shown a photo of Richard Nixon and answers that when Nixon left the White House, the Secret Service would count the silverware. But that was just a movie.

"I can only say that all the gifts were appropriately dealt with," Hillary explained to reporters, "and we followed the same procedures that all presidents have followed."[19] Morally anesthetized Clinton explainers, such as John Podesta, shrugged off the episode as trivial, a last gasp from the Clinton haters and scandalmongers. But the attempt to plunder the White House caused consternation among Clinton observers of all types. Some wondered why during the past eight years so few had been willing to say, "Wait a minute, this is wrong."

Remarked conservative columnist George Will, "I love liberals! They put up with this guy through perjury, suborning perjury, obstruction of justice, use of the military to cloud discussion of his problems. He steals the toaster and they say, 'That's it. We've had it with this guy.'"[20]

Few observers noticed yet another self-administered Clinton gift: the farewell party. The final day in office was a work day for both Clintons. Hillary had Senate work from her three new committee assignments, and the president had scores of last-minute pardons to sign. They then greeted George and Laura Bush at the White House for coffee and a ride with them to the swearing in at the Capitol. Then the Clintons departed the White House together. To do otherwise might have sent the wrong signal.

"It's a powerful symbol for them to leave together as a united front," said Columbia University political science professor Esther Fuchs. "It says to all these people who tried to destroy them that they're still standing. They came together; they're leaving together."[21] The Clintons boarded a Marine helicopter on the White House lawn and waved goodbye to staff and the waiting bank of television cameras. After an agonizingly endless televised orgy of goodbyes at Andrews Air Force Base, they flew to John F. Kennedy Airport in New York.

There, at TWA Hangar No. 12, three thousand people greeted the Clintons. A high-school marching band performed and a big-screen television beamed the now-former president's image to those on the periphery. Speakers blared the proceedings.

Such events do not happen spontaneously, nor without considerable cost. Who had sprung for this one? Even those who had flown to New York with the Clintons had no idea. When Jim McTague of *Barron's* decided to look into it, he found that the New York State Democratic Party hadn't paid, nor had any of the national Democratic organizations. Both TWA and the New Jersey Port Authority, which runs the airport, told him to ask Bill Clinton.

Clinton spokeswoman Julia Payne, hired after working on the failed presidential campaign of Al Gore, explained that "friends" of Bill Clinton had paid for it. When McTague asked if the friend had been Denise Rich, he was told flatly, "You have no need to know."

Hillary and her office did not return calls from reporters.[22]

"Stroke of the Pen, Law of the Land" | 7

Executive Power

Article II of the Constitution vests all "executive power" in the president and obliges him to "take care that the laws be faithfully executed." The Supreme Court has held that the "take care" clause not only directs the president to enforce the laws that Congress has passed, it authorizes him to use his inherent constitutional authority with respect to any "rights, duties, and obligations growing out the Constitution itself... and all the protections[s] implied by the nature of government under the Constitution."[1]

This broad grant of constitutional discretion has been invoked by presidents to justify the issuance of executive orders implementing laws or general presidential authority. The power was used sparingly by presidents until the twentieth century. For example, our first five presidents—Washington, John Adams, Jefferson, Madison, and Monroe—issued only an aggregate of fifteen executive orders.[2] The practice soared during Franklin Delano Roosevelt's administration when a staggering 3,522 executive orders were issued.[3] President Reagan issued 409 in eight years; President Bush 165 in four years.[4]

What is interesting about William Jefferson Clinton's use of executive orders to make law is not the number of executive orders, but their content, objectives, and timing—and the employment by President Clinton of executive orders to reverse or repeal orders issued by prior presidents.

One of Ronald Reagan's very first executive orders, EO 12291, required cost-benefit analyses for new government regulations. Clinton repealed it. Reagan's EO 12612 urged bureaucrats to exercise restraint in taking action that would result in federal preemption of state laws. This, too, was revoked by Clinton, as was EO 12606, concerning laws or regulations interfering with the traditional family. A Clinton EO also struck down a 1988 Reagan presidential order stressing the constitutional guarantee against uncompensated taking of private property. Another struck down a 1991 Bush EO about unclear rules that led to costly and unnecessary lawsuits.

One of Bill Clinton's first EOs, 12836, dealt with union-only federal contracts and union dues, a preemptive strike at *Communication Workers v. Beck*, a U.S. Supreme Court ruling that limited the unions' ability to confiscate the money of workers for political purposes. That form of forced worker contribution to Democrats, particularly Bill Clinton, is a blatant intrusion on the political rights of union members in favor of union bosses. A Clinton executive order also changed federal policy on the use of replacement workers for strikers, a bid to end a practice allowed by the courts.

Within days of being sworn in as president, Clinton also issued an order about homosexuals in the military, changing existing policy to what became "don't ask, don't tell." That order responded to pressure from Clinton's homosexual supporters, who had raised $3.5 million for him. In the words of Clinton's openly homosexual adviser David Mixner, "Clinton became the Abraham Lincoln of our movement."[5]

Bill Clinton's feminist cheerleaders and the abortion lobby had to wait only two days into the Clinton presidency before a memorandum was issued allowing abortions on U.S. military bases overseas, another reversal of Reagan and Bush policy.

The 1995 *Adarand v. Pena* case was a landmark Supreme Court ruling against government racial preferences and quotas. Prior to *Adarand*, the government sponsored in one form or another more than 160 racial preference programs allocating some $10 billion through overt racial spoils systems. Those submitting the lowest bid, for example, would not get certain jobs or contracts unless they or their companies fit certain racial or ethnic profiles. Bill Clinton responded to the *Adarand* decision with a slogan he must have borrowed from the Reverend Jesse Jackson. He said he wanted to "mend not end" these discriminatory programs, benignly labeled "affirmative action," and used an executive order to continue the profiling.

"Stroke of the pen, law of the land. Kind of cool," said Clinton strategist Paul Begala.[6] No debate, no hearings, no cumbersome votes by elected lawmakers—just an executive edict. Just like the tsars of Russia. Clinton loved the feel of this kind of power, and he continued to warm to the process as his remaining days in office diminished. January 2001, Bill Clinton's last three weeks in office, turned into a gusher of executive orders and presidential decrees.

On January 10, 2001, appropriately enough for one of the final flights of a lame duck, Clinton signed EO 13186, "Responsibilities of Federal Agencies to Protect Migratory Birds." This measure calls for the secretary of the interior to establish an Interagency Council for the Conservation of Migratory Birds. The council will include representation from the departments of Interior, State, Commerce, Agriculture, Transportation, Energy, and Defense, EPA, and other agencies. A peculiar action for a president about to leave office—

creating a brand new bureaucratic entity that would be part of a new president's government. But Bill Clinton was consumed with leaving his mark on the government he was about to leave.

That same day, Clinton signed EO 13187, "The President's Disability Employment Partnership Board," which amended one of his previous EOs that had countermanded one by George H. W. Bush. Boards, commissions, councils, committees, tribunals, and agencies are so plentiful in Washington that no one can even identify them all. This new executive order established yet another, with fifteen members appointed for two years. Above all, Bill Clinton believes in government, and whatever he said about the era of big government being over, he was endlessly creating more and more of it.

On January 12, Clinton signed EO 13188, Extension of the Advisory Committee on Expanding Training Opportunities, another amendment of an earlier order, breathing more life into another dreaded advisory committee. On January 15, he signed EO 13189, creating the "Federal Interagency Task Force on the District of Columbia." He also created the "President's Commission on Educational Resource Equity," EO 13190, yet another new commission with members appointed by the president. Its ostensible purpose was to study resource "gaps," one of the concerns of teacher unions that see education "problems" as excuses to ask for more money.

Two days later came the "Implementation of the African Growth and Opportunity Act" order and the "United States-Caribbean Basin Trade Partnership Act" order and the "Lifting and Modifying Measures With Respect to the Federal Republic of Yugoslavia (Serbia and Montenegro)" order. You may have thought that the president's hand was getting writer's cramp from signing so many executive orders, but he does not suffer from that form of disability. He was just getting started.

On January 18, with two days to go in his presidency, Clinton signed an executive order for "Federal Leadership on Global

Tobacco Control and Prevention." This gives the Department of Health and Human Services (HHS) a larger role in combating the "global epidemic of diseases caused by tobacco use." Also on January 18 came orders entitled "Prohibiting the Importation of Rough Diamonds from Sierra Leone," "Trails for America in the 21st Century," "Final Northwestern Hawaiian Islands Coral Reef Ecosystem Reserve," and "Governmentwide Accountability for Merit System Principles; Workforce Information."

Bill Clinton also found time for an executive order for his own family. Before leaving office he signed an executive order extending Secret Service protection for his daughter, Chelsea, for an additional six months. Thus, when Chelsea went to Aspen on a ski trip in March 2001, she was accompanied by a detail of no fewer than six secret service agents. The agents arrived five days before Chelsea and her friends and checked into condos renting for $300–$500 a night.[7]

"Everybody in America either wants somebody pardoned or a national monument," said Bill Clinton, when his remaining presidency was measured in hours rather than days.[8] This was classic Clinton. Of course there is a latent demand for pardons. Try to find a felon who believes he shouldn't be pardoned. But, as we were to learn, Clinton was so eager to exercise that particular presidential power, he (and his family) actually went into the pardon solicitation business. And, as for monuments, no one was more anxious for a monument than Clinton, and he continued to find ways to create literal monuments to his own excessive exercise of presidential power.

Monument Mania

In May 1997, Clinton presided at the opening of the new memorial to Franklin Delano Roosevelt at the border of the Tidal Basin in Washington. The memorial shows the New Deal founder and wartime leader seated in a wheelchair, a reality that was studiously hidden from the American people by FDR and his aides. And gone were Roosevelt's omnipresent cigarette and cigarette holder. Wheelchairs are in; cigarettes are out.

Clinton made sure that everyone who visited the FDR memorial would also think of William Jefferson Clinton. The plaque in the information center prominently features the name WILLIAM J. CLINTON etched just below that of Franklin Delano Roosevelt. Clinton's dedication is above and in larger characters than the names of the FDR Memorial Congressional Committee members, architect Lawrence Halprin, who worked on the project for more than twenty years; private donors; and the citizens of the United States who made it all possible.[9]

When it came to national monuments, however, Clinton's regal style soared into the reaches of pharaonic megalomania. He launched a vast land grab that made a mockery of limited powers that had been granted to the president under the Antiquities Act of 1906. That act requires that the amount of federal land embraced within a national monument consist of "the *smallest* area compatible with the proper care and management of the objects to be protected." Congress did not intend that vast areas be set aside under this act. An example of the intended scale was the Statue of Liberty. But the concept of "smallest" is not in keeping with the Clinton character, appetite, or vision of himself.

The most controversial of his additions to the nation's monuments came with his proclamation on September 18, 1996, when Bill Clinton, with virtually no public warning, congressional consultation, or concern for either due process or the rights of those directly affected, established the Grand Staircase-Escalante National Monument in Utah. At a whopping 1.7 million acres, it was the largest monument outside of Alaska. It was a blatant reelection campaign stunt. Clinton knew that environmentalists in the east would applaud his action. The sparsely populated areas in Utah hurt by his decision were not going to support him anyway.

As he neared his last day as president, Clinton went on a virtual monument binge. On January 11, 2000, he established Grand Canyon-Parashant National Monument consisting of 1,104,000 acres, and Agua Fria, in Arizona, adding another 71,000 acres. On that same day, he also made a national monument out of the entire California coast, all 840 miles from Mexico to Oregon. This coastline already comes under the protection of the state of California, fifteen county governments, and the California Coastal Commission. But Bill Clinton wanted his name associated with the preservation of this glorious area.

Earlier in April 2000, Clinton had established Grand Sequoia Monument in California on 327,769 acres of federal land. In June, he followed with 164,000 acres for the Canyons of the Ancients, in southern Colorado; the 52,000-acre Cascade Siskiyou and 195,000-acre Hanford Reach; and the Ironwood Forest, with 128,917 acres.

On November 9, 2000, two days after the election, Clinton proclaimed the Enlargement of the Craters of the Moon, adding 661,287 acres, along with the 293,000 acres of Vermilion Cliffs.

On January 17, 2001, in the midst of a pardon frenzy, he found the time to create nine more new national monuments: Buck Island Reef, 135 acres; the Carrizo Plain, 204,107 acres; Kasha-Katuwe Tent Rocks, 4,148 acres; Minidoka Internment, 72.75 acres; Pompey's Pillar, 51 acres; the Sonoran Desert, 486,149 acres; the Upper Missouri Breaks, 377,346 acres; the Virgin Islands Coral Reef, 12,708 acres; and finally Governor's Island, a scant 20 acres but which brought the Clinton grand total to an astounding 5,686,767 acres. And, for one last measure, he declared some sixty million acres, about one-third of the national forests, off limits to logging and road building.

It is difficult to assess the impact Clinton's actions will ultimately have. So much of the West is controlled by the federal government that these states have come to resent the immense federal presence and influence exercised from thousands of miles away. There was no effort to balance the interests and economies of the areas most directly concerned. The raw exercise of single-minded authority, without hearings or public notice, did not leave any room or time for careful planning or balanced deliberations. The only certain effect of these actions was an immense personal legacy for Bill Clinton.

Pact Man

President Clinton also exercised his authority in an area where presidents enjoy great personal power. Unfortunately, he not only wanted to put his name on treaties, he seemed to have a lust for bad ones. Clinton signed the 1997 Kyoto Protocol on global warming, ostensibly committing the United States to a draconian program of energy reduction while leaving huge nations such as China and India exempt. He also signed the 1992 Biodiversity Treaty, which threatens American innovations in agriculture and pharmaceuticals.

Then there was the UN Convention on the Rights of the Child, a measure that reads as though drafted by Hillary Clinton and her mentor Marian Wright Edelman of the Children's Defense Fund. In arms control, Clinton signed the 1997 amendments to the ABM Treaty. His administration even claimed the United States was still bound by the Comprehensive Test Ban Treaty, which had been rejected by the Senate in 1999.

In the global reality of today's world, few international organizations can succeed without the participation of the United States. The United Nations, for example, would wither away without American financial support and active involvement. International organizations, even those with American support, unfortunately all too frequently degenerate into forums for denunciations of American interests unless carefully overseen. The United Nations is a prime example, but international organizations and professional diplomats are constantly spawning others.

The International Criminal Court (ICC) was established by the 1998 Rome Statute and designed to deal with "international" offenses such as war crimes, genocide, and crimes against humanity. Bill Clinton initially opposed the ICC, recognizing its many flaws.

It may sound like a noble endeavor, but it is fraught with peril for Americans and American interests. The ICC creates an international bureaucracy, based in the Netherlands, empowered to arrest, prosecute, and punish individuals, whatever their country, accused of international offenses. Constitutional rights that Americans take for granted—the right to a jury trial, protection from double jeopardy, the right to confront accusers, for example, as well as the protection afforded by life-tenured independent American jurists—would not exist as we know them under the ICC.[10] Comparable provisions would be included in some form, on paper at least, but, as we have learned over the course of two hundred years, there are no real freedoms in countries or courts with paper bills of rights, without the American system of separated powers to enforce them.

Critics of the ICC note that some of the twenty-seven governments that have signed the ICC treaty show what a hypocrisy it is. For example, the government of Sudan, an Islamic military dictatorship, continues a savage war against its own Christian citizens, and virtually all black Africans. What will an ICC do that consists of countries such as Sudan?

It is entirely possible that the ICC could impede the activities of the United States military. Could former senator Bob Kerrey, who has acknowledged participating in the killing of women and children in Vietnam, be brought before the ICC?

Unfortunately, Bill Clinton forgot his earlier opposition to the treaty as the deadline for his legacy project approached. On December 31, 2000, he authorized an American representative to sign the ICC's statute, thereby approving American endorsement of the tribunal he previously saw as antithetical to American interests.

The date was significant in that it was the very last day countries could become parties to ICC without having ratified it. Though it would have to be approved and ratified by the Senate, President Clinton's eleventh-hour decision sent the message that the United States was on board, increasing the chances that another international bureaucracy would soon be causing mischief, threatening American sovereignty, and relieving Americans of their rights.

"Many in the Senate are rightfully concerned that under the United Nations–mandated ICC system, the United States military would not be ensured adequate protections," observes Susan Bradford, who serves on the International Law Committee of the Federalist Society. "With hundreds of thousands of military personnel operating in dozens of countries globally, it would appear that it is only a matter of time before Americans are found to violate international law and summoned to appear before the ICC."

Another concern for the U.S. military, says Bradford, "is that it will likely [call for] United Nations personnel to investigate matters pertaining to human rights violations." This could "undermine the legitimacy of military operations by raising questions about the American use of force, particularly with regard to such issues as the proportional use of force, legitimacy of its targets, and civilian casualties."[11] Former senator Kerrey might be well advised to start shopping for a lawyer.

The president takes a special constitutionally prescribed oath to defend the Constitution, which guarantees to American citizens the rights that the ICC would deny to them. President Clinton's sudden reversal on the ICC revealed his unfortunate preference for international bureaucratic arrangements at the expense of American national interests and security. Of course, the president's New Year's Eve action on the ICC will bolster his reputation with the international elite among whom he is much more comfortable than the home-grown variety, and from whom, not so coincidentally, he began to receive valuable speaking engagements and pleasant foreign travel almost from the instant he left office.

Rules and Regulations: Clinton's Contribution to the Federal Register

During the Clinton years, few areas of life remained off limits to the visible and intrusive hand of federal regulation. Clinton rhetoric, as in so many areas, was the reverse of Clinton policy and practice. Clinton talked about reducing the size of government, but he is of, by, and for big government. He once told the American people that he opposed a tax cut because he did not trust citizens to spend their money sensibly. Of course he would create more government, more rules, and more federal standards because he believes that government is wiser than its citizens.

"We say to America's taxpayers, when you deal with the IRS, you also have privileges and we respect them," said Bill Clinton. "You have protection and we will help provide it. You have rights and we will shield them."[12]

Yet in 2000, the Clinton administration proposed the biggest IRS budget increase since the 1980s. Under Margaret Richardson, the IRS became a Clinton attack dog, with underlings letting slip that the conservative victims of audits were special "political" cases. A remarkable number of Clinton opponents found that they were being watched—and investigated.

And the hypocrisy marches on. While the Clinton administration sided with strident advocates of gun control, on Clinton's watch even the Environmental Protection Agency started arming its agents. The administration also politicized the Immigration and Naturalization Service, hurrying in 1996 to legalize 75,000 immigrants with arrest records, thus fattening the voter register with potential Democratic votes.

In its spare time, Clinton's Justice Department sent 139 heavily armed federal agents into a private home without a warrant on April 22, 2000, to make sure that a young child, Elian Gonzalez, whose mother had died trying to flee the tyranny of communist Cuba, was returned to the arms of Fidel Castro.

"There was no alternative but to enforce the decision of the INS and the federal court," said Bill Clinton. But Harvard Law School professor Laurence Tribe, often mentioned as a potential Clinton appointee to the Supreme Court and Al Gore's Supreme Court lawyer during the Florida recount litigation, said that the action struck at the heart of constitutional government.[13]

In these final days, Clinton added hundreds of federal rules on issues ranging from encryption radionuclides, drinking water, mining cleanup, and airport security to the banning of snowmobiles in national parks. The volume was such that three months after he left office, Clinton rules were still awaiting publication in the Federal Register, which his last minute contributions would ultimately enlarge by an estimated 4,000 pages. An analysis of all would require a separate book, but some examples stand out.

Bill Clinton had eagerly adopted a Republican program and proudly proclaimed the end of "welfare as we know it." During his tenure, this legislation helped move large numbers of people from welfare to work. But Clinton turned back the clock with eleventh-hour regulations that undermined those very successes by lowering food-stamp eligibility requirements.

Clinton also initiated changes that facilitated class-action lawsuits launched by groups funded by the Legal Studies Corporation, the government-funded legal service network that nurtured Hillary Clinton on her way to the top. These groups exist to bring lawsuits, often accomplishing nothing but forcing up the costs of goods and services and keeping lawyers fully employed.

Several days before he left office, Bill Clinton imposed a full 608 pages of "ergonomic" rules, aimed at complaints of repetitive motion injuries that saddled business with compliance nightmares. The Small Business Administration estimated that the ergonomics rules would have cost American businesses $60 billion to $100 billion a year. These rules would have opened the door for government inspectors to intrude on those who work at home and telecommute, a group on the increase in the information age. The new rules went far beyond the scope of those proposed by federal safety agencies and discussed with the public. And they had little or no scientific or medical justification. Fortunately, Congress repealed the ergonomic rules soon after President Clinton moved out of the White House.

Clinton's EPA worked feverishly in January 2001 with environmental groups and farm-worker unions to produce new regulations for the first time in sixty years, to require substantially lower quantities of arsenic, a naturally occurring substance, in drinking water. The new rule reduced the standard from 50 parts per billion to 10 parts per billion. There is no scientific consensus about levels of arsenic, and neither the need for nor ultimate cost of the new rule was apparent. This was a clear example of the "ready-fire-aim" approach pursued by Clinton's regulators as they packed their bags to leave office. The only clear need for the rule was the need for the Clintonistas to enact rules.

If implemented, the Clinton rule would have required hundreds of towns to install new filtration systems on wells, doubling or even tripling water rates. Overall costs would run in the billions and, since water systems are almost entirely public, the taxpayers, not "industry," would be stuck with the tab. The incoming Bush administration rejected the measure along with the ergonomic rules.

But the political damage was done. Like a land mine that explodes as it is being removed, the arsenic rule and other Clinton rules had unpleasant political consequences for Bill Clinton's successor. No matter how unnecessary the arsenic rule was, no matter how costly it would be to implement, revocation of the rule put President Bush in the untenable political position of being opposed to reducing the level of arsenic—a poison in the public's mind irrespective of amount—in the water we drink. No amount of explanation could take away the image—or the opportunity for environmentalist demagoguery and cartoonist punditry.

So the rules and monuments left Clinton in a position of doing noble-sounding things, leaving all the unpleasant consequences and costs to play out on his successor's watch, and causing damaging political consequences if his actions—however ill-advised—were repealed.

But Clinton was still not finished. On January 19, with one day to go, Clinton put into effect a rule that strengthened the ability of the federal government to blacklist government contractors based on alleged noncompliance with federal regulations. This rule began with a pledge in 1997 by Al Gore to leaders of the AFL-CIO. When it was formally proposed in July 1999, and again in June 2000, letters opposing the rule exceeded those in favor of it by a margin of nine to one.

The General Services Administration was of the view that the Clinton measure was not needed and that existing rules were more than sufficient to protect the interests of the public and the taxpayers. Under the Clinton rule, a missed paperwork deadline would be sufficient violation for the government to reject a contractor, and firms could lose a contract due to spurious charges by unions.

Randel Johnson, vice president for labor policy at the U.S. Chamber of Commerce, which filed suit against the rule, said that under the Clinton rule, "Government agents would have had virtually unlimited, arbitrary power to decide who could compete for the government's business. . . . We have fought this political payback to the unions every step of the way."[14] "This was midnight-hour, back-room policymaking at its worst," said Representative Thomas M. Davis of Virginia.

Another eleventh-hour rule—launched on January 17, 2001—required thirty percent reductions in the amount of power used by air conditioners, washers, and water heaters. Bill Richardson, Clinton's energy secretary, hailed these measures as the greatest environmental achievement of the Clinton administration. Congress, however, had flatly rejected the measure in 1999 on the grounds that it would involve excessive costs and constitute a "cruel penalty" on consumers, according to the Air Conditioning and Refrigeration Institute.[15]

Another January 17 rule actually altered the definition of who qualifies for the status of human being. The rule, intended to make it easier for pregnant women to participate in scientific studies, describes a child as a "fetus, after delivery, that has been determined to be viable." Thus, instead of regarding an unborn child as a human being, the Clinton rule adopted the feminist language that characterizes a child as a fetus. This will come as a surprise to most people, particularly mothers, accustomed to using the term "baby." This rule is an eleventh-hour edict that is intended to destigmatize partial-birth abortion, a brutal, gruesome practice that even many in the pro-choice ranks oppose. In the Clinton rules, even after birth, a child is still a fetus, with a right to live subject to the whims of someone else.

It is both appropriate and lawful for a new administration to review half-baked rules dumped on an unsuspecting public by an outgoing, soon to be utterly unaccountable, administration. Clinton's last-minute avalanche left the new administration with a huge workload of latent time bombs and land mines. The Bush administration suspended some of the rules and began the process of reviewing others. By early April, the new administration had withdrawn 124 Clinton rules and was taking aim at forty-five others.[16] But, as with the arsenic rule, the political cost of making sensible decisions was in many instances quite severe.

Midnight Appointments

One of the president's most important powers is to appoint judges, executive branch officials, and members of countless boards and commissions. Here again, Bill Clinton went into a feeding frenzy as his presidency slipped away.

Most important governmental positions, including judges, are presidential appointments with the "advice and consent of the Senate." A president may not act unilaterally. However, the Constitution gave presidents the power to fill key positions, if vacant, by himself, during a congressional recess for one session of Congress. Because the Senate jealously guards its confirmation power, "recess" appointments have been used sparingly by presidents. Antagonizing the Senate in this fashion can have unpleasant repercussions. Senators have many ways to retaliate.

But it is hard to retaliate against a president who has left Washington to join the rubber-chicken speechmaking circuit. President Clinton saw an opportunity, and he took it.

On December 27, Clinton used a recess appointment to put Richmond lawyer Roger Gregory on the United States Court of Appeals for the Fourth Circuit. He had previously used a recess appointment to name Bill Lann Lee, a supporter of race and gender quotas, to the leading civil-rights post in the Department of Justice.

In addition to Gregory, Clinton resubmitted to the Senate the names of North Carolina State Court of Appeals judge James A. Wynn, for the Fourth Circuit; Enrique Moreno, a lawyer from El Paso, Texas, for the Fifth Circuit; H. Alston Johnson III, a lawyer from Baton Rouge, Louisiana, for another seat on the Fifth Circuit; and Judge Helene White, who serves on the Michigan State Court of Appeals, for the Sixth Circuit. He also resubmitted the names of Kathleen McCree-Lewis, a Detroit lawyer, for the Sixth Circuit; former Iowa attorney general Bonnie Campbell, for the Eighth Circuit; San Francisco lawyer Barry Goode, for the Ninth Circuit; and James Duffy, a lawyer from Honolulu, for the Ninth Circuit.

These nominations continued the Clinton pattern of appointing activist judges of liberal persuasion, often with dubious qualifications. And they were all being sent to a United States Senate controlled at that time, although barely, by Republicans. It was unlikely that any, aside from Judge Gregory—for complicated political reasons—would be confirmed, but Clinton was making a political statement.

Clinton nominee James Duffy is a former president of the Hawaii Trial Lawyers Association, and trial lawyers were among Clinton's strongest supporters. Barry Goode, nominated to the already very liberal Ninth Circuit, was cofounder of Northern California Lawyers for Clinton-Gore. The other nominees provided a nice gender/ethnic mix of potential liberal jurists—sure to be withdrawn by President Bush or rejected by the Republican Senate. But like the politically motivated rules and regulations, they were win/win propositions. Either the judges were allowed to take office and Clinton would get the credit—or they would be rejected and Democrats could scream about racism and gender discrimination. Who says that presidents should not play politics with judges?

Clinton also took advantage of his remaining days as president to stack various boards and commissions. The Kennedy Center for the Performing Arts is a center of Washington social and cultural life, and the president gets to pick thirty of the center's 130 board members. In January 2001, major contributor Ronald Dozoretz, husband of former Democratic National Committee finance chair Beth Dozoretz, and a *very* good friend of Bill, graciously resigned as a board member of the Kennedy Center shortly before his term was about to expire—which would have occurred after Clinton had left office. President Clinton immediately appointed him to a new six-year term. According to Kennedy Center insiders, the move was unprecedented.

Clinton rewarded Bill Daley—his commerce secretary, Mr. Fix-it from the Chicago Daley political family, and Al Gore campaign manager—by putting him on the Kennedy Center board, and reappointed Jean Kennedy Smith, the former envoy to Ireland, to the board as well. Before he left office, Clinton also appointed to the Kennedy Center board Vinod "Vin" Gupta, the CEO of InfoUSA, who donated $1 million to Clinton's presidential library foundation, slept in the Lincoln Bedroom, and hosted Clinton on a visit to Nebraska. After the appointment, just to satisfy appearances, the Clintons returned a $7,000 treadmill Gupta had given the first family.[17]

Bill Clinton then appointed his inaugural poet Maya Angelou to the board of the United States Holocaust Memorial Museum. In 2000, Angelou had been awarded the National Medal of the Arts, but her appointment to the Holocaust Museum did not sit well with beltway commentators such as Richard Cohen of the *Washington Post*, who noted Angelou's uncritical participation in events staged by Louis Farrakhan of the Nation of Islam. Although Clinton had administered a stern tactical reprimand during his first presidential campaign to Sister Souljah, a rapper who suggested that blacks consider killing whites instead of each other, Clinton never repudiated Farrakhan and his Nation of Islam theology, which puts out papers saying that white people are the result of a failed scientific experiment on the Isle of Patmos by a mad scientist named Yacub.

"She [Angelou] bestowed her name and prestige upon a man whose antisemitism and racism were by then unquestionable, and who referred to the murder of Europe's Jews as 'the so-called Holocaust of the so-called Jew, the imposter Jew,'" said Cohen. "Maya Angelou doesn't belong in its [the Holocaust Museum] board room," Cohen concluded. "She belongs, instead, in the museum's exhibition rooms. She has lots to learn."[18] Curious choice for the Holocaust Museum, but then Clinton claims to be the first black president, not the first Jewish president.

On the party front, Bill Clinton installed the slippery and heavily investigated fundraiser Terry McAuliffe as head of the Democratic National Committee. Also slated for a DNC post was Jake Siewert, Clinton's press secretary. As anyone experienced in Washington politics could readily see, the DNC was to be a wholly owned subsidiary of the Clinton family. And don't you forget it, Mister Gore and Senator Lieberman.

Cumulative Effects

The eleventh-hour appointments, executive orders, monuments, and regulations repeated patterns long evident in the Clintons' presidency, and reflected some of his most unfortunate traits. He showed disdain for the rights of private property owners and vastly expanded federal government control over the economy and environmental policy.

Clinton rules and executive orders expanded an already intrusive and onerous federal regulatory power. They promoted the role of organized unions, who represent approximately 15 percent of the work force but remain key Democratic Party clients. And they reflected blatant disregard for the expense of government and financial burdens on consumers.

The outgoing president's appointments bent the rules and rewarded friends and contributors. The favoritism and partisanship was this time completely undisguised. Wolves in wolves' clothing.

"The principle of government supremacy is Clinton's clearest legacy," wrote libertarian commentator James Bovard. "Clinton did more than any recent president to place the federal government above all laws—above the Constitution—and beyond effective restraint."[19]

Sex, Lies, Audiotape, and DNA | 8

The President's Plea Bargain

Though he wields immense power, the president of the United States is not above the law. Richard Nixon discovered the hard way that the president is not a king and that the rule of law prevails in this nation. So did Bill Clinton.

Robert Ray, Kenneth Starr's successor as independent counsel, a New York prosecutor with a reputation for integrity and fairness, pledged that he would enforce the principle that even the president must obey the law. On his last full day in office, Clinton entered into a plea bargain with Ray to avoid prosecution for his knowingly false testimony under oath. On January 19, 2001, President Clinton finally conceded that he had broken the law.

David Kendall, Clinton's personal lawyer, had been negotiating with Ray for weeks. Ray wanted to settle, but the Arkansas bar wanted to disbar Clinton for false testimony. On December 25,

Kendall, Ray, and Clinton met in the White House Map Room, so named because it bears on the wall a 1945 military map that was there when Franklin Delano Roosevelt left the room for the last time. The Map Room also was the location of scores of Clinton's notorious White House fundraising coffees. If Mr. Ray was served coffee that day, he presumably did not have to pay for it. And Bill Clinton gave no fundraising speech. In fact, he refused even to speak a single word to Ray during the final meeting on January 19 when he signed the plea. Kendall spoke as Bill Clinton sat with a frozen grin on his face.

The Map Room first became famous during the Clinton administration as the venue for Hillary's 1997 session-in-pink, in which she bobbed and weaved her way through 148 Whitewater questions in thirty-six minutes. It was quite a tour de force—performance-wise, that is. She did not, of course, fool everyone. *New York Times* columnist William Safire was prompted to label Hillary a "congenital liar." In any event, she certainly put the Map Room, so to speak, on the map.

Her husband inspired reactions much like Safire's. "Most reporters were convinced that Clinton had an almost congenital inability to tell the unvarnished truth," wrote Howard Kurtz of the *Washington Post*.[1] Then-senator Bob Kerrey of Nebraska, later to become the center of a much discussed Vietnam War experience, pronounced Bill Clinton an "exceptionally good liar." And the *American Spectator* magazine put out a bumper sticker that read, simply, "They're Lying." No one seemed to have any doubt who "they" were.

Notwithstanding questionable testimony, missing billing records, inexplicable coincidences, and other suspicious circumstances that would have brought down less accomplished dissemblers, the Clintons managed to survive Whitewater, Travelgate, and Filegate. Robert Ray closed out all of these investigations and, while not pronouncing Bill and Hillary innocent of criminal wrongdoing, declined to prosecute, allowing them to retain their constitutional presumption of innocence. His Travel Office report, however, indicated that Hillary had made "factually false" statements to a grand jury. Other delicate matters remained, such as Bill Clinton's lies under oath during the Paula Jones/Monica Lewinsky matter. The president did not want to take those troubles with him to private life, and risk a prosecutor without the protection of the mantle of the presidency.

On January 10, David Kendall flew to Little Rock to confront Marie-Bernarde Miller, who had been appointed to prosecute the Arkansas Bar Association case against Clinton. Miller was not about to be pushed around by Clinton's emissary, whom she kept waiting for hours while she and her colleagues hashed out the matter. Then Miller laid down the law to Kendall. To join the plea offer in this case, Bill Clinton had to accept a five-year suspension of his license to practice law in Arkansas and pay legal fees of $25,000. Second, Clinton would have to acknowledge that he knowingly violated a judge's order to tell the truth—a duty the President of the United States and Yale Law School graduate should not have needed a special judicial decree to remember.

When Kendall broke the news, Clinton was furious. For years special prosecutors had made his life miserable. Now, in the last hours of his presidency, they were trying to rub his face in it and spoil his departure, what should have been a happy and historic occasion. White hot with rage, Clinton nonetheless knew that it was an offer he could not refuse. On January 19, he formally accepted Ray's deal and the galling statement that went with it. Clinton had been the second president to be impeached, the first to be hauled before a grand jury, the first to have to give a blood sample for a DNA match, and the first to be held in contempt of court for lying to a federal judge. He just couldn't stand to be disbarred, to be found unworthy of practicing the profession of law, to be singled out for that lawyer's ultimate disgrace—up there with Richard Nixon. So he swallowed this bitterest of pills:

Today I signed a consent order in the lawsuit brought by the Arkansas Committee on Professional Conduct, which brings to an end that proceeding. I have accepted a five-year suspension of my law license, agreed to pay a $25,000 fine to cover counsel fees, and acknowledged a violation of one of the Arkansas model rules of professional conduct, because of testimony in my Paula Jones case deposition. The disbarment suit will now be dismissed.

I have taken every step I can to end this matter. I have already settled the Paula Jones case, even after it was dismissed as being completely without legal and factual merit. I have also paid court and counsel fees in restitution, and been held in civil contempt for my deposition testimony regarding Ms. Lewinsky, which Judge Wright agreed had no bearing on Ms. Jones' case, even though I disagreed with the findings in the judge's order.

I will not seek any legal fees incurred as a result of the Lewinsky investigation, to which I might otherwise become entitled under the Independent Counsel Act. I have had occasion, frequently, to reflect on the Jones case. In this consent order, I acknowledge having knowingly violated Judge Wright's discovery orders in my deposition in that case.

I tried to walk a fine line between acting lawfully and testifying falsely, but I now recognize that I did not fully accomplish this goal, and that certain of my responses to questions about Ms. Lewinsky were false.

I have apologized for my conduct, and I have done my best to atone for it with my family, my administration and the American people. I have paid a high price for it, which

I accept, because it caused so much pain to so many people.
I hope my actions today will help bring closure and finality
to these matters.

According to insiders, Bill Clinton had been involved in shaping "every clause, every word and every comma."[2] His lawyer, David Kendall, tried to put the best spin on it, saying that the president had not actually admitted that he had lied. On the Sunday *Meet the Press* program two days later, Clinton's all-purpose apologist James Carville had the indescribable temerity to say: "Never, ever was there any allegation about the president's testimony before the grand jury; never, ever anything about obstruction of justice."

But take a moment and carefully examine the Clinton admission, using simple English, rather than Clintonspeak, to interpret it. Clinton was charged by Arkansas bar authorities with making false statements of material facts in a federal legal proceeding and engaging in conduct that was dishonest, deceitful, and prejudicial to the administration of justice, and an obstruction of justice. He did not even appeal when a federal court held him in contempt of court and fined him for that conduct. In his plea bargain Bill Clinton acknowledged "knowingly violating" the judge's order to testify truthfully and accepted a five-year suspension of his license to practice law. This is a humiliating disgrace for an ordinary lawyer. It is appalling for one who is the president of the United States and who has taken the nation's highest office along with a solemn oath to "take care" that federal laws are faithfully executed.

But Clinton simply could not be forthright about it with the American people. He stated that he "tried to walk a fine line between acting lawfully and testifying falsely," but that he "did not fully accomplish this goal, and that certain of [his] responses... were false." In other words, with the agile rationalization capabilities and elastic moral code of a Bill Clinton, he *accidentally* testified falsely.

The president earlier had tried to justify his lying because he was "motivated...by a desire to protect himself...from embarrassment." In short, the president's defense was—and remained even after his plea—that, because of a desire to serve his personal interests, he had failed to accomplish his goal of not breaking the law. As a bank robber might fail to accomplish his goal of not sticking up a bank because he wanted the money.

But neither the law nor Arkansas's standards for lawyer conduct are so ingenuous. The Arkansas Supreme Court's disciplinary committee had recommended disbarment because, as the Arkansas Supreme Court had ruled in a 1998 case, "There is simply no place in the law for a man or woman who will not tell the truth even when his interest is involved."[3] So, David Kendall and James Carville to the contrary notwithstanding, the president accepted a five-year suspension of his license to practice law for lying under oath instead of disbarment just as a man who robs a bank will accept a five-year sentence to avoid a longer one. And both plea bargainers know in their hearts that they are guilty.

Bill Clinton glossed over a few other inconvenient facts in his public statement. He did indeed settle the Paula Jones case, which he characterized as without merit. It had been dismissed, but Ms. Jones had appealed—to an appeals court that had repeatedly ruled against Clinton in other aspects of the case. Clinton paid $850,000 to get rid of the case. A rather steep price for a meritless case.

It is true that Bill Clinton did not seek legal fees under the independent counsel law, but he never would have prevailed had he done so. The court that oversees the independent counsel law does not award fees to persons who admit that they have knowingly violated the law.

In short, the Clinton statement, while a shameful admission of guilt for a president of the United States, was also an artful, evasive, and self-pitying defense of his conduct. Bill Clinton had escaped indictment but at quite an expensive and revealing price.

Ray considered the matter closed, and there would be no prosecution for perjury or obstruction of justice. But others were not so willing to drop the subject. Nat Hentoff of the *Village Voice* took Ray to task. "Clinton did commit perjury and obstruction of justice, and Robert Ray has let him off the hook on his testimony before the grand jury," wrote Hentoff, who cited the opinion of Richard Posner, chief judge of the federal Seventh Circuit Court of Appeals, that Clinton had clearly perjured himself in the Paula Jones case. "By clearing Clinton of this more serious act of perjury, Ray failed his own responsibility to make sure that Clinton—as president and chief administrator of the law—was not above the law."

Hentoff added that "for the convenience of George W. Bush, who doesn't have to worry about pardoning Clinton, and to fulfill the desire of many in this country to let all of this ignominy come to closure, Ray has carved an exception into that mantra, 'the rule of law.' So Clinton will escape. An ordinary citizen who obstructed justice—even the CEO of a major company who committed serial perjury—would have to face a trial."[4]

But most people were anxious to move on to a new president, and not many were anxious to live through a criminal trial of Bill Clinton—and potentially another O. J. Simpson verdict. Besides, Clinton was bringing so much disrepute upon himself during his last weeks in office that his Paula Jones testimony was fast becoming just another tawdry Clinton memory.

Third-Rate Romance, High-Rent Rendezvous

In retrospect, it seems utterly predictable that the most humiliating and disgraceful scandal of Bill Clinton's presidency would involve a wanton and juvenile sexual romp. Perhaps no one could have been expected to guess that the president would develop a running, sophomoric, oral sex affair in the Oval Office with a twenty-one-year-old intern who showed up in the West Wing one night wearing a thong and bearing a slab of pizza. That would have been pretty hard to see coming. But Bill Clinton gave his friends and enemies plenty of advance warning that if there were mistakes to be made during his years in the White House, at least some of them would involve women, and words such as "style," elegance," and "class" would not be part of the story.

Of course, Bill Clinton should have known better. By the time Clinton ran for the presidency, his idol, John F. Kennedy, had been exposed as a reckless and apparently uncontrollable satyr with a craving for prostitutes, starlets, and gangsters' molls. JFK had managed to get away with it thanks to an adoring and complicit press, but times had changed—big time.

The youngest Kennedy destroyed his chances to be president because of womanizing. In July 1969, after an evening of booze and women, he drove one of them to her death off a bridge on Chappaquiddick Island in New England.

The incident rocked the nation, the press, the Kennedy family, and a young Bill Clinton. He seemed to see a lesson in Chappaquiddick. "Politics gives guys so much power and such big egos they tend to behave badly toward women," he told his friend Mandy Merck. "And," he added, as if sex were a virus that traveled through the air, "I hope I never get into that."[5] Well, he did get into that. In fact, he was always getting into that. He once remarked that one of the neat things about politics—and power—is that it seemed to be something of a chick magnet. And young Bill Clinton seemed to need that form of gratification even more than most politicians.

The real warning that times had changed came in 1984 when young, liberal, smart, good-looking presidential candidate Gary Hart was snared by the press cavorting with a young, part-time model named Donna Rice. Hart made it worse, of course, by having pictures taken with the long-legged Ms. Rice in swimming attire aboard a yacht named, appropriately enough, *Monkey Business*. That was the end of Gary Hart's bid for the presidency. Indeed, it killed his political career altogether. Hart had literally dared the press to catch him up to something like what they almost immediately caught him up to. For that alone, he impressed the public as so blindly stupid and reckless that he is widely regarded today as little more than a silly political footnote.

Bill Clinton has been called a sex addict, and pop psychologists have offered a number of typically vacuous excuses for his behavior. Some theorize that Clinton's apparent compulsive sexuality could be the result of growing up with an alcoholic stepfather. Even Hillary speculated that her husband's randy behavior must have been rooted in his exposure to tension between his mother and grandmother. "A psychologist once told me that for a boy, being in the middle of a conflict between two women is the worst possible situation. There is always the desire to please each one."[6] This sounds like the country and western music explanation for chronic promiscuity: "Torn Between Two Women." Can't blame Bill for needing to bring happiness to so many women given that history. But no one has explained it better than Clinton's cocaine-addict half brother, Roger, who observed, "Anyone who watches an addiction develop has seen how predictable stupid behaviors are."[7]

Roger was certainly on target with that analysis. Clinton was once so smitten by an attractive woman named Cyd Dunlop that he called her late at night in her hotel room, while she was in bed with her husband. That minor impediment did not deter the eager Clinton, who attempted to talk her into slipping away from her husband and coming to his room, right then. Failing that, could she meet him the next day, early? Dunlop made the keen observation that Clinton was acting like an oversexed adolescent. "I just thought he was an idiot," she said.[8] But when Clinton had sex on his mind—apparently all the time—his brain was not the organ involved in controlling his actions.

Young Bill Clinton was so consumed with sex that, as he joked later to radio host Don Imus, he outfitted the back of his pickup with Astroturf. The commander-in-chief of America's armed forces apparently thought that this revelation would ingratiate him with enlisted men whom he sensed, rightly, did not respect him as commander. "It was a real sort of Southern deal," Clinton said. "I had Astroturf in the back. You don't want to know why, but I did."[9] Clinton never learned what John Barrymore said: "Sex is the thing that takes the least amount of time and causes the most amount of trouble."

The governor of Arkansas apparently has a lot of time on his hands, so Governor Clinton was able to pursue his passions with enthusiasm and growing notoriety. One longtime object of his affections was introduced to the American public by a supermarket tabloid called the *Star*. The stories about this liaison were predictably lurid. Clinton apparently told anyone who would listen in colorful imagery about Gennifer Flowers's skills at oral sex. She responded in kind regarding his talents in that same department in *Penthouse* magazine, in an issue that hit newsstands in November 1992, the month Bill Clinton was elected president.[10]

The Flowers liaison had come very close to derailing the Clinton bid for the presidency. The story became so public, including an audio tape of a Clinton-Flowers telephone call in which Clinton told Flowers—as he was to tell a young White House intern several years later—to just deny the whole thing, that the Clintons were forced to address the issue on national television.

The two of them negotiated a *60 Minutes* interview, in which Hillary took charge, to the point where she seemed to be both actor and director. That evening, the program threw its reputation for tough, investigative journalism out the window. Interviewer Steve

Kroft acted as if he were a pitcher in a slow-pitch softball game, smiling with amusement—and no follow-ups—as the Clintons knocked his offerings out of the park. They told some incredible whoppers in the process. The segment became, in effect, a video of "Stand by Your Man."

But Clinton's reputation as a chronic philanderer concerned even some of the most sympathetic of journalists. "It would bother me greatly if Clinton was still messing around after the *60 Minutes* interview—let alone after the election," wrote Michael Kinsley, *New Republic* editor at the time and longtime cohost of CNN's *Crossfire*. "That would reveal a brutal willingness to deceive the public—way beyond the normal politician's cynicism—as well as a frightening lack of self control."[11]

Kinsley managed to get over his concerns. He had to if he was to continue to support Clinton, because Clinton was not about to stop craving women—and giving in to his instincts. Clinton not only kept "messing around," but he was to prove that Kinsley's assumption about a hypercynical, brutal willingness to deceive the press was an understatement.

After the election, Arkansas troopers told reporters for the *American Spectator*, the *Los Angeles Times*, and CNN that they had procured more than one hundred women for Bill Clinton, at his request, during the campaign and after the election. One of those mentioned turned out to be Paula Corbin Jones, a twenty-four-year-old secretary for the Arkansas Industrial Development Commission. On May 8, 1991, Jones caught Clinton's eye at a governor's conference on total quality management. The governor directed a trooper to bring her to his hotel room where Clinton made an indecent and lewd proposition, complete with lowered trousers. Jones claimed that she was shocked and embarrassed, declined the governor's invitation, and left the room. After seeing her name in one of the "Troopergate" stories, she brought suit in federal court for sexual harassment by her then-superior, the governor of Arkansas.

Needless to say, the stakes were now astronomical. Clinton was president, and he could not afford to answer questions about liaisons with women, particularly unwelcome approaches to young public employees. He fought the suit all the way to the United States Supreme Court, losing 9-0.

The Clinton camp also indulged in what Clinton adviser Dick Morris was later to describe as a standard Clinton "secret police" smear campaign. Jones was portrayed as a promiscuous practitioner of oral sex, white trash, a cheap slut, and a dupe of radical-right Republicans bent on destroying the president by any and all means necessary. But Jones pressed on.

The Paula Jones case and rumors swirling around it may have reached the pinnacle of absurdity when Clinton's lawyer, the experienced and respected criminal lawyer Robert Bennett, found himself on national television having to respond to questions about the president's anatomy, actually proclaiming that Clinton was "a normal man" in terms of "size, shape, direction."[12]

Nothing like that had ever happened in any modern democracy. Foreigners watched in complete bewilderment. In America, during the Clinton years, everything went.

Yet Clinton seemed oblivious to the damage he was doing to himself and his country by making both objects of international ridicule. For example, when an ancient mummy was found in Peru and brought to the Smithsonian Institution for viewing, Clinton quipped that it was "a good-looking mummy," adding, "If I were a single man, I might ask that mummy out." Americans had to wonder why the president, for just a little while, could not act and talk like the leader of the most powerful nation in the world and not a carnival worker or amateur stand-up comic. Come to think of it, this may be a little unfair to carnival workers.

And Clinton's undisciplined thinking seemed to be contagious. When asked about the mummy quote, press secretary Mike McCurry, an otherwise highly respected spokesman, responded, "Probably she does look good compared to the mummy he's been [sleeping with]."[13]

McCurry's vulgar reference to Hillary seemed particularly outrageous and gratuitously unfair given all that Hillary had done to stand by her husband during his compulsively errant behavior.

Presiding over the Paula Jones lawsuit was Little Rock, Arkansas, federal judge Susan Webber Wright, ironically a law school student of Clinton's during his brief stint as a law professor. There is no record of Professor Clinton making a pass at the future Judge Wright, but he did manage to lose her criminal law exam along with a number of others.

In early 1998, Clinton gave sworn testimony in a deposition—in Judge Wright's presence—in the Jones case. Shorn of his customary backdrop of presidential symbols and his protective entourage, momentarily just an individual caught up in the civil justice system, answering awkward questions, Clinton did not do well. He was evasive, lied, licked his lips, squirmed, and generally did a tolerable imitation of someone who had been caught in flagrante delicto, and was trying to explain the inexplicable. In short, he looked like what he was.

The big news of the deposition was the number of highly specific questions to Clinton about his relationship with someone new: Monica Lewinsky. She was a White House intern from Beverly Hills, and a psychology graduate of Lewis and Clark College. Raven haired, lantern jawed, with prominent eyebrows, a full-figured, twenty-two-year-old peach, Monica was barely older than the Clintons' daughter, Chelsea. She gained her internship on the recommendation of millionaire businessman Walter Kaye, a heavy Clinton contributor. President Clinton met Monica in November

1995 during a government shut down over a budget dispute between the president and Congress. She showed up bearing pizza. She already had a crush on the president and now demonstrated her maturity by showing the president her thong underwear. She was soon showing her talent at the president's favorite form of sexual gratification—although he was later to claim that that particular activity somehow did not fall within his definition of the term "sex."

The relationship continued until late May 1997 and included marathon sessions of phone sex, exchanges of gifts, and a semen-stained blue dress that Monica preserved for posterity. And, of course, the now famous presidential cigar trick. Lewinsky came to see her role as "assistant to the president for blow jobs."[14] He indulged her fantasies about a life together after his presidency, but she tired, grew suspicious of his evasions, and came to call him the "Big Creep."

News of the Monica affair was leaked to the press in January 1998, and the nation began a bizarre roller-coaster ride of politics, sex, and lying. On January 26, 1998, in the Roosevelt Room, Clinton made his famous finger-wagging statement that "I never had sexual relations with that woman, [pause] Miss Lewinsky." The president seemed to be making three points: It wasn't sex; it was a "woman"—not an intern; and he wasn't too sure of her name.

Bill Clinton later repeated the same lie to a full meeting of his cabinet. Although some of his inner circle apparently believed him, and many others pretended that they did, it was obvious to most of the world, including some of his intimates, that he was lying. "This was Clinton at his cold-blooded worst," said George Stephanopoulos, the Rhodes scholar who had pulled plenty of duty defending Clinton. "Gone were the guilty tics of his past denials— the downcast eyes, the stutter, the dry throat and pale face that displayed a sense of shame and sorrow and vulnerability. Now, full of self-righteous fury, he was lying with true conviction. All that mattered was his survival. Everyone else had to fall in line; his staff, his cabinet, the country, even his wife."[15]

As it had from the beginning, the Clinton spin machine went into high gear. The word went out that Monica was a mentally unstable, stalking, Valley Girl sexual predator. Hillary went on national television and blamed it all on a "vast right-wing conspiracy."

Independent counsel Kenneth Starr, asked by Clinton attorney general Janet Reno to investigate whether Clinton had violated federal laws including perjury and obstruction of justice, was demonized as a Bible-thumping, sex-obsessed kook. The personal lives of lawyers on Starr's staff were smeared. The Justice Department was persuaded to set in motion criminal investigations of Starr and the *American Spectator*—a magazine that had dared to be one of Clinton's major accusers.

At the end of the day, there were too many lies for Clinton to conceal, too many tapes of Monica describing details that only someone engaged in sex with Clinton could know, and too many attempts by Clinton to suborn perjury or obstruct justice. And, most of all, there was the one thing Clinton could not deny. His DNA all over Monica's souvenir blue dress. Even Johnnie Cochran wasn't going to be able to explain that.

The result was the 445-page Starr Report, which made the Gennifer Flowers episode seem like the memoir of a Victorian lady. On December 19, 1998, Bill Clinton became only the second president of the United States to be impeached. That day he vowed to serve "until the last hour of the last day of my term."[16] And he kept his promise because the senators of his own party did not believe that lying under oath, witness tampering, and obstruction of justice constituted impeachable offenses if the motive for doing all that was to cover up sleazy sex in the White House.

It took the spring and summer of 2001 and stories of missing intern Chandra Levy and Representative Gary Condit to remind these senators and the American public that lying, cover-ups, and witness tampering—especially if it involves sex—can have serious consequences. And it is seldom benign.

But Judge Wright was not as easily duped as the senators who voted to acquit Bill Clinton of the impeachment charges. She found Clinton in contempt of court for his lies and interference with the justice system. Clinton paid $850,000 to get rid of the Paula Jones suit. That still left open whether he had violated criminal laws and whether he should lose his license to practice law—matters which were not to be resolved until that last Friday of the Clinton presidency.

So Much Forgiveness, So Little Time | 9

The Pardon Process

Even before the 2000 presidential election, Bill Clinton was showing symptoms of the early stages of pardon fever. The White House informed the Office of the Pardon Attorney at the Justice Department that the president wanted more cases in the pipeline for his review. For some reason, Clinton apparently thought his record on clemency did not match those of previous presidents, and he wanted to be remembered as at least as compassionate and magnanimous as his predecessors.

"The White House was yelling and screaming for more cases," said Margaret Love, a former pardon attorney. "But at Justice they didn't have anything more to give to the president. So the White House told Justice to go find some more cases, to search around in old clemency files. So, they just gave them a list of 30 or more cases that had already been denied by Clinton so that the White House could pad its numbers."[1]

Under normal circumstances, the pardon process is highly regularized—to protect against corruption and improper influence. Pardon applicants may utilize the services of an attorney or act on their own. The applicant files his clemency petition, addressed to the president, with the Office of the Pardon Attorney. The standard form requests information about the offense, the petitioner's criminal record, his employment and residence history subsequent to his conviction, other biographical information, and his or her reason for seeking a pardon. The application must be signed and notarized and the applicant must submit notarized affidavits and character references who support the request for executive clemency.

When the Office of the Pardon Attorney receives a petition, it screens it for eligibility. The crime for which the pardon is sought must be a federal offense (the president cannot grant clemency for state law offenses) and, under Department of Justice regulations, a five-year period must have elapsed, beginning on the date of the individual's release from confinement. If no condition of confinement was imposed as part of the applicant's sentence, the date of conviction is used.

According to the DOJ regulations, a pardon will not be granted to a person who is on probation, parole, or supervised release. A person who has not yet been convicted or has not fully served the sentence for the federal crime for which pardon is sought is also generally considered ineligible for a pardon. The president, of course, has the power to waive or override these conditions. For example, President Ford pardoned ex-president Nixon even though there had been no prosecution and thus no conviction. But such a deviation from standard practice is quite rare.

As an initial investigative step in a pardon case, the Office of the Pardon Attorney contacts the probation officer for the federal district in which the petitioner was prosecuted to obtain copies of the pre-sentence report and the judgment of conviction, as well as information regarding the petitioner's compliance with court supervision. The pardon attorney also typically seeks the views as to the merits of the pardon from the probation office, the prosecutors, law enforcement officials, and the sentencing judge. In appropriate cases, the FBI, other federal agencies such as the IRS or the Immigration Service, and even victims, may be consulted.

If review of the petition and the information obtained as a result of the investigation warrants denial of clemency, the pardon office prepares a report to the president to be signed by the deputy attorney general recommending that the pardon be denied. The deputy attorney general may seek further investigation or changes in the proposed presidential action. Ultimately, the report and recommendation are forwarded to the president through the Office of White House Counsel. That office reviews the report further, may seek more information, and ultimately forwards the file and recommendations for action to the president.

For his part, the president may take whatever action he deems appropriate. The president's authority under the Constitution is unlimited: "[H]e shall have Power to grant Reprieves and Pardons for Offenses against the United States...." The president retains the authority under the Constitution to consider a pardon request from an individual who is ineligible to apply under the regulations or who has not applied at all. He can grant clemency to this person if he believes the action is appropriate. As explained by Alexander Hamilton in *The Federalist Papers* (No. 74), the Framers intended the president's power to grant pardons to be essentially absolute, in part because they believed that "the sense of responsibility is always strongest in proportion as it is undivided" and also because the unfettered nature of this authority would "inspire scrupulousness and caution." Mr. Hamilton, needless to say, had never met Mr. Clinton.

When the president decides to grant clemency, whether in the form of a pardon or a commutation of a sentence, the counsel to the president asks the Office of the Pardon Attorney to prepare the appropriate clemency warrant. If the president intends to pardon a number of applicants, a master warrant of pardon will be prepared for his signature. The signed master warrant bears the seal of the Department of Justice, lists the names of all of the individuals receiving the president's grant of clemency, and directs the pardon attorney to prepare and sign individual warrants of pardon to be delivered to each pardon recipient.

Bill Clinton had promised to respect the regular pardon process that had been carefully developed and refined by his predecessors. During a 1996 PBS interview about possible pardons for his former Whitewater business partners, James and Susan McDougal, the president said, "My position would be that their cases should be handled like others. There's a review process for that, and I have regular meetings on that, and I review those cases as they come up, after there's an evaluation done by the Justice Department. That's how I think it should be handled."[2] That commitment, like many others, was forgotten or ignored as Clinton's term of office neared completion.

Christmas Pardons

As the holiday season of 2000 approached, the clamor for presidential pardons in high-profile cases grew in intensity. The pardons Clinton had granted to the Puerto Rican FALN terrorists gave hope to a variety of convicted criminals and attorneys hoping to benefit from what soon became known as Clinton's desire to turn pardon-activist during his last days as president.

Strenuous lobbying was done on behalf of Jonathan Jay Pollard, who had exploited his position as an intelligence research specialist for the navy to pass along important and highly classified defense information to Israel. The Pollard story had broken in November

1985 and shaken U.S.-Israeli relations. Pollard's pleas that he had only been trying to help an ally of the United States ultimately carried little weight, as did a Justice Department agreement that it would not seek a life sentence in exchange for a Pollard guilty plea to espionage. He was nonetheless sentenced to life in prison.

Pollard had been elevated to hero status in Israel, and a number of support groups pressed the case that his punishment had been too harsh, arguing that by the late 1990s he had already served longer than others who had given secrets to an ally. In 1998, at the Middle East Peace talks at Wye Plantation in Maryland, Israeli prime minister Benjamin Netanyahu attempted to secure a pardon for Pollard from President Clinton. The Israeli government took responsibility for Pollard's actions, argued that Pollard had acknowledged that he was wrong and had been severely punished, and made the case not for a pardon but for a reduction in Pollard's sentence to the time that he had served.[3]

In the end, despite high expectations, Pollard failed to make Clinton's Christmas clemency list. So did another candidate, this one the subject of worldwide lobbying and with Cold War connections. Leonard Peltier is serving two life sentences in Leavenworth, Kansas, for the murder of FBI agents Ron Williams, twenty-seven, and Jack Coler, twenty-eight. The two agents had been involved in a shoot-out with some thirty heavily armed men on the Pine Ridge reservation in South Dakota on June 26, 1975. Peltier's supporters came to include the Dalai Lama, Desmond Tutu, Nelson Mandela, government officials in Canada, Italy, and France, United States senators Daniel Inouye and Paul Wellstone, former attorney general Ramsey Clark, the Reverend Jesse Jackson, Rigoberta Menchu, and movie stars Robert Redford, Susan Sarandon, Danny Glover, and others. They contended that Peltier had not received a fair trial, and the push for the president to pardon Peltier mounted during Clinton's final year.

Then–FBI director Louis Freeh and FBI agents strongly opposed the Peltier pardon. He, along with Pollard, ultimately did not make the Clinton clemency list.

Another unsuccessful supplicant was Michael Milken, who, during the 1980s, made billions for himself and others in the high-risk ("junk") bond business. Milken was convicted of securities fraud, served twenty-two months of a ten-year sentence, and paid more than $1 billion in fines, restitution, and legal settlements. After serving his sentence, Milken involved himself in charitable activities, including a search for a cure to prostate cancer, from which he suffered. Those supporting a pardon for Milken included New York mayor Rudolph Giuliani, the man who, as United States attorney in New York, had prosecuted Milken.

President Clinton was also considering pardons for Whitewater veteran Susan McDougal (her husband James McDougal had died in prison on March 8, 1998) and Webb Hubbell, the former associate attorney general who pleaded guilty to felony income tax evasion and mail fraud in December 1994. Susan McDougal, whose Arkansas nickname was "Hot Pants," lucked out. Webb Hubbell, Hillary's former colleague at the Rose law firm, did not.

On December 22, 2000, President Clinton granted executive clemency to fifty-nine persons, including a pardon for Illinois congressman Dan Rostenkowski, a thirty-year veteran of the House of Representatives. Rostenkowski had been chairman of the powerful House Ways and Means Committee and widely viewed as a symbol of big government and pork-barrel spending. Rostenkowski had been charged with using public funds to buy personal gifts and to pay employees who did little or no work. In 1996 Rostenkowski pleaded guilty in federal court to two counts of mail fraud and was sentenced to seventeen months in prison and $100,000 in fines.

Rostenkowski had not asked for a pardon, and five years had not elapsed since the completion of his sentence, as Department of Justice regulations required as a condition of eligibility for a pardon. Clinton's action thus came as something of a surprise. But, when viewed as a partisan payoff, it made sense. So did some of the other pardons.

Independent counsel Donald Smaltz's investigation of former agriculture secretary Mike Espy resulted in the conviction of Archie Schaeffer III, chief spokesman for the Tyson corporation, a major force in Arkansas, and a source of many favors for the Clintons. It was a Tyson official, after all, who had helped Hillary score $100,000 in phantom cattle futures trading. Schaeffer had been convicted for attempting to influence Espy, who had been acquitted in late 1998. Clinton had made no secret of his view that the Smaltz investigation was abusive and intrusive. The Schaeffer pardon thus killed two birds with one stone: It undid the work of an independent counsel, whom Clinton regarded as a Kenneth Starr clone, and paid in part a personal debt to the Tyson's Foods empire.

Clinton also pardoned Joseph R. Hendrick, a North Carolina automobile dealer who was convicted of mail fraud involving a scheme in which he gave millions of dollars in cash, jewels, and expensive cars in exchange for favors from executives at the America Honda Motor Company. There may have been legitimate reasons for the Hendrick pardon, but there were questionable aspects as well. Hendrick is a friend and former business associate of Hugh L. McColl, chairman of the Bank of America. Two weeks before the December 23 pardon, the Bank of America's charitable foundation pledged $500,000 to the Clinton Library. Bank officials denied any connection between the pledge and the pardon, but it smelled peculiar, especially since Hendrick, like Rostenkowski, had not met the five-year-after-completion-of-sentence provision in Justice Department regulations.

Most of Clinton's other pardons were for drug, tax evasion, and fraud charges, several in situations where sentences had seemed disproportionately harsh.

The Christmas 2000 pardons—and denials—showed that Clinton was capable of resisting intense lobbying but that he was also capable both of bending the normal rules and procedures and acting in a way that seemed to satisfy personal, as opposed to presidential, impulses. And there was obviously more to come.

"I expect to do another round of pardons," President Clinton told reporters. "I haven't had any meetings or made any decisions about the others yet. I just expect to do some." These words provided considerable encouragement to those who still expected to benefit from Clinton's desire to leave a memorable pardon legacy. But they vastly understated the spree on which Clinton was about to embark. And those who knew Bill Clinton best, and how to take advantage of his needs, were hard-pressed to conceal their glee. The feast was about to begin.

A New Round of Pardons

Hillary's brother, Hugh Rodham, a rumpled, overweight, Webb Hubbell type, enjoyed "nearly unfettered" access in the White House. Aides said that his penchant for spouting "half-baked" policy, business, and legal notions "always made our alarms go off when he was around." Roger Clinton was another such. A family member, undisciplined, apparently incapable of accomplishing anything constructive on his own, there was little aides could do to limit his access.[4] According to one report, a White House official pinned the blame squarely on Clinton and those on his staff who catered to him. By the end of his term, the official said, Clinton was "surrounded by enablers" and had "no one around him strong enough to say no."

Phones rang constantly, as if the White House was conducting some kind of pardon telethon. Letters flowed in from everywhere. The word was out. Partisan Democrats were desperate to get what they wanted before the reins passed to a Republican. Campaign contributors queued up anxious for one last return on their investment. Cronies and political pals saw one more chance to get another "yes" from the president who wanted so desperately to please.

The mounting cases led to friction with pardon attorneys at the Justice Department. The White House resolved this by simply bypassing the Department of Justice altogether. Clinton granted at least twenty-six clemency applications not vetted by the DOJ. He also decided to plunge on with pardons over the department's objections or where he knew that there would be objections if he had let career prosecutors know what he was doing.

The pressure became white hot as Bill Clinton attempted to pack four more years of the presidency into four days on the calendar. Madame de Pompadour, a favorite of Louis XV, said, *"Après nous le déluge"* [After us the deluge]. Bill Clinton planned to have the deluge before he left office. On January 20, his last day in office, Bill Clinton issued 140 pardons and commuted thirty-six sentences.

Very few publications printed the full list. It is a story that should be told. The commutations included: Benjamin Berger, Ronald Henderson Blackley, Bert Wayne Bolan, Gloria Libia Camargo, Charles F. Campbell, David Ronald Chandler, Lau Ching Chin, Donald R. Clark, Loreta De-Ann Coffman, Derrick Curry, Velinda Desalus, Jacob Elbaum, Linda Sue Evans, Loretta Sharon Fish, Antoinette M. Frink, David Goldstein, Gerard A. Greenfield, Jodie E. Israel, Kimberly Johnson, Billy Thornton Langston Jr., Belinda Lynn Lumpkin, Peter MacDonald, Kellie Ann Mann, Peter Ninemire, Hugh Ricardo Padmore, Arnold Paul Prosperi, Melvin J. Reynolds, Pedro Miguel Riveiro, Dorothy Rivers, Susan Rosenberg, Kalmen Stern, Cory Stringfellow, Carlo Anibal Vignali Jr., Thomas Wilson Waddell III, Harvey Weinig, Kim Allen Willis.

Pardons included: Verla Jean Allen, Nicholas M. Altiere, Bernice Ruth Altschul, Joe Anderson Jr., William Sterling Anderson, Mansour Azizkhani, Cleveland Victor Babin Jr., Chris Harmon

Bagley, Scott Lynn Bane, Thomas Cleveland Barber, Peggy Ann
Bargon, David Roscoe Blampied, William Arthur Borders Jr.,
Arthur David Borel, Douglas Charles Borel, George Thomas
Brabham, Almon Glenn Braswell, Leonard Browder, David Steven
Brown, Delores Caroylene Burleson aka Delores Cox Burleson,
John H. Bustamante, Mary Louise Campbell, Eloida Candelaria,
Dennis Sobrevinas Capili, Donna Denise Chambers, Douglas
Eugene Chapman, Ronald Keith Chapman, Francisco Larois
Chavez, Henry G. Cisneros, Roger Clinton, Stuart Harris Cohn,
David Marc Cooper, Ernest Harley Cox Jr., John F. Cross Jr.,
Rickey Lee Cunningham, Richard Anthony De Labio, John
Deutch, Richard Douglas, Edward Reynolds Downe, Marvin Dean
Dudley, Larry Lee Duncan, Robert Clinton Fain, Marcos Arcenio
Fernandez, Alvarez Ferrouillet, William Dennis Fugazy, Lloyd Reid
George, Louis Goldstein, Rubye Lee Gordon, Pincus Green, Robert
Ivey Hamner, Samuel Price Handley, Woodie Randolph Handley,
Jay Houston Harmon, John Hemmingson, David S. Herdlinger,
Debi Rae Huckleberry, Donald Ray James, Stanley Pruet Jobe,
Ruben H. Johnson, Linda Jones, James Howard Lake, June Louise
Lewis, Salim Bonnor Lewis, John Leighton Lodwick, Hildebrando
Lopez, Jose Julio Luaces, James Timothy Maness, James Lowell
Manning, John Robert Martin, Frank Ayala Martinez, Silvia Leticia
Beltran Martinez, John Francis McCormick, Susan H. McDougal,
Howard Lawrence Mechanic, Brook K. Mitchell Sr., Samuel Loring
Morison, Charles Wilfred Morgan III, Richard Anthony Nazzaro,
Charlene Ann Nosenko, Vernon Raymond Obermeier, Miguelina
Ogalde, David C. Owen, Robert W. Palmer, Kelli Anne Perhosky,
Richard H. Pezzopane, Orville Rex Phillips, Vinson Stewart Poling
Jr., Norman Lyle Prouse, Willie H. H. Pruitt Jr., Danny Martin
Pursley Sr., Charles D. Ravenel, William Clyde Ray, Alfredo Luna
Regalado, Ildefonso Reynes Ricafort, Marc Rich, Howard Winfield
Riddle, Richard Wilson Riley Jr., Samuel Lee Robbins, Joel

Gonzales Rodriguez, Michael James Rogers, Anna Louise Ross, Gerald Glen Rust, Jerri Ann Rust, Bettye June Rutherford, Gregory Lee Sands, Adolph Schwimmer, Albert A. Seretti Jr., Patricia Campbell Hearst Shaw, Dennis Joseph Smith, Gerald Owen Smith, Stephen A. Smith, Jimmie Lee Speake, Charles Bernard Stewart, Marlena Francisca Stewart-Rollins, John Fife Symington III, Richard Lee Tannehill, Nicholas C. Tenaglia, Gary Allen Thomas, Larry Weldon Todd, Olga C. Trevino, Ignatious Vamvouklis, Patricia A. Van De Weerd, Christopher V. Wade, Bill Wayne Warmath, Jack Kenneth Watson, Donna Lynn Webb, Donald William Wells, Robert H. Wendt, Jack L. Williams, Kevin Arthur Williams, Robert Michael Williams, Jimmie Lee Wilson, Thelma Louise Wingate, Mitchell Couey Wood, Warren Stannard Wood, Dewey Worthey, Rick Allen Yale, Joseph A. Yasak, William Stanley Yingling, Phillip David Young.

The list of beneficiaries of Clinton's last-minute clemency orgy was as eclectic as one could imagine: small- and big-time crooks, con men, bank robbers, terrorists, relatives, ex-girlfriends, a cross section of the Clinton cabinet, a former director of the CIA, perjurers (appropriately enough), tax evaders, fugitive money lenders, Clinton campaign contributors, former members of Congress, and friends of Jesse Jackson. The sheer number of pardons and clemency grants, coupled with their timing—the last day of the Clinton presidency and the first day of Bush Two—staggered the press and smothered the story. Details would have to come later, and they were both hard to uncover and slow to be revealed.

The most outrageous pardons were also concealed by a considerable number of pardons and clemencies of minor drug offenders who had received disproportionately harsh sentences and undoubtedly deserved some sort of break. These were the presidential actions that had been properly staffed and vetted. But salted within this list of "normal" grants of executive clemency were some extraordinary and very unusual and interesting stories. One of these was Hearst media empire heiress Patty Hearst.

In February 1974, a violent left-wing militia called the Symbionese Liberation Army (SLA) kidnapped the famous publishing family heiress, Patricia Hearst, nineteen years old. Hearst apparently fell in love with her captors and turned into an amateur debutante terrorist herself. Two months after her abduction she had transformed herself into SLA soldier "Tania" and was photographed, decked out in revolutionary costume, submachine gun in hand, taking part in a bank holdup in San Francisco. After her capture, Hearst claimed that the SLA had brainwashed her, but the jury did not buy her story. She was convicted and sentenced to seven years in prison. She served two years before President Carter commuted her sentence.

Hearst subsequently married one of her guards, told her story in a book, *Every Secret Thing*, and launched an acting career, appearing in such films as *Cecil B. Demented*. She further capitalized on the wool she had pulled over Jimmy Carter's eyes, convincing him to bring up the matter of a pardon with Bill Clinton when Clinton awarded the Georgia Democrat the Presidential Medal of Freedom in Atlanta in August of 1999.

Carter, however, first broached the matter with the Department of Justice. "When President Carter mentioned Patty Hearst to President Clinton, it wasn't out of the blue," Carrie Harmon, a spokeswoman for Carter, assured reporters. "The issue here is, is there is a process and did we follow the process, and the answer is 'Yes.'"[5]

Patty Hearst thus pulled off a presidential daily double—executive clemency from two Democratic presidents. Heiress, to terrorist, to prison, and back. But, as mentioned earlier in this book, Clinton had a soft spot for white suburban female terrorists.

But Clinton's biggest surprise was not Patty Hearst. On the day Clinton acted, the luckiest pardonee was listed on the website of the Clinton Department of Justice as number six on the Justice Department's most-wanted list of international fugitives. He had never served a day in jail because he fled the country and renounced his citizenship—a previously unexplored route to a presidential pardon.

If I Were a Rich Man | 10

The Man on the Run

On March 10, 1984, Craig Copetas was seated at a table in a restaurant in the Swiss canton of Zug. Seated nearby, at a corner table, wearing a black suit, was Marc Rich. He was tall, with spidery legs, sinewy fingers, and the kind of striking tan one gets on the ski slopes. Seated with him was his partner Pincus "Pinky" Green. Copetas had long sought an opportunity to speak with Marc Rich and knew this might be his only chance.

The previous year, Copetas had gone underground as a commodities trader in order to write a *Harper's* article, and eventually a book, about the "metal men," the elite group of traders who control rare commodities, including strategic metals, and deal in everything from corn to armaments. Rich was king of the metal men who believed, "There's always a way to make money on a deal if you are in total and absolute control."[1] He was known as a financial gladiator, ruthless tycoon, and in the words of one trader, the "prince of fucking darkness."[2] It would have been impossible, the author knew, to write about such a person from the outside. His movements, companies, and dealings were all shrouded in secrecy.

In due course Rich stood and passed by Copetas's table. Here was the undercover writer's big chance.

"Mr. Rich," he said. But he never finished the sentence. As Copetas described the scene: "He looked at me, frightened, his chill brown eyes flashing the agony of ripped flesh."[3]

Rich fled through the restaurant kitchen to a bathroom, where he escaped through a window, leaving behind a blue cashmere overcoat, a Florentine leather briefcase, and an unfinished lunch of capellini d'angelo and fileto del pomodoro. Marc Rich was avoiding unwanted inquiries, as he had been doing for some time. The Copetas incident was, in fact, one of his more unobtrusive exits.

Rich was born in Antwerp, Belgium, on December 18, 1934, the only child of David Reich and Paula Wang. Like many other Jewish families, they fled to the United States in the early 1940s, first to Philadelphia, then to Kansas City, Missouri, where they changed the family name to Rich.

Marc Rich became an American citizen in 1947. His father became a millionaire dealing in fashion jewelry, car parts, and speculating in tobacco. He ultimately moved his family to Queens, New York, where Marc enrolled at the Rhodes School in Manhattan and, later, the marketing program at New York University.

On October 30, 1966, Marc Rich married Denise Joy Eisenberg, a woman ten years his junior whose family had also fled Europe in 1941. There was more to it than physical attraction. Denise's father was Emil Eisenberg, chairman of Desco Inc., one of the nation's largest manufacturers of shoes. To one observer, "Their wedding appeared more of a merger than a marriage."[4]

At the time Marc was working for Philip Brothers, the biggest metals and commodities buyer and seller in the world. An aggressive trader, Rich thrived, to the point that he wanted to strike out on his own. The result was Marc Rich International in New York, the American subsidiary of Marc Rich & Co. AG, the Swiss parent company. Rich would soon command more than forty offices in thirty countries.

Rich relentlessly raided other companies, especially Philip Brothers, for traders. He worried that someone might outdo him while he slept and even took telexes with him to the bathroom. He played rough and expected his traders to do the same. One of his field agents in Asia, Edmund Mantell, was brutally murdered, an event that Craig Copetas says added more drama to the Marc Rich legend.

"To the metal men who knew Mantell, his death suggested that negotiations with Marc Rich once settled with handshakes were now being settled with hit men."[5]

By 1977 Rich was the biggest aluminum trader in the world. At one point, he became a fifty percent partner with oilman Marvin Davis in Twentieth Century Fox studios. For this purpose he founded Richco Holdings, a Netherlands Antilles corporation. Rich looked at the Hollywood move as part real estate, part tax shelter. It delighted his wife, Denise, who had started to write songs, loved attention and movie society, and thought Marc was too secretive.

"Denise wanted to be known in society, dance under some lime-light," said a Rich executive. "She wanted to get out and do some things a woman with money can do. . . . Denise just wanted a chance to strut her stuff."[6]

Her husband, Marc, was much more interested in money. How he got it was of secondary importance. One of his associates said, "Marc never once reflected on the moral implications of a deal."[7]

Rich told the Nigerians he was selling their oil to Spain when he was actually shipping it to South Africa, then a pariah nation because of its apartheid policies. A bribe of $1 million to Nigerian officials fixed the problem. Between 1979 and 1990, Rich shipped about eleven million tons of oil to South Africa, some eight percent of that nation's supply.[8]

Rich struck lucrative oil deals with Iranian Ali Rezai who, like many others, fled when the Ayatollah Khomeini seized power and began a campaign of anti-American hatred. America was now the "Great Satan." The Ayatollah seized and held American diplomats as hostages.

U.S. president Jimmy Carter and other Western leaders slapped a trade ban on Iran. Trading with the Khomeini regime thus became a criminal offense, but that caused not the slightest hesitation for Marc Rich. Rich's own traders warned him about doing business with Iran, but Rich and partner Pinky Green took such cautions as signs of weakness. They continued dealing with Iran, paying for oil in weapons, automatic rifles and rockets, shipped from Thailand, which the Ayatollah needed for his war with Iraq, as well as for the suppression of his own countrymen.

Americans were also barred from trading with Libya because of Colonel Gaddafi's sponsorship of international terrorism. It was Gaddafi's regime that bombed the PanAm airliner over Lockerbie, Scotland. The Libyan dictator was a rabid anti-American and foe of Israel. These inconveniences proved no obstacle to Marc Rich, who bought Libyan crude oil through European third parties. He also shipped barley and soybeans to Libya when those commodities were under U.S. embargo.

Marc Rich also helped to prop up the Castro dictatorship in Cuba. Rich's operation set up sugar-for-oil deals between the USSR and Cuba. Jose Oro, a Cuban defector and onetime director of mining exploration on the island nation, revealed that Rich's firm traded metals in Cuba as well. Rich also dealt in Soviet crude oil during the Cold War and expressed interest in buying oil from Iraq when it was under an international embargo for the 1990 invasion of Kuwait.[9] For Rich, dealing with pariah nations and terrorist dictators became a lucrative way of life.

These actions, especially the Cuba deals, made Rich eligible for stiff penalties, as much as ten years in prison and huge fines. But Rich was a gambler, willing to take the risk for the handsome payoffs that made him a billionaire. Never mind the moral questions involved.

"Mr. Rich and Mr. Green have apparently made vast sums of money over the past twenty years by trading with virtually every enemy of the U.S.," said Morris "Sandy" Weinberg, who during the 1980s prosecuted Rich's stateside exploits in oil that got him in trouble.[10] These involved a practice known as "daisy chaining," bogus trades that avoided regulations by relabeling old oil as new. This enabled Rich to sell oil for $25 to $40 a barrel that could be sold legally for only about $6 per barrel. "Marc and Pinky saw others making a fortune out of daisy chaining and decided that they'd be able to get away with it," said one trader.[11]

Rich and Pinky Green were also adept at "calving," an illegal practice in which a subsidiary based in the United States pays inflated prices for materials from another of its subsidiaries based elsewhere, thereby avoiding taxes. Rich's operations were a sham inside a fraud.

Morris Weinberg headed a team of prosecutors from New York's elite southern district U.S. Attorney's Office that eventually brought charges against Rich in a fifty-one-count indictment, in part under RICO, the Racketeer Influenced and Corrupt Organization statutes.

"It was a truly extraordinary case," Weinberg told a congressional committee in 1991. "The evidence was absolutely overwhelming that Marc Rich, in fact, committed the largest tax fraud in the history of the United States."[12]

Weinberg subpoenaed 200,000 pages of documents, and a judge slapped a $50,000-per-day fine on Rich for failing to produce them.

In what became known as the "steamer trunk affair," Weinberg's men halted a Swissair 747 about to take off and seized two steamer trunks full of documents that Rich had promised to produce to Weinberg. A paralegal from a New York law firm was trying to spirit the evidence out of the country.

Rich fought back with a high-powered team of lawyers, including Edward Bennett Williams, elite New York and Washington law firms, several Swiss firms, and Michael Tigar, defender of the Chicago Seven and Seattle Eight. In Switzerland, Rich was represented by Rudolf Moismann, chief prosecutor for the canton of Zug and a director of Marc Rich AG.

This all-star lineup tried to portray Rich as a victim of a persecution campaign by Weinberg. Rich made it clear that he wanted closure, by any means necessary. As usual, money was no object, but imprisonment was not an option he would consider.

Edward Bennett Williams came into Weinberg's office, put his feet on the desk, and offered to settle the case for $100 million. Weinberg said no. Rich and Green fled the country.

A "Red Notice" by INTERPOL failed to apprehend them despite a number of leads. Rich became a citizen of Spain on July 26, 1982, and a citizen of Israel on July 18, 1983, a day after Pincus Green, born in New York on January 3, 1934, also became an Israeli citizen. Craig Copetas believes that Pinky Green became a Bolivian citizen as well.

"I want those boys in jail," said Morris Weinberg. "Marc and Pinky will try to come back. Bet on it."[13]

Meanwhile, life on the lam proved little different than it had been before. In fact, Rich maintained "contact" with millions of Americans in a creative way.

Rich changed the name of Marc Rich International to Clarendon, Ltd. This firm then sold $1.3 million in nickel and $4 million worth of copper to the United States Mint, a major purchaser of metals and a division of the very Treasury Department that Rich had defrauded.[14] This discovery led to hearings by the House Committee on Government Operations, then chaired by Michigan Democrat Bob Wise. The 272-page printed proceedings were titled *The Strange Case of Marc Rich: Contracting with Tax Fugitives at Large in the Alps.* Subsequent hearings by the Committee on Government Operations were titled *They Went Thataway: The Strange Case of Marc Rich and Pincus Green.*

"Can there be little wonder why Americans have lost confidence [in] this government's ability to enforce the laws?" said Congressman Mike Synar. "And can there be little wonder why most Americans believe there are two sets of laws in this country, one for the rich, no pun intended, and one for the rest of us?"[15]

"This isn't your miscreant who has fled the country for knocking over fifteen 7-Elevens and is kicking around the dock at Marseilles," said then-representative Wise. "This is Marc Rich operating with total impunity out of a tall office building in Switzerland. And why hasn't this been made a priority?"[16]

Howard Safir, former associate director for operations at the U.S. Marshals Service, was convinced that, given the political will and the proper resources, Rich and Green would have been apprehended, just like other international fugitives. One of these, CIA renegade Ed Wilson, had been lured out of Libya and apprehended in the Dominican Republic.

Safir and his men missed Rich by a few hours in England and a matter of days in Jamaica. They also came close in Switzerland. The case left the marshal incredibly frustrated.

"Are the defendants in the largest tax case ever in the history of the United States to be allowed to sit virtually in luxury in a very nice country and thumb their nose at the United States?" he said.[17]

Rich, who speaks English, German, and Spanish, continues operating from a six-story glass and marble building near the railway tracks in Zug. He occupies a spacious corner office on the top floor, with a white leather sofa, walls hung with white fabric and Spanish abstract paintings. A fervent cigar smoker, he keeps his supply in a wood box on his desk. A Plexiglas crate is also filled to the brim with cigars. Rich keeps a ship's clock on a small filing cabinet, a reminder of the tanker fleet over which he presides. During the year 2000, Rich's operations took in a reported $7 billion.

Rich's Swiss mansion is filled with fine art, including works by Picasso. He also owns a villa on the slopes of St. Moritz and a $10-million home in Marbella on the Spanish coast. He flies the world in a private jet. The "long arm of the law" was never quite long enough to grab him. Rich even continued to travel on a U.S. passport, in addition to the others he uses, after he had renounced his American citizenship.

But Marc Rich wanted something else, a pardon, which only one person in the world could grant. That person was the president of the United States. This presented a challenge, but Rich seemed to sense that William Jefferson Clinton could be had. He was right.

For Marc Rich, the question became how to manipulate Bill Clinton. He needed a plan and ultimately conceived one that involved two of Clinton's most notorious passions: women and fundraisers. His ex-wife, Denise, was both; he soon decided to let her strut her stuff, as she very much liked to do. To paraphrase James Carville, troll through the White House with a voluptuous woman and a lot of money, and who knows what you will pull in.

In Israel, which like Switzerland and Spain refused to extradite the fugitive, Marc Rich gained a reputation as a philanthropist, giving a reported $80 million to a number of causes, including the rescue of Jews from Ethiopia. The Rich Foundation, headquartered in Tel Aviv, gave $2.6 million to the Tel Aviv Museum of Art. The Israel Philharmonic and the Birthright Israel were also recipients of Rich largesse, the latter to the tune of $5 million. No one seemed to mind that these donations were likely the gains from his trading with South Africa, Iran, Libya, Iraq, Russia, and Cuba.

These and other charitable ventures gained him a number of prominent powerful allies, including Elie Wiesel, Shimon Peres, Ehud Barak, Abe Foxman, executive director of the Anti-Defamation League, and Abner Azulay, a former high operative of the Mossad, Israel's intelligence service. Azulay is also the director of the Rich Foundation. Representatives of Marc Rich also offered a donation to the American Jewish Congress if the AJC would support his application for a pardon.

"It was made known to us that if we were to speak favorably of Mr. Rich, we would be the beneficiary of a gift," said Phil Baum, executive director of the AJC. Mr. Baum was an exception. The AJC did not write a letter supporting Rich, and Rich did not make a donation. But Marc Rich's foundation pledged $100,000 to the Anti-Defamation League, and Foxman did write a letter supporting Rich.[18]

Rich also wisely hired former White House counsel Jack Quinn. Quinn is a smart and smooth Washington lawyer who had been not only counsel to President Clinton but chief of staff to Vice President Al Gore. He knew better than to submit the usual pardon application which would have generated an outpouring of adverse publicity and an avalanche of opposition from prosecutors, law enforcement agencies, and Congress. So he filed his applications directly with the White House and casually mentioned his approach to Eric Holder, deputy attorney general, who was hoping to be named attorney general if Al Gore were elected president. Holder apparently did not see fit to mention the matter to the career prosecutors involved in the case.

Rich's advocates claimed that the indictment against Rich was flawed because the price control laws were confusing and of questionable soundness. But Rich and Green were able to understand the regulations well enough to exploit them for millions of dollars in profits. Regardless of whether they were wise or effective public policy, the measures in place at the time were law and prosecutors believed that Rich had a duty to play by the rules or face the consequences.

Quinn also contended that Rich's transgressions should have been civil rather than criminal matters. However, the prosecutors saw only classic criminal fraud involving phony invoices, a second, secret set of financial records, and false reports to the Department of Energy. Rich and Green willfully violated the price controls, the prosecutors argued, and their companies later pled guilty to doing so. Only Rich and Green had escaped justice.

Rich's lawyers claimed that the prosecutors were overzealous, ambitious, and had refused to negotiate. But the Department of Justice and its prosecutors in New York maintained a longstanding policy of not negotiating with fugitives. They recited Rich's long history of acting in bad faith, his refusal to obey grand jury subpoenas, and his attempt to avoid a massive contempt of court fine by purporting to sell his corporation in a sham transaction. Nevertheless, in the early 1990s, U.S. Attorney Otto Obermaier took the extraordinary step of flying to Switzerland and meeting with Marc Rich to attempt to negotiate a resolution to the case. Although he was willing to pay staggering sums in fines, Rich refused any deal that would involve surrendering to federal authorities and submitting to the U.S. justice system. As it turned out, he would never need to do so.

Looking Out for No. 1

"The present impasse," said former Mossad operative Azulay in an e-mail, "leaves us with only one other option: the unconventional approach which has not yet been tried and which I have been proposing all along." Azulay then wrote about the idea of sending "DR on a personal mission to No. 1 with a well-prepared script."

Rather amateurish code for a former Mossad official; DR was obviously Denise Rich, and "No. 1" was Bill Clinton, the president of the United States,[19] or, as Monica Lewinsky put it in a similarly crude attempt at cryptography, "the big He." Denise Rich was apparently willing to undertake such a personal mission. The only question is what—or how much—it took to convince her.

Denise Rich lived with Marc and their children in Switzerland before their marriage ended in divorce. The details of the divorce are sealed, but as attorneys in New York discovered, there is evidence that Denise remained an informed and active player in the Marc Rich empire.

In 1993 she filed a lawsuit against her former husband and in the court filings admitted that she got lost in the "dizzying corporate network" of her husband's business dealings. "Until 1990, I was a shareholder of MRCH," she wrote, adding, "and I still maintain an interest in the company." Indeed, in 1990 she owned 13.91 percent of Marc Rich and Company, shares she apparently subsequently sold for $165 million.

Denise Rich lost the lawsuit, but the documents, explored by prosecutors in New York, include a discussion of how Rich officials, to achieve a lower tax rate, wanted to keep Denise as a part owner of one of Marc Rich's U.S. subsidiaries.[20] Given those realities, it requires no stretch to see Denise Rich as useful to her former husband in many other ways. To whom much is given, much is expected. The same formula seemed to work with "No. 1."

Denise Rich gave at least $1.5 million to causes related to the Clintons. The majority of it, nearly $1 million, came near the end of Clinton's second term, when Rich's lawyer and former White House counsel Jack Quinn were pressing No. 1 for a pardon. Denise Rich gave $450,000 to the Clinton Library foundation, including $100,000 on May 11, 2000, two months after the Azulay plan for her "personal mission" had been launched.

Denise also gave $100,000 to the Democratic National Committee, at least $109,000 to Hillary Clinton's senatorial campaign and paid a full $40,000 for entertainers to perform at Hillary's birthday party on October 25, 2000. She even gave a $25,000 donation to the Gore-Lieberman Recount Committee.

It is no coincidence that Prime Minister Barak brings up a Marc Rich pardon to Bill Clinton on December 11. Clinton assures Barak that he knew "all about the case" from Denise.

To top it all off, she gave more than $7,000 in furniture to the Clintons as they moved into their post–White House homes, and in November 2000, at her cancer benefit, she presented Clinton with a gold saxophone.

"Thank you, Denise," said Bill Clinton after receiving the instrument. "Thank you for everything you have done to make it possible for Hillary and me to serve."

As if that were not enough, she also wrote letters. Robert Fink, one of Marc Rich's lawyers, suggested that Denise Rich write a cover letter to POTUS including a request that "you wisely use your power to pardon Marc."[21] Denise first wrote to Clinton on December 6, saying that she supported the pardon for Marc Rich "with all my heart" and asking the president, as if he needed any coaxing, to consider "what it feels like to see the press try and convict the accused without regard for the truth."[22]

Two weeks later Denise agreed to deliver another copy of her letter to the president by hand, on December 20 at the White House. This part of her "personal mission" involved separating Bill Clinton from Barbra Streisand, one of his most vocal—and clinging—Hollywood supporters. That must have been an interesting sight to see.

Marc Rich's attorneys also wanted to reach out to Senator Hillary Clinton, which became known as the "HRC option." On December 26, Robert Fink e-mailed Jack Quinn to say, "I think the best person to call Hillary... may well be Denise." But cooler heads prevailed, and the HRC option was apparently scrapped. HRC thus dodged what would have been a very unfortunate—for her—paper trail.

On January 10, Azulay excitedly e-mailed Jack Quinn. Denise had called from Aspen, where she owns a home. Denise was with "B," Beth Dozoretz, a woman with access to the president. Dozoretz served as the chief fundraiser for the Democratic National Committee in 1999. She hosted a fundraiser at her Washington mansion that raised $1 million. In May 2000, Dozoretz herself pledged to raise $1 million for the Clinton Library. And she had done countless other fundraising and miscellaneous acts of kindness for Bill Clinton. He had even become godfather to her child—presumably promising to see to the infant's moral and ethical upbringing. Dozoretz asserted her Fifth Amendment right not to testify before the House Government Reform Committee in order to avoid any further explanation of her role in the pardons.

Dozoretz had received a telephone call from POTUS, who said he was impressed by Jack Quinn's latest letter. POTUS "wants to do it" and was doing all he could "to turn around the WH [White House] counsels," she reported. Two days later Marc Rich met with Israeli prime minister Ehud Barak. Barak had the second of three calls with Bill Clinton on January 8. Clinton assured him he was "working on" the Rich pardon and asked him not to talk about it with others.

Jack Quinn's January 16 e-mail to Robert Fink, subject "Denise," said "I am advised that it would be useful if she made another call to P," meaning "No. 1" or POTUS. (It is not clear whom they were expecting to fool with these grade-school codes.) The message would be simple. "I'm not calling to argue the merits. Jack has done that and we believe a pardon is defensible and justified. I'm calling to impress upon you that MR and our whole family has paid a dear price over eighteen years for a prosecution that should never have been brought and that singled out MR while letting the oil companies he dealt with go scot free. Please know how important this is to me personally."[23]

On January 19, Arthur Levitt, chairman of the Securities and Exchange Commission, received a call from a White House official. The official explained that Bill Clinton was preparing a last-minute pardon for Marc Rich and wanted to know what Levitt thought about it.

For a Clinton appointee, Levitt exhibited unusual fastidiousness. He checked with his staff and called back.

"The man's a fugitive," he said. "This looks terrible." The White House official agreed.[24] It would be interesting to know what the unknown White House official meant. It should not have been hard to find responsible government officials—even in the Clinton administration—who would have known that it would look, and be, terrible for the president to override a Department of Justice process and secretly pardon a "most wanted" fugitive. Perhaps they were trying to find people who did not think it would be terrible.

But time was running short, and if they were looking for a high official who would not turn on a red light, they succeeded with Eric Holder. On that same January day, Quinn called Holder informing him that he would be getting a call from the White House asking about his position on Marc Rich. Later that night, Beth Nolan, the White House Counsel to President Clinton, called Holder. Holder accommodatingly told her he was "neutral, leaning towards favorable" to the Rich pardon if it had foreign policy benefits.

The next morning, hours before he was to leave office, President Clinton approved the pardon.

Denise Rich had accomplished her mission, showing what a woman of generosity can accomplish with Bill Clinton. Marc Rich found that the same "honey trap" schemes the Soviets employed so effectively, making ample use of women, resonated well with Clinton's most publicized weakness. The Rich campaign also played on the president's resentment of prosecutors, a particularly effective strategy in light of Clinton's contemporaneous plea agreement with Robert Ray, finalized the day before.

Law enforcement authorities were outraged, particularly those who had been chasing Rich around the globe. Rich of course was delighted, and the man who had once dived through a bathroom window to escape a journalist was now feeling liberated enough to speak out.

"I do not consider the pardon granted by President Clinton as an eradication of past deeds—but as the closing of a cycle of justice and a humanitarian act," Rich said, in a statement distributed by a Tel Aviv public relations agency. "The indictment against me in the United States was wrong and was meant to hurt me personally—the pardon granted by President Clinton remedied this injustice eighteen years later."

Those familiar with both the Rich case and the normal procedures for presidential pardons were flabbergasted. New York mayor Rudolph Giuliani, formerly the U.S. attorney responsible for the Rich prosecutions, was told of the pardon on January 20 while attending the Bush inauguration. He did not believe his ears. "Check again," he told the aide bringing him the news, "they must mean Michael Milken." When the aide confirmed that it indeed was Marc Rich, taking pains to spell out "Marc," Giuliani was dumbfounded. He said that it was "impossible, the president would never pardon a fugitive, especially Marc Rich. It cannot have happened." But it did.

Once again, Bill Clinton had done the unthinkable. A lawyer who fielded many of the pardon applications told *Newsweek* that "I think Clinton wanted to pardon all of them" and that "he just can't stand law enforcement."[25] But that was by no means the full story. An examination of the other pardons reveals a much more complex story.

Empty the Prisons | **11**

She Takes a Village

After World War II, a group of Russian Jews established a self-sustaining farming community in New York State. The Skevere Hasidic group in Rockland County, also known as the New Square community, lived in relative peace and harmony until the late 1990s. At that time, some of its members diversified into the education industry.

Benjamin Berger, Jacob Elbaum, David Goldstein, and Kalmen Stern set up a religious school in Brooklyn. They listed more than 1,500 students who were to receive federal funds known as Pell Grants. However, the project was a scam; the students were fictitious. The four were convicted in 1999 of swindling $40 million in federal funds and sentenced to prison terms of up to six and a half years. Almost immediately, their tight-knit community began a campaign for their release.

Efforts were made to recruit New York mayor Rudolph Giuliani to the cause, pressing him to write letters supporting clemency for the convicted felons. In return, they offered to stage a special event for his expected Senate campaign. Giuliani declined, making clear he would not even discuss the fate of the four convicted swindlers.

Enter Hillary Clinton. In August 2000, Hillary visited New Square. Showing once again her talent for setting the right sartorial mood, she was wearing a long skirt and a modest head covering for her private meeting with Rabbi David Twersky. We're not sure what was discussed, but subsequent events provide some telling clues.

In the election of 2000, Hasidic groups in New York showed remarkable diversity, some with a pronounced inclination toward Rick Lazio, Hillary Clinton's Republican opponent. Lazio was more conservative and friendlier to Israel. He had not, for example, spoken out in favor of a Palestinian state, as had Hillary. And he had not hugged Yasir Arafat's wife in the wake of virulent anti-Israeli rhetoric as Mrs. Clinton had famously done. The Hasin vote historically went Republican in years past, with margins reaching the 90th percentiles. Two Hasidic groups neighboring New Square voted, as expected, overwhelmingly for Lazio, 3,500 to 150.

But New Square itself voted for Hillary Rodham Clinton by a count of nearly 1,400 to 12. For seasoned political analysts, it was a stunning development.

"Not since the 1982 presidential election in Albania in which the Stalinist dictator Enver Hoxha won by 1,627,959 to 1—the one is still at large—have so many people agreed so wholeheartedly on the virtues of one candidate," wrote Charles Krauthammer of the *Washington Post*.[1] (Mr. Krauthammer did not know it at the time he wrote, but "the one" apparently migrated to Palm Beach, Florida, where he is still having trouble with ballots.)

For those with suspicious minds, Act I was the August meeting between Hillary and Rabbi Twersky. Act II was the 99 percent victory by Hillary on election day. Act III was a December 22 meeting in the White House Map Room with Bill and Hillary Clinton in attendance. (The Map Room should be renamed for the Clintons in honor of all their memorable moments in that venue.) The New Square Hasidim pleaded with the first couple for clemency for their colleagues. Berger, Elbaum, Goldstein, and Stern, were dubbed the "New Square Four"—nomenclature usually reserved for martyrs, not con men. Act IV was January 20, when president Bill Clinton commuted the sentences of all four, from a maximum of seventy-eight months—more than six years—to thirty months. Curtain closes.

The right-wing conspiracy, and even a few commentators not theretofore identified with that group, saw the New Square grants of clemency as a clear case of a pardon in exchange for votes. Hillary Rodham Clinton, needless to say, claimed to know nothing about any reciprocity.

"I did not play any role whatsoever," she said. "I had no opinion about it."[2] Hillary watchers have heard this refrain before, most notably when she swore that she had had "no role" in the vicious purge and smear of the career White House Travel Office employees early in her husband's first term. Hillary even stuck with that story in the face of the unforgettable "hell to pay" Travelgate memo in which White House aide David Watkins described the consequences if Hillary's desires were not implemented promptly. But it worked then and she wasn't about to change her modus operandi now.

Hillary even denied that she had uttered a sound in the December 22 meeting when the case for clemency was made to her husband. The demure first lady and senator-elect had apparently pushed the mute button—at least in the meeting. "She wants the credit for going into the—into the meeting with New Square, but she doesn't say a word," said former Clinton aide George Stephanopoulos, in his new role as ABC commentator. "The fact that she didn't say a word shows that she knew something was wrong with the meeting."[3]

Representative Chris Shays, Republican from Connecticut, said that "the bottom line, this is just one of a number of very, very questionable pardons, in which in this case the first lady was a participant."[4]

In late February, Mary Jo White, President Clinton's U.S. attorney for the Southern District of New York, said she would consider the New Square case as part of her investigation of the Clinton pardons.

"There is no way to prove a *quid pro quo*," wrote Krauthammer, "but then, the Clintons have been especially diligent in covering their tracks in similar dealings over the past twenty years."[5] Maybe there was no proof of a *quid pro quo*, but maybe there does not need to be. Another Latin legal phrase seems to cover it: *res ipsa loquitur*—the thing speaks for itself.

Roger and Me

William Jefferson Clinton is not the first president to find that the first family can be troublesome, particularly brothers. Lyndon Johnson's younger brother, Sam Houston Johnson, had a drinking problem. Richard Nixon's brother, Donald, borrowed $205,000 from Howard Hughes to save his fast-food chain that featured triple-decker Nixonburgers. Nixon had the Secret Service keep Donald under surveillance to avoid embarrassing incidents. Billy Carter, Jimmy's brother, smoked marijuana on the White House roof, urinated in public, and even became a foreign-policy problem when he tried to curry favor with Libya's Colonel Gaddafi.

Roger Clinton was all of the above—and more. Bill Clinton's father died three months before Bill was born. Roger Clinton, ten years Bill's junior, was the son of Roger Clinton, Senior, the car dealer who married Bill's mother. According to Bill Clinton, Roger Sr. was an abusive drunk, and it often fell to the future president to protect Roger Jr., who called him "Big Brother." Bill Clinton, said Roger, "was almost obsessive about wanting me near him and was my best friend, my guardian, my father, and my role model."[6] Roger may have had a role model, but he did not share his big brother's talent for getting out of trouble.

Bill Clinton played tenor saxophone in a jazz combo called "Three Blind Mice." Roger also had musical aspirations, but his first group was tellingly named "Dealer's Choice," supposedly after a pinball machine, but actually somewhat more prophetic. In his autobiography, Roger explains how he was introduced to a Colombian who became his "partner in dealing" and how he would get "hammered, just stoned out of my head."[7] Roger bragged about wild cocaine binges at the Governor's Mansion in Little Rock when Hillary was away.

Governor Bill Clinton authorized a sting operation that led, ironically, to Roger's arrest on drug charges. In 1985, Roger pleaded guilty to conspiring to distribute cocaine and was sentenced to two years in prison. He served one year at the Federal Correctional Institution in Fort Worth and was released to a halfway house in Dallas.

Roger testified in a cocaine prosecution that led to a six-month term of incarceration for Dan R. Lasater, financier, hamburger magnate, racehorse owner, and major contributor to the campaigns of Bill Clinton. Lasater had flown the Clintons to the Kentucky Derby on his corporate jet, and Bill Clinton had lobbied the Arkansas legislature to give Lasater's firm a contract to sell bonds for a state police radio system.

Lasater had been Roger Clinton's cocaine supplier, and Roger Clinton had been Lasater's driver. In 1990, Governor Clinton issued a pardon to Lasater. While Lasater was in prison, his bond business was handled by his executive vice president, Patsy Thomasson. In a move that never did receive anywhere near the attention it deserved, President Clinton brought Patsy Thomasson to Washington, where she became director of the Office of Administration. In a masterstroke of personnel placement, Ms. Thomasson was put in charge of the notoriously nonfunctional White House drug-testing program. A Clintonesque version of type-casting.

Roger, of course, remained a faithful supporter of Big Brother and accused radio talk-show host Rush Limbaugh of treason for criticizing the president. Limbaugh, in turn, called him a half-witted half brother. Roger may have been inept and somewhat dim-witted, but he was not so stupid that he was unable to figure out that his brother's success would be his meal ticket. He bragged of his influence when his brother was governor. He continued to take advantage of his familial connections when his brother moved to Washington.

When Alabama businessman John Katopodis was promoting a new regional airport, he wanted to bring a federal official to a conference on the project. Larry Wallace, an Arkansas lawyer, offered to bring in Rodney Slater, secretary of transportation. The tradeoff was to be a job for one Roger Clinton.

According to law enforcement records cited by *Newsweek*, Bill Clinton had expressed concern for the welfare of his "baby" brother. Wallace proposed that Roger receive a "consulting" contract of $35,000 a month from a foundation connected with Katopodis. Katopodis expressed dismay that he was being milked for $35,000 a month for "consultation" with a cipher who played in a third-rate rock band. He dropped the whole thing when the FBI asked him to wear a wire.[8] Roger Clinton was not charged with anything, but in the hectic final days of the Clinton White House, Roger was again pushing to use his extraordinary access for favors from his brother that would pay him dividends.

Roger remained friends with men he had met in prison, and he promised half a dozen of them that brother-president would grant them pardons before he left office. In a campaign that apparently began midway through the Clinton presidency, Roger helped his pals find lawyers and fill out pardon applications and made sure all the paperwork was filed "timely and properly" with the Justice

Department. He seemed to believe that the actual pardon part was going to be easy.

Roger had convinced himself that a pardon was a matter of right, something like a free suit or a bus ticket at the end of a prison sentence. "Everybody wants a pardon," Roger has explained. "When you get out of prison and you've done your time and all the paperwork and you've been a productive, beneficial part of society and you've obeyed the law, you're entitled to it."[9] It's a good thing the people elected the older brother president.

Access to the president was, of course, important, and Roger certainly had that. In the latter days of the Clinton presidency, Roger, Bill, and Hugh Rodham, Hillary's brother, frequently golfed and went on outings together. On one of his frequent White House visits, Roger put a list of his friends' names in a place where Big Brother would be sure to see it.

"I put it into a stack of papers on a table in the White House where he would see it," Roger Clinton told the *Los Angeles Times*. "I put the names on it. I put down their relationship to me. And I said they had all gone through the Justice Department and they were deserving." Sort of like the list he must have prepared for Santa Claus when he was a kid.

About a week later, Roger asked the president what he thought of the list, and the president responded that he "would look into it."[10] How carefully the president looked into it, like so much surrounding Clinton's pardon grants, remains unclear. But we know he was looking for people to pardon and we know he tried whenever he could to help his little brother. And he was certainly contemplating a pardon for Roger. Roger could be forgiven for thinking he might get presidential pardons for his prison buddies.

The standard procedure for granting a pardon includes a criminal background check conducted by the Federal Bureau of Investigation. Roger Clinton, however, was able to avoid that inconvenience.

White House Counsel Beth Nolan requested that, instead of the FBI, higher levels of the Justice Department should handle this duty. A DOJ official told *Newsweek* that "they wanted this done outside the ordinary course of business."[11] Of course they did. Such a move would prevent then–FBI director Louis Freeh, not Bill Clinton's favorite official, from knowing about, and possibly interfering with, plans for Roger's pardons.

On January 20, an eager Roger Clinton was stunned to find that his prison buddies, whom he declined to name, did not make Big Brother's final pardon lineup. "It sort of caused a rift," he said. "My feelings were hurt. It was a disaster."[12]

For two weeks Roger refused to speak to Big Brother, notwithstanding that he, himself, had made the list, the first pardon ever by a president to a family member.

"You want it for your namesake, for your children, for your record," said Roger.[13] But Roger Clinton's difficulties did not end with his pardon. Roger was apparently so crass, heavy-handed, and unsubtle in his efforts to sell influence, and ultimately so ineffective in delivering, that he seriously angered both his business partners and those who paid him good money for pardons and, it has been alleged, things like diplomatic passports. The government's tough prosecutors in New York launched a serious investigation, still unresolved as of this writing.

Hugh Rodham and the Cocaine Kingpin

For reasons that we can only speculate about, Clinton's rush of last minute pardons tipped heavily in favor of persons who had used or distributed cocaine. Carlos Anibal Vignali, of Los Angeles, for example, was a high-volume cocaine trafficker convicted of shipping nearly half a ton of the drug to Minneapolis. There the cocaine was turned into crack and sold in poor neighborhoods at a substantial markup. Convicted and sentenced in 1994 to fifteen years, Vignali got lucky on January 20. Bill Clinton commuted his sentence to time served.

Carlos Vignali was a big boy, not one of the low-level types jailed for a long term under mandatory sentencing laws or on vague conspiracy charges. He was a cocaine trafficker of the very type that the Clinton administration had made such efforts, at least rhetorically, to stop.

"He was not a minor player; he was not a street-level dealer," former U.S. attorney Todd Jones, who helped prosecute the case, said in an interview. "This guy was a major source in keeping a drug organization here being fed with dope from California." Jones said that the U.S. Attorney's Office in Minneapolis strongly recommended that Vignali not be released early from prison because of the scope of his crime and his unrepentant attitude. "We considered it a no-brainer," Jones said. "I did not believe that there was any way [clemency] was going to be granted in this case."[14] Jones, of course, was not aware that brains had nothing to do with the Vignali commutation. Like many others, he did not figure on the leverage being applied on behalf of the unrepentant drug dealer.

Carlos Vignali is the son of Horacio Vignali, a wealthy Los Angeles property developer, parking-lot owner, and used-car dealer. After his son went to prison, Horacio decided to become a major donor to politicians in California, mostly Democrats. His donations to Democrats around Los Angeles exceeded $150,000, and in the fall of 2000, he gave $10,000 to the Democratic National Committee. As the Clinton administration wound down, the politicians whom the elder Vignali had befriended became a veritable phone bank and letter-writing committee on behalf of the son, the imprisoned drug smuggler.

Those who wrote or called the White House on the Vignali matter in the waning days of the Clinton presidency included Representative Xavier Becerra, Los Angeles county supervisor

Gloria Molina, former representative Esteban Torres, state senator Richard Polanco, and former state assembly speaker and Los Angeles mayoral candidate Antonio Villaraigosa. Los Angeles county sheriff Lee Baca also pitched in.

Horacio Vignali also asked Clinton's U.S. attorney appointee in Los Angeles, Alejandro N. Mayorkas, to intervene. Remarkably, Mayorkas called the Clinton White House on behalf of the convicted felon. The action prompted an angry resignation by Assistant U.S. Attorney Duncan DeVille, a Los Angeles–based prosecutor engaged in fighting organized crime. DeVille's letter captured the spirit of frustration that law enforcement officials felt over the commutation of Vignali's sentence.

"I frequently place in danger both my life and, more importantly, the lives of law enforcement agents, in the pursuit of drug dealers. Accordingly I cannot support your recent actions in assisting in the pardon," said DeVille. "I'd been a proponent of the rule of law and preaching the gospel of the rule of law in Eastern Europe for the past few years," he added. "Now suddenly I started getting asked by prosecutors about this pardon. . . . I kept being called a hypocrite."[15]

When asked how he got out, Vignali said, "Word around prison was that it was the right time to approach the president."[16] Shamefully, the cocaine kingpin was right. The American public did not know it, but America's prison population had better insight into what was going on in the White House than the leading journalists who were there every day. The president was in the mood to grant favors—and pardons. And the usual procedures were being bypassed. The stars were in the proper alignment. Hugh Rodham, Hillary Clinton's brother, President Clinton's frequent golf partner, and White House guest and resident in the final days, charged the Vignali family $200,000 for Carlos's ticket to freedom.

Quack Clemency

Hillary's brother Hugh was a particularly busy prospector in the mother lode created by Bill Clinton's pardon frenzy. A supermarket tabloid—and tabloids tended to be a good source for information on "Friends of Bill"—was the first to report the news. Earlier, the *Star* had broken the Gennifer Flowers story and also the news of Clinton campaign adviser Dick Morris's love affair with a prostitute's toes. The *National Enquirer*, America's "leading" tabloid, with a circulation of two million, specializes in celebrity scandal—was first to publish the news that the Reverend Jesse Jackson had fathered a child with a staff member of one of his organizations. Weeks later, the same tabloid scooped the mainstream media on the Hugh Rodham pardon scam.

"Clinton Pardon Payoff Exposed," read its February 22, 2001, front-page headline. Inside, readers were shown a copy of a $200,000 wire transfer from a G.B. Data Systems of Marina Del Rey, California, a company owned by Almon Glenn Braswell, to the law firm in which Hugh Rodham was a partner. Here was yet another unsubtle Clinton/Rodham family operation. The payoff was sent on January 22, the first business day after Bill Clinton pardoned Braswell, a quack and a convicted swindler.

Among other highly marginal and bad-smelling ventures, Braswell had peddled a fake cure for baldness, with ads claiming "Eighty percent success rate in experiments conducted by noted European doctors!" He was convicted of mail fraud and perjury in 1983 and sentenced to three years. He was subsequently sued by race-car driver Richard Petty, football player Len Dawson, and baseball legend Stan Musial, whose pictures Braswell had used in ads for a prostate remedy. During a two-hour deposition in the fall of 2000, Braswell took the Fifth Amendment 196 times.

Although Braswell had been a contributor to Republican causes, when the Bush campaign learned of his felony record, his donation of $175,000 was promptly returned.[17] Moreover, Federal prosecutors had also been investigating Braswell for tax evasion.

So Braswell was a convicted felon, a well-known shady operator, the defendant in civil suits for improper business practices, a Fifth Amendment taker in order to avoid talking under oath about his conduct under oath, and under investigation for cheating on his taxes. In short, a perfect client for Hugh Rodham, and a natural candidate for a William Jefferson Clinton pardon. Of course, this pardon, like fifty or more others, did not go through Department of Justice channels. But that was not the Hugh Rodham or Bill Clinton way. Rodham reportedly received a total of $434,000 for his "work" on the Braswell and Vignali pardons. When the story broke, Hillary publicly stated that she had insisted that her entrepreneurial brother return the money. He promised to do so, but it is unclear whether he fulfilled his promise.

The Carnies and the Nut Cases

Hillary's two brothers seemed to have a nose for trouble. Like the pigs in France who hunt for truffles, they were constantly digging up something that smelled.

In 1999, Hugh and brother Tony tried to put together a multi-million-dollar deal to export hazelnuts from the former Soviet republic of Georgia. The proposed deal set off rivalries between political factions in the Georgian republic, and White House officials, including former national security adviser Sandy Berger, who begged, pleaded, and pressed the Rodham brothers to drop the venture. Tony, the more defiant of the two, continued to pursue it.

Tony Rodham had married and divorced Nicole Boxer, daughter of California senator Barbara Boxer. Like his brother, he was a graduate of the University of Arkansas. He, too, took a ride on the pardon gravy train, helping to obtain a pardon for Edward and Vonna Jo Gregory, carnival promoters.

The Gregorys, from Brentwood, Tennessee, are the owners of United Shows of America and were convicted in 1982 on charges of bank fraud. That, of course, was no impediment to presidential access in the Clinton years. They spent time at Camp David with Bill Clinton, and at the Clintons' request, with Tony Rodham handling the arrangements, they staged carnivals on the White House lawn for parties in 1998 and 2000. Over the strenuous objections of the Department of Justice, President Clinton pardoned the pair in March 2000. The pardon came during Hillary's hotly contested Senate campaign, to which the Gregorys, naturally, had contributed.

According to campaign watchdog groups, the Gregorys gave $2,000 to Hillary's campaign committee and another $11,000 in soft money donations to her New York Senate 2000 committee. For good measure, they also gave $4,000 to the presidential campaign of Vice President Al Gore. United Shows, the Gregorys' carnival company, gave $50,000 to the Democratic Congressional Campaign Committee for the 2000 elections, and, in 1998, $25,000 to the Democratic National Committee and $10,000 to the Democratic Senatorial Campaign Committee.[18]

The carnival owners were naturally pleased with the work of Tony Rodham, a Washington-based consultant whom they had approached after they failed to secure a pardon from President Clinton during Christmas 1999. This seemed quite logical to the Gregorys. "His brother-in-law is the president of the United States," said Gregory. "And I asked if he could help me."

Tony Rodham denied asking for or receiving any money for his efforts, and he and Mr. Gregory maintained that no pardon-related payments had been concealed under Mr. Rodham's consulting contract for the carnival business. "We have a business contract with Tony Rodham," Mr. Gregory said. "The compensation definitely fits the work he's done. He has not been overpaid."[19]

To summarize: Brother-in-law Hugh sought and received money for obtaining pardons. There are witnesses who say that they paid brother Roger for pardons never received. Brother-in-law Tony obtained pardons for people who paid him money for "consulting." And we are told and expected to believe that neither Bill nor Hillary had the slightest idea that all three brothers were seeking pardons for friends, pals, and business partners. Nor did the first couple know that money was a common denominator in these pardon requests. They never thought to ask, we are told. Of course they didn't ask. They didn't need to.

Yet More Friends of Bill

Harry Thomason, the big-time television sitcom producer and longtime friend of both Clintons, had produced *The Man from Hope*, the hagiographical video shown at the 1992 Democratic national convention. Thomason now marshaled his influence in favor of executive clemency for Robert Clinton Fain and James Lowell Manning, Arkansas restaurateurs, convicted on tax charges in the early 1980s.[20]

Thomason spoke directly with the president on behalf of the pair, and also approached Harold Ickes, a White House mainstay since 1994. Ickes is also the law partner of William Cunningham III, Hillary Clinton's Senate campaign treasurer. Ickes referred the matter to Cunningham, who drew up the pardon paperwork and sent it to the Department of Justice on January 16, 2001, four days before the president was to leave office. It is usually impossible to obtain pardons on this kind of schedule, but the unusual became the usual, and the irregular became the regular, during the final days of the Clinton administration.

Another Clinton friend, the Reverend Jesse Jackson, also became an active pardon lobbyist. The Reverend Jackson was embroiled in a tricky paternity flap with a former employee of one of his companies, but he too had friends who needed pardons, and he could not very well wait until his paternity controversy went away. He intervened on behalf of Mel Reynolds, the former Democratic congressman from Chicago who resigned in 1995 after a state court conviction for having sex with a sixteen-year-old campaign worker.

In 1997, Reynolds was convicted of separate federal fraud charges stemming from concealing debts in order to obtain bank loans and laundering union political donations that were intended for voter registration drives but were directed instead to his election campaign. Reynolds was also found guilty of enlisting aides to cash at least $164,000 in campaign contributions at currency exchanges and banks, apparently to make the money difficult to trace. He had two more years to serve on his federal charges when Clinton commuted his sentence.

The president offered no explanation for this act of executive grace. But that was true of most of the other grants of pardons and commutations. In most cases, there wasn't much that could be said. In this case it is reasonable to assume that a request by the Reverend Jackson was all the reason Clinton needed. Jackson had provided extraordinarily useful support during the Lewinsky scandal. He helped save Clinton's presidency.

Jackson also played a role in the pardon for Dorothy Rivers, a Democratic Party loyalist, former executive director of the non-profit Chicago Mental Health Foundation, and a top official of Jackson's Rainbow/PUSH Coalition.

Rivers pleaded guilty to stealing $1.2 million in government grants following a forty-count indictment on charges of fraud, theft, tax evasion, obstruction, and making false statements. She used federal money slated for homeless children to buy, among other things, a $35,000 fur coat, a Mercedes-Benz for her son, clothes for her live-in boyfriend, landscaping, and $250,000 for a record company. She used the cash to hire a chauffeur and to throw parties. At one of these events, she ordered a champagne glass six feet tall. She also used federal money for political donations and to make payments on a six-unit apartment and a home on Lake Michigan.

Rivers, a kind of reverse Robin Hood who stole from the poor and gave to herself, showed absolutely no remorse at any time but received relatively lenient treatment by the court anyway. She faced more than ten years in prison, but in November 1997, she received the least amount of time allowed under federal sentencing guidelines—five years and ten months. President Clinton reduced it to time served, which came to about three years.

Analysts could come up with no explanation for this pardon. For, to repeat, Rivers had taken money intended to help poor homeless children and used it instead to enrich herself. But she had a friend in the Reverend Jackson. And President Clinton owed an immense political debt to Jackson. That seemed to be all that was necessary.

Another Jackson crony was John H. Bustamante who pleaded guilty to fraud in 1993. Jackson sought a pardon for Bustamante, and Clinton, of course, delivered. Fortunately for the country, Jackson apparently knew when to stop asking, or else we might have had to close some federal prisons.

The president also pardoned Lloyd Reid George who had been mentioned to him in passing on January 17, 2001, on his hurry-up trip to Arkansas. George had been convicted in 1997 of mail fraud for selling an overpriced irrigation system to a state prison. Fraud against the government was a crime that President Clinton seemed peculiarly anxious to forgive. Of course, if your name was mentioned to President Clinton during his last week in office, whether you were Mother Theresa or Charles Manson, whether you needed it or not, you were likely to get a pardon. As the *New York Times* observed, the George case confirmed that applicants could get "quick results, as long as they had the right connection to Mr. Clinton."[21]

Clinton also bypassed the Justice Department in issuing a pardon for Edward Downe Jr., a publishing and financial executive from Connecticut who in 1993 pleaded guilty to insider trading. Downe, naturally, was a contributor to Hillary Clinton's campaign. The pardon drew criticism from the Securities and Exchange Commission, but then the SEC is against insider trading. Insider trading, as we learned, was precisely how to get a pardon from Bill Clinton. So the behavior that got Mr. Downe into prison was also his ticket out.

Douglas Eakley, a former roommate and classmate of Bill Clinton at both Oxford University and Yale Law School, represented the case of Salim B. Lewis, a takeover specialist who pleaded guilty to stock-price manipulation in the late 1980s. Lewis received a pardon. One more successful use of a Clinton connection.

Charles W. Morgan III of Little Rock, whose crime had been conspiracy to distribute cocaine, received a January 20 pardon. Morgan received help from William H. Kennedy, the former associate White House counsel and partner of Hillary Clinton at the Rose law firm in Little Rock. You might remember Kennedy as the author of the note about "vacuuming the files" at the Rose law firm after Hillary departed. He failed to have any memory of that writing as well as the question of who hired Craig Livingstone

Clinton connections even worked for Republicans. David C. Owen, a former aide to Clinton's 1996 opponent Bob Dole, had been busted for filing a false tax return. Owen procured a January 20 pardon with help from Clinton adviser James Hamilton, the lawyer for Vincent Foster, the Rose law firm veteran who became White House counsel and whose sudden death in 1993 caused so much controversy. Hamilton also refused to divulge his final conversations with Foster to the independent counsel.

The list of Clinton friends and contributors who helped get last minute grants of executive clemency seems to go on forever. Adolph Schwimmer, who violated the Neutrality Act to ship arms to Israel, secured a January 20 pardon through the efforts of Brian Greenspun, a Democratic contributor and overnight White House guest of Bill and Hillary Clinton.

Some names on the list proved no new surprises. Susan McDougal, the president's former Whitewater business partner and alleged occasional girlfriend (at least her late husband thought so), had been convicted of misusing a federally backed $300,000 loan and went to jail for eighteen months on a contempt of court citation for refusing to give testimony under oath about the Clintons. An Arkansas federal grand jury had ordered her to testify. And an Arkansas federal judge had denied her claim that there was something improper about the subpoena. On his last day in office, her Arkansas friend in the White House wiped her slate clean.

Others in the Whitewater case also received pardons. The president granted a pardon to Robert W. Palmer, a Little Rock appraiser who pleaded guilty to conspiracy in the Whitewater case. Clinton also pardoned Stephen A. Smith, a former aide to Clinton when he was Arkansas governor, who had been convicted of a misdemeanor in the Whitewater probe.

Webster Hubbell, the ex–Rose law firm partner who had become Clinton's associate attorney general—and later pleaded guilty to taking money from clients and his law firm—did not get a pardon and was quite bitter about it. After all, he had remained loyal to President and Mrs. Clinton despite considerable pressure from prosecutors. A Hubbell pardon may have been just too much even for Bill Clinton. But still, one has to wonder why. The public outcry would not have been any greater if Hubbell had been pardoned. He had, to use his own words, "rolled over" again and again for the Clintons. His frustration seemed justified.

But other political allies made the final list. During his FBI background check for his job as secretary of housing and urban development, former San Antonio mayor and rising Democratic Party star

Henry Cisneros was less than candid about $250,000 in hush money he had paid to Linda Jones, a former mistress, between 1979 and 1984. Facing an aggressive prosecutor who obtained an eighteen-count federal felony indictment for his various false statements, Cisneros cut a deal and pleaded guilty to a misdemeanor count of lying. President Clinton issued him a pardon and tossed one in for the mistress. President Clinton obviously has a soft spot for mistresses. As well he should.

Richard Wilson Riley Jr., son of Bill Clinton's secretary of education, got a pardon for a conviction for conspiring to sell cocaine and marijuana in 1993. Clinton pardoned John Deutch, his former director of the Central Intelligence Agency, who transferred classified intelligence documents to unsecured home computers, a rather disturbing practice for the keeper of the nation's secrets. It was especially egregious at a time when American nuclear secrets were showing up in China, and CIA and FBI agents were selling material to Russia. Samuel Loring Morison, a former navy intelligence analyst convicted of leaking sensitive, classified photographs to the media, also received a pardon from the president.

Ronald Henderson Blackley, chief of staff for former agriculture secretary Mike Espy, received a Clinton commutation. He had been convicted of making false statements regarding $22,000 he accepted from agribusiness friends. Clinton also issued a pardon to John Hemmingson, convicted in 1996 of laundering money to cover a campaign loan for Mike Espy's brother. The Clinton pardons, in fact, included all but one of those convicted in the Espy investigation.

In all, Clinton pardoned three of his cabinet level appointees (Espy, Cisneros, and Deutch), one son of a cabinet member (Riley), one brother, and one of his alleged ex-girlfriends, along with terrorists, swindlers, and con men. A curious menagerie of others still remained to receive pardons and commutations.

Good Old Boys, Druggies, Odometer Frauds, and Anteater Smugglers

In keeping with his promise to prioritize drug convictions, President Clinton commuted the sentences of Donald R. Clark, convicted in 1991 of conspiracy to grow and sell an especially potent type of marijuana; Antoinette M. Frink, who served eleven years of a fifteen-and-a-half-year sentence for selling cars to a drug trafficker who used them to run cocaine; Billy Thornton Langston Jr., sentenced to thirty years in prison for conspiracy to manufacture PCP; and Cory Stringfellow, sentenced to 188 months in federal prison in 1995 for conspiring to sell LSD. Mitchell Couey Wood, convicted of conspiracy to possess and distribute cocaine, also received a pardon.

In all, Clinton commuted the sentences of twenty-one drug offenders including Marcos Arcenio Fernandez, Gloria Libia Camargo, Velinda Desalus, Jodie E. Israel, Kellie Ann Mann, Peter Ninemire, Kim Allen Willis, Gerard Greenfield, and other relative unknowns. In some of these cases the offenders had received long sentences for minor offenses. The case with the most merit was likely that of Derrick Curry, a promising high-school basketball player with a college scholarship. For a minor role as a courier Curry was charged with conspiracy to distribute crack cocaine and sentenced to nineteen years, his age at the time. But not all cases fit this profile. Many seemed impossible to justify.

For example, Bill Clinton commuted the sentence of Harvey Weinig to only 270 days served. Weinig was a Manhattan lawyer who had been convicted of participating in one of the largest drug money-laundering cases in New York history. Weinig had helped the Cali cartel and had even played a role in a kidnapping. Both the Department of Justice and the U.S. attorney in New York were stunned by Clinton's action, which, to date, has never been explained. A reaction of outrage came from Columbia's government officials, calling Clinton's actions "sordid." Clinton connections were involved, of course. Weinig was related by marriage to a former Clinton White House senior communications aide. And his attorney was cosy enough to the White House to take the matter over the heads of prosecutors directly to White House counsel Beth Nolan, chief of staff John Podesta, and Clinton crony-in-chief Bruce Lindsey. In the end, the connections with Clinton trumped the connections with the Cali cartel.

Ernesto Samper, the former Colombian president who saw his country decertified and facing sanctions for lack of cooperation with Washington against drugs, described the Weinig clemency as "repugnant." Asked Samper, "What would have happened if, with just a few days left in my presidency, I had set free several drug traffickers arrested in Bogota, and if those same people were found to be helping people in my government?"

Colombian general Rosso Serrano, formerly the nation's top antidrug agent, said the Clinton action would have the drug traffickers laughing. He said that it "sent the wrong message to the antidrug struggle, because it negates the suffering of all the families of those who died to fight trafficking."[22]

In his pardon binge, the president of the United States showed a particularly soft spot for frauds.

Clinton pardoned William Sterling Anderson, former South Carolina House Speaker pro tem. Anderson had been sentenced to fourteen months in prison in 1987 for charges stemming from the falsification of customer credit records for his mobile home business. David Marc Cooper pled guilty in 1992 in a federal fraud case involving faulty brake shoes for army jeeps. He received a pardon along with one William Dennis Fugazy, a limousine mogul guilty of perjury and various scams to avoid paying creditors.

Former Democratic senatorial candidate Charles D. Ravenel participated in the looting of the Citadel Federal Savings Bank, one of the biggest bank frauds in the history of South Carolina. He pleaded guilty in 1995 and received a pardon from Bill Clinton on January 20, 2001. Christopher V. Wade, a real estate agent involved in Whitewater, hid assets in a bankruptcy case and pleaded guilty to fraud charges not related to Whitewater. Wade, too, received a last-minute pardon. Stanley Pruet Jobe, convicted in a check-kiting scheme, was pardoned on Clinton's last day. Stuart Harris Cohn, guilty of a 1979 commodities violation and pardoned by Bill Clinton, is the brother-in-law of a former Democratic representative, Sam Gejdenson.

Richard Pezzopane and William Arthur Borders were both convicted of bribing a judge. No problem. Both received pardons. Jimmy Rogers, a South Carolina county sheriff, pleaded guilty to taking bribes to allow gambling by organized crime. He received a pardon along with fellow South Carolinian Leonard Browder of Aiken, sentenced to five years' probation for Medicaid fraud and illegally dispensing controlled substances. Robert Michael Williams was convicted of conspiracy to transport in foreign commerce securities obtained by fraud. He was also pardoned. Pardon recipient Joseph A. Yasak was a Chicago police sergeant convicted of lying to a grand jury.

While the "big" pardons of Marc Rich and Carlos Vignali got the most attention and prompted the most indignation, some of the "smaller" pardons showed that there were few depths to which Bill Clinton would not descend.

On his last day in office the president of the United States pardoned Art and Doug Borel, a pair of Arkansas good old boys who were caught rolling back the odometers on used cars, a federal crime and an offense that obviously victimizes poor people. The Borels had been rolling back odometers for years but got caught in 1991 when the FBI sent an attractive female agent to their Auto Clock and Speedometer Shop in Little Rock, asking to have her odometer rolled back. The brothers obliged.

The Borels' main complaint about their record was that it prevented them from buying firearms for hunting. Remarkably enough, the Borels were not the only used-car odometer cheats to benefit from the presidential pen.

Larry Lee Duncan of Branson, Missouri, was also busted for rolling back odometers. He hired a Little Rock attorney to file his request and also received a pardon from Bill Clinton, on his last day in office.

So did Billy Wayne Warmath, sixty-two, of Walls, Mississippi, who went to prison for a year and a day after a September 1965 conviction in federal court for using a Texaco credit card that came addressed to a man who had previously rented Warmath's house. Warmath used the card nineteen times, running up purchases totaling $123.26. Warmath was totally stunned by the presidential pardon. "It won't really change a thing," he said. "I'm going to be mean no matter what happens. But damn, I'm happy about this."[23] Mr. Warmath may, as it turns out, have been the most honest man to receive a Clinton pardon.

If Bill Clinton was hoping his pardons would secure his place in history, he certainly gained a sort of distinction by becoming the first president to pardon an anteater smuggler. In 1988, a federal grand jury indicted Howard Winfield Riddle in a scheme to smuggle the skins of endangered anteaters from Thailand to Texas, where anteater skin is prized for cowboy boots. Riddle was sentenced to ten months in jail, community service, and a $30,000 fine. He first applied for a pardon in 1995. The president rejected the bid in 1998, but on January 20, 2001, opted to pardon Riddle, who said his only connection to Clinton was that he voted for him twice.[24]

Bill Clinton's pardon pen seemed to favor criminals from the South and Southeast. Pardon recipients included four Floridians, four Oklahomans, seven South Carolinians, and twenty-four Arkansans.

Money Plus Access Equals Pardon

Bill Clinton granted forty-seven clemencies without any examination or review by the pardon attorney of the Department of Justice. This was nearly a third of the total and nearly twice as many as the two dozen originally reported. The cases that bypassed normal channels included brother Roger, Susan McDougal, Henry Cisneros, and many others.

To all but the willfully blind, money, power, connections, and, above all, access had been key factors in obtaining pardons and commutations from Bill Clinton. That was clear even to still imprisoned spy Jonathan Pollard, who told the Israeli newspaper *Yedioth Aharonoth* that he had made a mistake trying to catch the attention of Israeli politicians by "waving the flag of Israel." Instead, he said, "I should have waved a dollar bill in front of them and convinced them that I had a lot of money."[25] But why odometer fraud Larry Lee Duncan, among countless thousands of convicted felons nationwide, should have received a pardon from the president of the United States, the most powerful man in the world, was one of the lingering mysteries. And how had an obscure anteater smuggler and a small-time credit-card cheat made the list?

Another mystery was whether pardoned drug kingpin Carlos Vignali and his handlers had leaked news of Hugh Rodham's service to the *National Enquirer* as a way to get back his $200,000 fee.

As spectacular and audacious as it was, the president's last-minute pardons of drug smugglers, terrorists, crooks, quacks, scammers, frauds, tax cheats, money launderers, politicians, thugs, international fugitives, arms dealers, and miscellaneous perjurers did not exhaust the possibilities of reprieve from the Clinton administration.

In 1999, the Treasury Department fined musician Ry Cooder $25,000 for failing to obtain the proper license to travel to Cuba and make the Grammy-winning recordings featured in the *Buena Vista Social Club*. In August of 2000, Cooder applied for a legal permit.

In September, he gave $10,000 to the Senate campaign of Hillary Clinton. On January 17, 2001, three days before Bill Clinton left office, he got his permit, with help from Secretary of State Madeleine Albright.

Cooder and Hillary denied there was any link between the permit and the contribution. Perhaps. You decide.

Bill and Hillary "Explain" the Pardons | 12

Of all the desperate sounds and fury of the final days of the Clinton administration—there was enough to keep reporters and congressional committees busy for weeks—none drew more attention and yells of outrage than the pardon of Marc Rich. Earlier Clinton misbehavior had first evoked the loud criticism of conservatives and Republicans. This time it was the Democrats, many of them liberal, leading the chorus.

"I think President Clinton made one of his most serious mistakes in the way he handled the pardon situation the last few hours he was in office," said Jimmy Carter in a speech at Georgia Southwestern State University. "A number of them were quite questionable, including about forty not recommended by the Justice Department." On Clinton's pardon of Marc Rich, Carter was more specific: "I don't think there is any doubt that some of the factors in his pardon were attributable to his large gifts. In my opinion, that was disgraceful."[1]

Paul Goldman of the Democratic National Committee, and former chairman of the Democratic Party in Virginia, called for censure of the former president, because he had "made hollow a key tenet of Democratic philosophy—that the president is the moral center of our political system and must lead by example to capture the power of America's principled idealism."

As Mr. Clinton left office, Goldman said, he pardoned an elitist who fleeced working people and then bought his way out of jail, adding, "Mr. Clinton didn't just take the White House china; he took its soul and flushed it down the toilet."

Democrats had to speak out, "to regain our party's soul," Goldman went on. Referring to the Democratic Party, and Clinton's departure as president, he invoked the Reverend Martin Luther King's famous "Free at Last" speech at the Lincoln memorial.[2]

This was powerful stuff, but it was echoed by the angst pouring from other Democrats and editorial pages everywhere. The combined censure finally got to Bill Clinton, whose blunted political sensibilities began to come back to life. Besides, the furor was not only damaging his treasured legacy, it was beginning to cut into his speaking fees. He addressed the issue on February 18 in the *New York Times*, in a defiant and fascinating 1,700-word op-ed piece entitled "My Reasons for the Pardons."

Eight Reasons, Four Lies

"Because of the intense scrutiny and criticism" of the Marc Rich and Pincus Green pardons, "I want to explain what I did and why," wrote Clinton.

After some trite, generalized comments about pardons and commutations of sentences, obviously pulled together by a speechwriter with a digest of American history at his fingertips, the former president explained that "the exercise of executive clemency is inherently controversial." Further, "the reason the framers of our Constitution vested this broad power in the Executive Branch was to assure that the president would have the freedom to do what he deemed to be the right thing, regardless of how unpopular a decision might be."

Clinton cited George Washington's pardons of leaders of the Whiskey Rebellion, Harding's commutation of the sentence of Eugene Debs, President Nixon's commutation of the sentence of James Hoffa, President Ford's pardon of former president Nixon, President Carter's pardon of Vietnam War draft resisters, and President Bush's 1992 pardon of six Iran-contra defendants, including former defense secretary Weinberger.

Having made the moral equivalency point, invoking not only George Washington but also the demon Richard Nixon—twice—Clinton got down to brass tacks. "On Jan. 20, 2001, I granted 140 pardons and issued 36 commutations," Clinton said, comparing his "total of approximately 450 pardons and commutations" to other presidents' totals.

"The vast majority of my Jan. 20 pardons and reprieves went to people who are not well known. Some had been sentenced pursuant to mandatory-sentencing drug laws, and I felt that they had served long enough, given the particular circumstances of the individual cases."

Many of these, Clinton argued were nonviolent and had been unfairly punished. Some had been treated badly by independent counsels, appointed, he did not mention, at the request of his own attorney general to investigate alleged misconduct by his appointees. The remainder of the pardons and commutations, he said, were granted for "a wide variety of fact-based reasons."

The common denominator, Clinton said, was that the recipients were "deserving of executive clemency." They had served their time, he added, and it was time to restore their civil rights.

He finally arrived at the central issue: Marc Rich and Pincus Green.

Ordinarily, I would have denied pardons in this case simply because these men did not return to the United States to face the charges against them. However, I decided to grant the pardons in this unusual case for the following legal and foreign policy reasons: (1) I understood that the other [similarly situated] oil companies [were] sued civilly by the government; (2) I was informed that, in 1985, in a related case against a trading partner of Mr. Rich and Mr. Green, the Energy Department... found that the manner in which the Rich/Green companies had accounted for these transactions was proper; (3) two highly regarded tax experts... reviewed the transactions in question and concluded that the companies "were correct in their U.S. income tax treatment of all the items in question..."; (4) in order to settle the government's case against them, the two men's companies had paid approximately $200 million in fines, penalties and taxes; (5) the Justice Department in 1989 rejected the use of racketeering statutes in tax cases like this one...; (6) it was my understanding that Deputy Attorney General Eric Holder's position on the pardon application was "neutral, leaning for"; (7) the case for the pardons was reviewed and advocated not only by my former White House counsel Jack Quinn but also by three distinguished Republican attorneys: Leonard Garment, a former Nixon White House official; William Bradford Reynolds, a former high-ranking official in the Reagan Justice Department; and Lewis Libby, now Vice President Cheney's chief of staff; (8) finally, and importantly, many present and former high-ranking Israeli officials of both major political parties and leaders of Jewish communities in America and Europe urged the pardon of Mr. Rich because of his contributions and services to Israeli charitable causes, to the Mossad's efforts to rescue and evacuate Jews from hostile countries, and to the peace process through sponsorship of education and health programs in Gaza and the West Bank....

I believe my pardon decision was in the best interests of justice. If the two men were wrongly indicted in the first place, justice has been done....

The suggestion that I granted the pardons because Mr. Rich's former wife, Denise, made political contributions and contributed to the Clinton library foundation is utterly false. There was absolutely no quid pro quo....

I am accustomed to the rough and tumble of politics, but the accusations made against me in this case have been particularly painful because for eight years I worked hard to make good decisions for the American people. I want every American to know that, while you may disagree with this decision, I made it on the merits as I saw them, and I take full responsibility for it.[3]

There you have it. Fugitive tax cheats were pardoned because prosecutors—under several different presidents, including his own Justice Department—had been wrongfully persecuting Mr. Rich and Mr. Green. No need for a trial to prove that. And there was no quid pro quo. And the ex-president was suffering from acute pain that anyone would think otherwise.

Reaction to the op-ed piece was swift and unfavorable. The *New York Times* offered an editorial response the following day. The editors found Mr. Clinton's explanation "unconvincing" as to the legal issues and "evasive in its failure to explain why Mr. Clinton was discussing Mr. Rich's case with major contributors to his party while he kept the Department of Justice in the dark about his consideration of a pardon for one of the nation's most famous tax fugitives."

Further, "we do not find his assertion that there was 'absolutely no quid pro quo' involving money to be a satisfactory explanation for the tangle of lobbying, public relations and legal activities depicted in e-mails among Ms. Rich, Beth Dozoretz, a former finance chairwoman of the Democratic National Committee, and Jack Quinn, the former White House counsel who became Mr. Rich's lawyer."

The editorial advised its readers to make up their minds whether they believed the former president. (Had he ever lied to them before?) However, "The plain fact is that Mr. Rich was an unsuitable candidate for a pardon. He fled the country rather than answer a legitimate summons to court. His wealth enabled him to claim citizenship in other countries and live in luxury abroad and then, with the help of friends and a lawyer with White House connections, to leap to the head of the pardon queue. Mr. Clinton conceded that a more typical pardon candidate would be someone who had served a prison sentence and thereafter lived within the law."

Mr. Rich and Mr. Green, of course, had not served a prison sentence. They had fled the country, removing themselves from the reach of the justice system to which all other Americans are subject. They then announced their distrust of that system. And President Clinton had just told the nation that they were right.

The editorial concluded: "The story of this pardon begins and ends with money and the access afforded by money. That is the unique circumstance that will linger in the minds of Americans whenever they contemplate this gross misuse of a solemn presidential responsibility."

One of the most biting and incisive reviews of Clinton's op-ed came from Michael Kelly, who had covered Clinton's 1992 campaign for the *New York Times* and was now the editor of the *Atlantic Monthly*. Kelly was one of the few journalists Bill Clinton had ever telephoned, weighing in with the writer to deny that Hillary had called a former campaign worker a "fucking Jew bastard." In the *Washington Post* on February 21, 2001, Kelly said that the former president's rationalization for the Rich/Green pardons is "in almost every important way a lie."

The first lie, Kelly wrote, was contextual. Yes, other presidents have issued pardons, and some of these were controversial. "But no other president ever did what Clinton did," wrote Kelly, and none "sought to corrupt the pardoning process on a wholesale basis. None set up a secret shop to bypass his own government and speed through the special pleas of the well connected and the well heeled. None sent the Justice Department dozens of names for pardon on inauguration morning, too late for the department to run even cursory checks."

A later version of the *Times* op-ed piece by Clinton, arranged by some of Clinton's handlers, toned down some of the president's assertions, but it was, at bottom, still the same grossly misleading, singularly unpersuasive, public relations ploy.

"Eight reasons; four lies," concluded Michael Kelly. "Not bad, even for the old master himself."[4]

No rejoinder appeared from the former president. Having made one effort to paper over the controversy, he apparently considered the matter closed. After all, he was no longer accountable to anyone and was not planning to run for office anytime soon. All he had to do was scratch out a living giving speeches, and further discussion of the pardons would not serve any constructive purpose. Clinton had been forgiven again and again by his liberal supporters. He knew they would get over this one too.

Hillary's Turn

But Hillary did not have it quite as easy. She was a new senator. It was decidedly unhelpful that her brother had been caught selling favors from her husband. She had to respond in some fashion. So she trotted out her tried-and-true "I am victim" script along with the always successful—for her—"I didn't have anything to do with it" mantra. The two approaches worked particularly well in combination, especially when seasoned with heavy repetition of the expression "you know," thus bringing the listener in on the act.

"Well, I was very disappointed and saddened by this whole matter. You know, it came as a surprise to me, and it was very disturbing. And I'm just very disappointed about it," she said in a news conference. "With respect to any questions about the pardons or the president's handling of the pardons, you'll have to ask him or his staff about that."

Hillary's entire press conference was one long plea for pity. She was surprised, you know, and disappointed, you know, and, you know, hurt. Poor, poor pitiful Hillary:

> "You know, I did not have any involvement in the pardons that were granted or not granted, you know, and I'm just very disappointed about my brother's involvement."

> "You know, as I have said in the past, when it became apparent around Christmas that people knew that the president was considering pardons, there were many, many people who spoke to me or, you know, asked me to pass on information to the White House Counsel's Office. I've already said that I did that, and I did. There were many, many people who had an interest, a friend, a relative, but it was all passed on to the White House Counsel's Office, and they, along with the president, made the decisions."

> "If I had known about this, we wouldn't be standing here today. I didn't know about it, and I'm very regretful that it occurred, that I didn't know about it. I might have been able

to prevent this from happening. And I'm just very disappointed about the whole matter."

"I don't know anything other than what has now come out, and I did not learn about that until very recently."

"I did not know my brother was involved in any way in any of this. I learned that there were some press inquiries, of a vague nature, last week sometime."

"I did not know any specific information until late Monday night. I was actually in a movie theater, and I was called and told that my brother had been involved and had taken money for his involvement.

"And as soon as I found out, I was very upset about it and very disappointed about it."

"[My brother] was a frequent guest at the White House. You know, he's my brother. I love my brother. I'm just extremely disappointed in this terrible misjudgment that he made."

"As soon as we found out Monday night, I was heartbroken and shocked by it, and, you know, immediately said this was a terrible misjudgment and the money had to be returned. And that's what we worked on."

"I was reacting as someone who was extremely disappointed in this whole matter. This was a very sad occurrence to have happen. And I wanted to be sure that the money was returned, and it has been."

"[L]et me use my own words, and my own words are that I'm very disappointed, I'm very saddened, and I was very disturbed when I heard about it."

"[It's] very regrettable, and it shouldn't have happened. And if I'd had any knowledge or notice of it, I believe I might have been able to prevent it. I don't think we'd be standing here talking about it. But I did not."

"[Y]ou know, I'm very disappointed about what's gone on for the last weeks. It is certainly not how I would have preferred or planned to start my Senate career, and I regret deeply that there has been these kinds of matters occurring."

"I have my hands full being a senator, learning the ropes, you know, working with my colleagues, dealing with my constituents, and I love doing it. I'm having a really good time doing it, but, of course, I'm disappointed and saddened that, you know, these matters are up."

"Obviously, I wish that the last weeks had unfolded differently, and I'm very sorry that they have not.

"But all I can say is now I've got a position and a responsibility that I'm going to do my very best to fulfill to the very best of my ability. And people will have to judge me at the end of my term based on what I do, and that's what I'm going to ask people to do."

"I really think that everything has to be put in context. And I know that that's often difficult to do, but I feel that our country is stronger and better because of the Clinton administration."

"You know, I don't have any memory at all of ever talking to my brother about this. You know, that's my best memory.

"But I have to say, and I will repeat once again, information was coming to me, information was passed on. So, you know, if I said information came, people wanted to look at, I might have said that. I just don't remember anything further than that."

"I knew nothing about my brother's involvement in these pardons. I knew nothing about his taking money for his involvement. I had no knowledge of that whatsoever."

"You know, I mean, I've said that I think my brother made a terrible misjudgment."

And for final emphasis:

"I don't personally have any information."

Remarkably, Hillary was able to stand before the press and the American public and deny—again and again—that she had ever spoken to her brother about his frantic efforts to secure pardons from her husband *and* that she *ever* spoken with her husband about pardons, a subject that consumed Bill Clinton over the last weeks of his presidency. Denise Rich, Jack Quinn, Beth Dozoretz, everyone in the White House Counsel's Office, prison grapevines, brothers, and mothers-in-law—everyone around Bill Clinton knew that he had pardons on his mind. Everyone spoke to him about it, except his beloved wife, his co-president. Remarkable. Just like the time Hillary sat in on the meeting to discuss the pardons on the Hasidic embezzlers and never uttered a sound—she repeatedly asserted that she acted as a conduit for pardon requests without saying a word about what she was doing. Hillary's version of the virgin birth.

HILLARY: You know, I never talk about conversations with my husband.

QUESTION: But this is a question that is being investigated. Have you sat down, at least—even if you don't want to say what you talked about—have you sat down with your husband and said, "What went on?"

HILLARY: You will have to ask the president and his staff any specific questions about any pardons that were or were not granted.

QUESTION: Senator, is Marc Rich among the people that he passed information on?

HILLARY: No. You know, I never knew about Marc Rich at all. You know, people would hand me envelopes, I would just pass them. You know, I would not have any reason to look into them. I knew nothing about the Marc Rich pardon until after it happened.

QUESTION: Had your brother been warned at all to avoid this kind of thing after the episode with the hazelnuts?

HILLARY: I don't know the answer to that. I believe so, but I don't know the answer to that.

QUESTION: Senator, do you think your husband made a mistake in pardoning Marc Rich?

HILLARY: I know that other senators have commented on this, and I think you might understand why I'm not going to have any comment on any of the pardons, on the merits or demerits that might surround any of these pardons.

QUESTION: Are you going over any of these pardons now, yourself, to see which one next could possibly create another political problem for you and/or your husband?

HILLARY: You know, I have no idea what is coming next. You know, I was talking to a friend of mine today, and you know, we were just amazed by what has unfolded over the past weeks. I don't have any information. I don't know anything about these.

And if issues are raised, I'm going to be in the same position as I've been in, which is to say that, you know, I was not involved in the decisions. I didn't even know about the vast majority of these things ever being considered. And you'll have to, really, ask the president and his staff who handled all of this.

QUESTION: ...the $400,000 your brother received had absolutely nothing to do with the president's decision to pardon these two men?

HILLARY: I believe that's the case. I absolutely believe that's the case. As far as I know, there was no connection whatsoever, and, you know, there was certainly no basis on which I even thought it was going on. And my husband has said that he didn't know that was going on. So as far as I know, there was no connection.

But again, with respect to any of these decisions. You'll have to talk with people who were involved in making them, and that leaves me out. I don't know enough to answer your questions. And I don't want to say anything that leads you to believe that I either know something or don't know something, because I don't. And so you'll have to ask people who were involved in them.

When Hillary was running for the Senate, she went to considerable lengths to portray herself as an active, involved partner in her husband's presidency. She claimed eight years worth of experience on the issues and ran her Senate race on the accomplishments of the Clinton administration, regaling reporters with the thorough, detailed discussions she had with "her husband." But now, in matters of huge importance involving her husband and brother, she claimed to know absolutely nothing at all. The first-rate scholar, veteran lawyer, graduate of Yale Law School, and eight-year resident in the White House, with her own office in the West Wing, had only lately even learned about the president's constitutional power to pardon.

Her press conference was a tour de force, something for the history books. It is not clear how much she had rehearsed, but she was incredibly consistent and focused on her dual message. She didn't know anything about what was going on. She said that or some variation of it more than *twenty* times. And she, herself, was the victim.

She was disturbed, disappointed (ten mentions of "disappointed"), saddened and sad, surprised, upset, heartbroken, shocked, and sorry. Oh yes, and the whole incident was deeply regrettable. And, finally, note the references to "the president." When Hillary wants to identify with what Bill Clinton does, he is "her husband." In this speech/press conference, except for one reference, the spouse of these many years became "the president."

In a sense, this breathtaking performance defied analysis or even satire. Christopher Buckley, author of comic novels and editor of *Forbes FYI,* made a gallant attempt with a *Wall Street Journal* opinion piece purporting to be by Hillary Clinton herself.

"I had hoped by now to be serving full-time the many citizens of New York State who elected me to be their senator," the piece opened. "However, because of certain actions undertaken by people whose name I appear to share, it is necessary to interrupt my important work on behalf of children, women, the elderly, minorities, the constituents of the Rev. Al Sharpton, the homeless, and certain communities in Rockland County, N.Y., to point out that none of these shocking, saddening, heartbreaking, deplorable, unspeakable, wretched, repugnant and personally disappointing things had anything remotely to do with me."

"Finally let me say that I was as surprised as anyone when I was informed that I have a brother named Hugh Rodham. He does not bear much resemblance to me. While I did grow up in a household with numerous other people, I was never informed that I had brothers. It was never discussed. If it was, I was not present. Clearly, exhaustive DNA testing is required before a conclusive biological link can be established between me and this alarming individual."[5]

The Buckley piece is indeed very funny but his effort at satire is a stretch because his imaginary column is only slightly more fantastic than the real thing. Michael Tomasky, author of *Hillary's Turn: Inside Her Improbable, Victorious Senate Campaign*, a work highly sympathetic to the senator, observed that "With Hillary, there was something about the way she answered questions that only raised other questions."[6]

That reality had seldom been showcased more graphically than with her press conference denial of any knowledge of her brother's and husband's pardon conspiracy. An equally dramatic showcase was her audacious play for sympathy for having, once again, been betrayed by those around her.

On February 14, the Senate Judiciary Committee held hearings on "Bill Clinton's Eleventh-Hour Pardons." "I certainly believe that in the case of criminal pardons a president should vet those pardons," said Democratic senator Dianne Feinstein of California, "not only with the Department of Justice, with the line prosecutor, with judges, with victims—and we saw that in the Puerto Rican case where none of the victims were consulted, and there was broad concern about those pardons. I have concerns not only about the Rich pardon but with a number of the criminal pardons."

Senator Charles Schumer, the senior senator from New York, also a Democrat, added, "To my mind, there can be no justification for pardoning a fugitive from justice. It does not matter that the fugitive believed the case against him was flawed or weak. It does not matter that the fugitive was enormously philanthropic. Pardoning a fugitive stands our justice system on its head and makes a mockery of it. One of the great strengths of our criminal justice system is that it is just that, a system. By allowing someone to choose to opt out of that system by fleeing and then opt into that system to get a pardon perverts the system entirely."

Department of Justice pardon attorney Roger Adams testified that when he was told that Marc Rich was "living abroad," he was not told that Rich was a fugitive, or under indictment.

"The President Was the President"

The House Committee on Government Reform under Indiana Republican Dan Burton also took up the pardon issue. The committee sought testimony from those who knew the most.

Television journalist Alan Colmes, the liberal half of Fox's *Hannity and Colmes*, questioned whether this was a legitimate inquiry for that committee, whose chairman was among the Clintons' staunchest critics. It should be recalled, however, that the Government Reform Committee had dealt with Marc Rich before, holding hearings led by Democrat Chairman Bob Wise in 1991 and 1992. While Marc Rich was a fugitive, one of his companies, Clarendon, had sold more than $4 million of nickel and copper to the United States Mint, a division of the very Treasury Department he had defrauded. Given this huge embarrassment, which deepened the case against Rich, the question for the committee concerned reforms that would prevent such a thing from happening again. So Marc Rich, the man the president had pardoned, was a very appropriate subject for this committee.

Here again the public heard a reprise of the now famous impersonal mistakes-were-made defense. "In hindsight, I wish that I had done some things differently with regard to the Marc Rich matter," testified Deputy Attorney General Eric Holder on February 8.

"Specifically, I wish that I had insured that the Department of Justice was more fully informed and involved in this pardon process." The Rich case, said Holder, did not stand out as one that was "particularly meritorious."

Consider that piece of innocent, understated plea for understanding. Mr. Holder pleaded guilty of having failed to ensure that his department had had greater involvement in a pardon that was not "particularly meritorious." Holder went on to recount his January 19 call from Jack Quinn and subsequent call from White House counsel Beth Nolan, and his "neutral, leaning towards favorable" opinion on the Rich pardon.

"Indeed it is now clear, and this is admittedly hindsight, that we at the Justice Department—and more importantly, former president Clinton, the American public, and the cause of justice—would have been better served if this case had been handled through the normal channels," Holder said. Here the number two person in the Department of Justice, who had knowingly stood silent while a major fugitive was pardoned, was able to get by with a simple misdemeanor plea for failing to observe "normal channels."

"DR," or Denise Rich, who was on such good terms with "No.1," Bill Clinton, was obviously an authority on Marc Rich and how he had received his pardon. The committee sent her a list of fourteen questions, including:

> ➤ Were all political contributions made by you between 1992 and the present made with your own money?
> ➤ Were you ever provided with money by any individual so that you could make a political contribution?
> ➤ How much money have you given or pledged to the Clinton Library?
> ➤ Describe all contacts you have had with President Bill Clinton regarding your former husband, Marc Rich.

➤ Did you ever discuss a pardon for Marc Rich with President Clinton? If so, describe the substance, place and time of such discussions.

➤ Did you ever discuss a pardon for any other individual with President Clinton or any other White House staff?

➤ Please list all gifts that you have given either to former president Clinton or to Senator Hillary Rodham Clinton.

These and other questions would have shed considerable light on many of the issues. But Denise Rich declined to testify, based on her Fifth Amendment right against self-incrimination. The Rubenesque songwriter, who had been seen on the cover of tabloids in the company of Bill Clinton, and who had been repeatedly shown on television presenting a golden saxophone to the president, and who launched a spectacular public relations campaign to explain her innocence of any wrongdoing, simply failed to show for the committee's March 1 hearing.

Beth Dozoretz did show up for the hearing, permanent smile on her face, but was just as unwilling to answer any questions. The Democratic fundraiser offered no opening statement, but committee members had a number of questions. "Now, what I would like to ask is the following," said Representative Christopher Shays. "Exhibit 63 is an e-mail which indicates that on January 10, 2001, President Clinton called you in Aspen, Colorado, where you were staying with Denise Rich. The e-mail indicates that the president discussed the Marc Rich pardon with you before he spoke with the Justice Department. My question is, at any time while you were discussing the Marc Rich pardon with President Clinton, did either you or the president mention Denise Rich's contribution to the Clinton Library or the Democratic National Committee?"

Dozoretz responded: "Upon the advice of my counsel, I respectfully decline to answer that question based on the protection afforded me under the United States Constitution." She added, "Sir, that will be my response to all questions."

Jack Quinn, who had testified once several weeks earlier, was quite willing to answer questions and did so skillfully and with considerable aplomb. But he could not offer much concerning the subjects that Denise Rich and Beth Dozoretz were unwilling to discuss.

"I informed Beth Dozoretz sometime around the Thanksgiving holiday that I would be pursuing a pardon for Marc Rich," Quinn testified. "I did so because she was a friend of mine, because she had a relationship with Denise Rich. She was in much more frequent communication with the president than I was."

Quinn's basic position had not changed.

"I did believe in the merits of the case I made," he said. "I still do. I don't expect to convince anyone of that, after all the publicity we've seen and all the questions that have been raised. But I believed in it and I do today. And I would not have misrepresented the facts, either to the people sitting alongside me or to the president."

Sitting alongside him were former Clinton staffers, who managed to shed some enlightenment but not on the key issues. Chief of Staff John Podesta and White House counsel Beth Nolan testified that they had considered the pardon request for Marc Rich dead. Nolan was speaking out publicly on the pardons for the first time. Nolan said she opposed a pardon for Marc Rich. Likewise, Bruce Lindsey, a former White House counsel and longtime friend of the president, said he opposed a pardon for Marc Rich because he was a fugitive.

So why, given all the opposition, did Bill Clinton grant the pardon? "The president was the president, sir," said Beth Nolan. "And I even had that discussion with him on the 19th, because we were in some heated discussion about one of the pardons, and I said, 'Look, my job is to tell you what I think about this and to tell you what my best judgment about it is, but I know who's president and who's not.' And he got to exercise the pardon power."

The syllogism was as starkly simple as it was irrefutable. The president has the power to pardon. Bill Clinton was the president. Bill Clinton granted the pardons because he had the power to do so. The president was the president.

Nolan said she was not aware that Denise Rich had contributed $1.2 million to the Democratic National Committee, $75,000 to Senator Clinton's campaign, and $450,000 to the Clinton Library. But it did emerge that former deputy counsel Cheryl Mills, who represented Clinton during the impeachment proceedings before leaving the White House for a job in the private sector, and who was, coincidentally, a fundraiser for the Clinton Library Foundation, was strangely present for a January 19 Oval Office discussion about pardons. When Justice Department pardon attorney Roger Adams called the White House Counsel's Office on January 20, it was Mills and not Nolan who answered the White House Office of Counsel to the President's phone.

Jack Quinn testified that he didn't know of Mills's involvement with the Clinton Library until Bill Clinton was out of office. Bruce Lindsey, who has a very close relationship with Mills dating back to 1996, testified that he was also a consultant for the Clinton Library while he was still in office, and still remained a consultant. But, of course, he denied discussing library matters with Denise Rich. It is truly remarkable how these things happen without people talking about them.

The $125-million Clinton Library is slated for a warehouse district called Murky Bottoms along the Arkansas River. It will be part of a $200-million complex that includes museums, a farmers' market, and headquarters for the regional library system. The library will reportedly include a 5,000-square-foot penthouse apartment.

Besides housing the Clinton memorabilia, the library plays a strategic role as a place to channel donations and reward friends. It would take the place of the Arkansas Highway Department and Development Finance Authority, which, as Roger Morris noted, became then-governor Clinton's "political piggy bank."[7]

The library foundation is dominated by close friends of the Clintons, including Terry McAuliffe, chairman of the Democratic National Committee; Ann Jordan, wife of Vernon Jordan, the Washington lawyer who helped find a job for Monica Lewinsky; and Cheryl Mills.

Time magazine reported that Beth Dozoretz and Denise Rich were among fifteen donors invited to one of the first library fundraisers, a 1999 meeting in a Manhattan hotel attended by Bill Clinton himself. It was Dozoretz, sources said, who introduced Denise Rich to the library effort.[8]

The Burton committee sought records of library donors. While Dozoretz refused to testify about the subject, the hearings provided a moment of illumination when Henry Waxman, California Democrat and a staunch defender of the president during the impeachment process, addressed the personal-versus-political issue.

"The president's relationship with a White House intern was a personal failing and a betrayal of his family. Everything that sprang from that scandal, including his false testimony under oath, came from that personal failure," said Waxman.

"In this case, however," he went on, "Mr. Clinton's failure to exercise sound judgment affected one of the most important duties of the presidency. Bad judgment is obviously not impeachable, but the failures in the pardon process should embarrass every Democrat and every American. It's a shameful lapse of judgment that must be acknowledged...."

Waxman noted that "the president could not grant a pardon in exchange for any personal benefit. A quid pro quo obviously would break the law. And although the president's pardon power is absolute, it is not above the law." While Waxman considered the pardon affair more bad judgment than illegality, he wasn't willing to let the issue drop.

Said Waxman, "[G]iven the extraordinary circumstances of the Rich pardon, it's important the U.S. Attorney's Office in New York fully, quickly, and impartially investigate this issue. The U.S. attorney is doing that, and its investigation should resolve any questions of illegality for the American people."

The Burton hearings ended late. The next day John Podesta unwound from his testimony at Stetson's, a Washington bar. There a dozen party goers compelled the former Clinton chief of staff to quaff various drinks in commemoration of his damage control work on various White House scandals. The libations included tequila for Travelgate, Jack Daniel's for Whitewater, Sex on the Beach for Monica Lewinsky, and last but not least, a Kamikaze for Pardongate.[9]

Meanwhile, Mary Jo White, the U.S. attorney for the Southern District of New York, a Clinton appointee, is investigating the pardons, and Attorney General John Ashcroft has decided to leave her in office until that odious political task has been completed. Ms. White was tagged "Mary Jo Whitewash" by one conservative commentator for a perceived failure to pursue Terry McAuliffe, the Clinton ally now head of the Democratic National Committee, in connection with a case involving a Teamsters Union kickback scheme.

But White was reportedly furious over the pardons, especially the one granted to Marc Rich. And she appears to be pursuing the pardon cases with vigor, working with the FBI and subpoenaing records from the Clinton Library as well as all government records on the cases. If she manages to win an indictment, it could lead to a sequel similar to Watergate. That scandal, which led to Richard Nixon's resignation, prompted many to conclude that, in the end, "the system worked." The same could be said if the courts act in accord with the principle that nobody, not even the president, is above the law.

But few see that prospect as likely. On the February 24 show of CNN's *Capital Gang*, Al Hunt said, "Look, I don't think that the U.S. attorney in New York or the congressional inquiry, certainly not the loopy Danny Burton, are going to ever prove a quid pro quo here. That's not the way the rot and money in politics works. It's not that explicit." All that is explicit is that rot, money, and Clintons go together.

The Toll Bridge to the Twenty-First Century | **13**

Money, Venality, Sacrilege

Two days after Bill Clinton's failed defense of the Rich pardon, Jimmy Carter's former chief of staff, Hamilton Jordan, explained the difference between Bill Clinton and other presidents in an op-ed piece entitled "The First Grifters."[1]

"It is difficult for the average citizen to comprehend how outrageous Bill Clinton's pardons are to those of us who have worked in the White House," wrote Jordan, who outlined the time-honored process followed by Jimmy Carter and other presidents for the issuance of pardons.... That process was quite intentionally circumvented," by President Clinton personally, in the Marc Rich case.

"We do know that Mr. Clinton found time to confer with his political advisers, party fundraisers, Denise Rich, her friends, and even foreign leaders about the pardon," wrote Jordan, but not the prosecutors and law enforcement officials responsible for protecting the integrity of the criminal justice system. Jordan declared that if he had approached President Carter for a pardon being sought by someone who had contributed to his presidential library, "he would have thrown me out of the Oval Office and probably fired me on the spot."

Hamilton Jordan could not conceive of any other chief of staff—Dick Cheney, Howard Baker, Jim Baker, or Leon Panetta—discussing with his president the political pros and cons of a pardon for a fugitive who had renounced his citizenship and fled the country to escape prosecution on tax fraud and racketeering charges.

"It is incredible that the ethical atmosphere of the Clinton White House had sunk to a level whereby the constitutional power of a president to issue a pardon was discussed among Mr. Clinton and his White House staff as just one more perk of office," Jordan wrote. Clinton, he said, had disgraced and demeaned his office by treating the pardon power in the same manner as giving campaign contributors overnight stays in the Lincoln bedroom or flights on Air Force One. How could this have happened?

Hillary had made the environment infinitely worse by exploiting "her public image of a wronged but loyal spouse to create a new persona for herself and win election to the Senate." The Clintons, he went on, "are not a couple but a business partnership, not based on love or even greed but on shared ambitions.... The Clintons' only loyalty is to their own ambitions." Every move they make, he went on, is "part of their grand scheme to claw their way to the very top." Jordan saw the Clintons as tawdry, unprincipled, opportunistic, taking advantage of anyone weak enough to fall for their stories. He called them "grifters...a term used in the Great Depression to describe fast-talking con artists who roamed the countryside, profiting at the expense of the poor and the uneducated, always one step ahead of the law, moving on before they were held accountable for their schemes and half-truths."

It was hard to conceive of any Republican delivering a tougher assessment than that. But Jordan was just one of many equally harsh bipartisan assessments of the Clinton character.

"I think people are beginning to feel that the bridge to the 21st century is a toll bridge that people have to pay to get across," said Arkansas governor Mike Huckabee, in a February 24 appearance on NBC's *Meet the Press*. He said that Clinton's last-minute flurry of pardons and the surrounding air of impropriety had caused embarrassment in Clinton's home state, where his previous scandals were well known. "If they [the pardons] look suspicious to James Carville, I think it's fair to say they look suspicious to everybody," said Huckabee.

Other governors, in Washington for the winter meeting of the National Governor's Association, used the occasion to speak out. "Like a lot of us, [Clinton] made mistakes and a lot of those pardons were clearly mistakes," said Governor Gray Davis of California, a Democrat widely believed to be considering a presidential bid. (Of course, Davis, who had presided over California's energy debacle, was only too pleased to point out mistakes by others. Governor Davis needed to look better than somebody.)

"Obviously there were serious issues raised by the pardons. It's troubling," said Governor Jim Hodges of South Carolina, also a Democrat. "I think it raises questions about the pardon process." (A gentle and misleading way of putting it. There was nothing wrong with the "process." The problem was that Bill Clinton had ignored the usual process. The problem was the president.)

"There's no excuse for what he did for Marc Rich. This should not have been done," said Senator Tom Harkin, Iowa Democrat.[2]

"I think either the president had an incredible lapse in memory or was brain dead," said Senator Joe Biden, a Democrat. For another Democrat, Senator Zell Miller, "It was a tremendous mistake on his [Clinton's] part, and I think it's something [that] will never go away."[3]

James Carville and Terry McAuliffe, two of the Clintons' loudest cheerleaders, went on record to say that the pardons were "a mistake" and raised "legitimate concerns." Al Gore, Clinton's vice president, though keeping a low profile, was reportedly "shocked."[4]

"It was a terrible thing he did," said Representative Barney Frank, the liberal Massachusetts Democrat, who staunchly defended Mr. Clinton during the Lewinsky scandal. "It was just abusive. These are people who forgot where the line was between public service and what was personally convenient for them."[5]

Congressman Frank, brother of one of the most reliable but generally inept Clinton apologists, Ann Lewis, and a member of the House Judiciary Committee, proposed a bill that would ban pardons between October 1 in a presidential election year and the end of a president's term.

In the Senate, Arlen Specter sponsored a bill that would require those pressing for presidential pardons and commutations to register as lobbyists. The bill would also require disclosure for those who donate more than $5,000 to presidential libraries. A spokeswoman for Hillary Clinton said the new senator from New York would support the measure, along with another by Mitch McConnell, chairman of the Senate Rules Committee, that would make senators-elect abide by Senate rules, rather than waiting until they are sworn in.[6] It was a measure, obviously, that would not apply retroactively to Hillary.

Hillary's support for these measures reprised a standard and regularly successful Clinton gambit. They would engage in some marginally lawful and blatantly abusive conduct, often actually violating existing laws. When caught in the act, they could call for new laws making their prior conduct illegal and decry the flaws in the system that allowed them to misbehave in the first place. It was like O. J. Simpson calling for an investigation to find the murderer of his wife. Except that the Clintons trotted out this maneuver again and again. While it had always worked for them in the past, even some of their most loyal supporters weren't buying it this time.

William M. Daley, who served as Mr. Clinton's commerce secretary and became Al Gore's presidential campaign chairman, called the pardons "terrible, devastating" and "rather appalling."[7] Spoken just like a candidate for his state's governorship!

Jerry Brown, mayor of Oakland and former governor of California, put it more bluntly. "He must have sugar plums dancing in his head," said Brown, who would know about such things. Brown, appearing on the February 21 broadcast of *Hannity and Colmes*, reminded the audience that "President Clinton didn't start out with a lot of scrupulosity." This is Californian Jerry Brown's way of saying, in more ordinary English, that Bill Clinton is, and always has been, unscrupulous. "Here we are talking money and venality," Brown, yet another unapprehended Yale Law School graduate, said, hinting that there might be "a criminal case."

Liberals were, finally, appalled. What Bill Clinton had done was in fact entirely predictable and entirely in keeping with his character and past conduct. But liberals seemed to think that something new, awful, quite completely unexpected, and "shocking, shocking" had occurred.

On the February 24, 2001, *Capital Gang* TV program, the eternally liberal Mark Shields asked Al Hunt of the *Wall Street Journal*, "What are these continuing revelations telling us about the legacy of Bill Clinton?" Replied Hunt, one of Clinton's staunchest defenders, "Mark, they leave a stain that is bigger than anything during impeachment which, despite the effort of Clinton-haters, really was all about awful personal behavior.... I think the damage is severe. I think it's lasting. It's on Bill Clinton's legacy. It's on Hillary Clinton, and it may well be on the Democratic Party."

Hunt had recently talked to two former cabinet members in the Clinton administration, two former top White House aides, and three lawmakers "who were very, very supportive of Bill Clinton." All, said Hunt, "used almost identical terms: disgusted, depressed, dispirited."

Somehow Hunt had rationalized lying under oath in a federal lawsuit and in front of a federal criminal grand jury by the president of the United States as nothing more than "awful personal behavior." But pardoning a tax-cheat fugitive—possibly for money—was disgusting.

This was the price that liberals paid for blinding themselves to the meaning of Bill Clinton's lawlessness and moral flaws. They had forgiven him so often for appalling personal—and legal—lapses, they were utterly at a loss to explain this latest abuse of power. They had convinced themselves that some lying, cheating, and lawlessness was tolerable without knowing that Clinton's brain just did not work that way. They could not bring themselves to understand that abuse of power and disrespect for the law and American institutions were real flaws, and that there were real consequences for these characteristics. They might have had to admit they had been wrong about the Clintons right from the beginning.

But the light did actually penetrate in a few quarters. *New York Times* columnist Bob Herbert is a left-winger known for vicious attacks on conservatives. On November 12, 1998, he wrote a piece titled "Run, Hillary, Run!" a plea for the first lady to enter the Senate race. Now Herbert felt betrayed and turned his late blooming sense of moral indignation on both Clintons.

"Mr. Clinton always had an easy, breezy relationship with wrongdoing," Herbert wrote. "But the Democratic Party overlooked the ethical red flags and made a pact with Mr. Clinton that was the equivalent of a pact with the devil. And he delivered. With Mr. Clinton at the controls, the party won the White House twice. But in the process it lost its bearings and maybe even its soul."

In the wake of the pardon scandal, "some of Mr. Clinton's closest associates and supporters are acknowledging what his enemies have argued for years—the man is so thoroughly corrupt it's frightening.... The president who hung a 'For Rent' sign on the door to the Lincoln Bedroom also conducted a clearance sale on pardons in his last weird sleepless days in the White House."

"The simple truth," he said, "is that the way in which some of the pardons were granted seems to fit neatly with the standard definition of a bribe, which is the promise of money or gifts—something of value—to influence the action or behavior of an official." He wondered in print whether the 1,400-12 count for Hillary from New Square, New York, was the result of a votes-for-clemency scheme.

Curiously, but characteristically, Herbert was outraged, not so much over what the Clintons had done to the country and to the rule of law, but over their having embarrassed and betrayed him personally and hurt the Democratic Party. "You can't lead a nation if you are ashamed of the leadership of your party. The Clintons are a terminally unethical and vulgar couple, and they've betrayed everyone who has ever believed in them.... As neither Clinton has the grace to retire from the scene, the Democrats have no choice but to turn their backs on them."[8]

Andrew Sullivan, writing in the *New Republic*, found something missing in the narrative of Bill Clinton. He, for one, did not think that President Clinton had been motivated by money or by the sexual charms of Denise Rich or Beth Dozoretz. He just couldn't find a rational explanation for the pardons of Marc Rich or Carlos Vignali.

"The rational answer is that there is no rational answer," wrote Sullivan in a "TRB From Washington" article titled "Psycho." The medical model of human behavior, which had been replacing the moral model for the past century, was now being invoked on behalf of the president of the United States. He just couldn't help himself.

"In Bill Clinton we had for eight years a truly irrational person in the White House, someone who, I think, lived on the edge of serious mental illness. He was and is a psychologically sick man."

Clinton, said Sullivan, was a man who abhors both silence and simplicity. "So the simple question of reviewing Justice Department recommendations turns into a months-long, rolling teach-in involving hundreds of people, envelopes, letters, personal requests, familial favors, and a homing signal to every sleazebag in the country that justice is for sale."

Sullivan concluded that "the behavior illustrated by his pardons is, I think, simply pathological. Psychologists can quibble over what exactly was awry with our ex-president's mind and soul. But no one can explain the sheer irrationality, the reckless, oblivious, careening narcissism of the last eight years without concluding that, at some level, Clinton was not psychologically healthy enough to have been president of the United States."

Sullivan reminded the loyalists, "We asked for it. We elected him. And truly gifted sociopaths have ways of inveigling those around them to participate actively in the sickness, to maintain denial, to keep up appearances. In the tragic figures of Hillary Rodham Clinton and the American electorate, we have two such enablers."[9]

Note again the recurring theme. Hillary and the people who stuck with and twice elected Bill Clinton to the presidency, in the face of overwhelming and recurring evidence of shameless, compulsive, immoral conduct, were the victims, the tragic figures. "Enablers" is a nice way of saying innocent coconspirators. It is the only way for liberals to rationalize their complicity in Bill Clinton's war on American values.

Liberal writer Jacob Weisberg came up with the idiotic notion that someone who isn't trustworthy neglects to mistrust others and that this was the case with Bill Clinton. Imagine that. Bill Clinton pardoned Marc Rich because he failed to distrust Denise Rich, Beth Dozoretz, and Jack Quinn. It was as though, Weisberg said, Clinton would rather have national attention for screwing up than not have our attention at all. This is yet another quirky modern excuse for Clinton's blatant misconduct.

The liberal London-based *Economist* came up with another explanation, notable at least for its originality. It said that "a commandment or two might have been broken...but it really depends on what you mean by 'broken.'" Recalling Clinton's "famed intellectual dexterity," the *Economist* "decided early on that Mr. Clinton was too dishonest an individual to be trusted with the presidency, however clever he might be." The former president "thrives on the limelight, on being a big beast in the political jungle.... Don't let him back—though God knows, we're sure you will."[10]

Bob Woodward, the famed author and *Washington Post* reporter, speculated that answers could be found: "If we had Clinton here on sodium pentathol—we might need a lot of the drug."[11]

Many African-Americans, aside of course from Jesse Jackson, also felt betrayed. But some of that sense of betrayal was a concern that Clinton's pardons were not allocated with sufficient attention to racial balance. In other words, the pardons did not look enough like America's prisons. Elijah Cummings, for example, a Maryland Democrat and member of the Congressional Black Caucus, saw in the pardons a double standard. So did Cynthia Tucker, a columnist for the *Atlanta Journal-Constitution*, a newspaper that called for Clinton's resignation during the Monica Lewinsky scandal.

"If Clinton cared about a legacy, he had a perfect opportunity to leave one," Tucker wrote. "Instead of granting clemency to just a few small-time drug offenders, as he did, he might have pardoned or commuted the sentences of thousands. He might have pointed out the folly of the so-called war on drugs.... With many African-Americans ensnared by the injustices of the system, he could have helped a black constituency that has been extremely loyal."

"Such clemencies would have sparked controversy," Tucker conceded with admirable understatement, "but it would have been a controversy over ideas instead of ethics. And history might have judged Clinton a courageous president who stood up for the common man rather than a money-grubber who favored the rich."[12] Alas, she concluded, these persons "didn't have $400,000 to give first brother-in-law Hugh Rodham."

Walter Reich, a psychiatrist and professor of international affairs, ethics, and human behavior at George Washington University, was director of the Holocaust Memorial Museum from 1995 to 1998. Reich saw the Rich pardon through his own lens. He thought the pardon touched "directly on some of the most incendiary stereotypes about Jews."

Reich was alarmed that Ehud Barak had lobbied Bill Clinton to pardon one of the Justice Department's most-wanted fugitives. Rabbi Irving Greenberg, whom Clinton appointed to chair the board of the Holocaust Museum, had urged the president to "perform one of the most God-like actions that anyone can ever do."

It was, Reich wrote, "in a way, as if the 6 million murdered Jews were beseeching the president, through their official spokesman, Greenberg, to pardon Rich.... This exploitation of the Holocaust in support of a billionaire on the lam is a grave cheapening of Holocaust memory and a devaluation of its moral force."

Reich was alarmed because all of this "plays into the oldest and most damaging stereotypes and canards, and it is likely to give aid and comfort to the worst varieties of anti-Semitism . . . the canard of the Jewish connection with money and power that's easily evoked in the public imagination." Reich found it ironic that one of those writing on behalf of Rich was Abraham Foxman, head of the Anti-Defamation League, "which is supposed to fight anti-Semitism, not provide fodder for it."[13] In late March, Abe Foxman admitted he had erred in writing a letter of support for Marc Rich.

Conservative commentator Charles Krauthammer condemned the Clinton pardons precisely because the power he had abused was so unique and absolute. "The pardon power is special," he wrote. "The American people feel it. Bill Clinton, oblivious as he was to the reverence due every other power of his office, from the Lincoln bedroom to the Oval Office, was supremely oblivious to the sacredness of this one." Because the pardon power is God-like, Krauthammer concluded, "It was not bad judgment. It was sacrilege."[14]

A Gangsta Love Story

Hillary Rodham Clinton's performance in the pardon scandal received heavy criticism as well. "There are far too many perplexities swirling around our new senator," wrote Ginger Munninger-Berlin in the *Times Union*, from the New York state capital of Albany. "One that stands out is the obvious incompetence to use good judgment and even positive influence—influence that benefits our state and the nation. Knowing this leaves us, the citizens of New York and numerous Democratic officials, to doubt her ability in total. Senator Clinton is not the victim," Munninger-Berlin concluded, "we the people she was elected to represent are."[15]

The *New York Observer* is a leftist publication that had defended the Clintons through thick and thin, with unflagging enthusiasm and moral blindness that bordered on the supernatural. The *Observer* now wanted the state's new senator, whom it dubbed "Slick Hillie," to resign. "Without New York, there is no Senate seat, there is no imperial post-presidency," the *Observer* said. But "the Clintons are playing New Yorkers for fools."

"It is clear now that we have made a terrible mistake," the *Observer* continued, "for Hillary Rodham Clinton is unfit for elective office. Had she any shame, she would resign. If federal officeholders were subject to popular recall, she'd be thrown out of office by springtime, the season of renewal."

Some epiphany had occurred to allow the *New York Observer* suddenly to see what it had steadfastly overlooked in the past. The Clinton critics had been dead right all along! "The Clintons have spent the last eight years treating the American electorate with dismissive contempt....Now, with Mr. Clinton stripped of the power and protection of the presidency, his supporters see him exactly as he is. And the image that presents itself is terrifyingly close to the caricature his enemies drew of him. They were right, after all. Mr. Clinton was, in fact, an untrustworthy low-life who used people for his own purposes and then discarded them."

The Clintons "remain smug and self-righteous, certain that New York will forget the early weeks of 2001, certain that New York will embrace its junior senator once again. They have fooled the public before. They believe they can do so again. Let's hope that this time, they are wrong."[16]

No one is making book as to how long it will take for the *New York Observer* to climb back onto the Hillary bandwagon. But it is certain to happen. There will be an election with a Republican in the race to help the *Observer* forget Hillary's past transgressions. Just as there always has been for her husband.

The pardons of the Hasidic swindlers in Rockland County drove *Newsday* columnist Jimmy Breslin over the edge. He observed that the husband of New York's new senator "was taking armchairs and coffee tables as he left the White House." However, "in the annals of thievery, there has been nothing like this: The New Square four, who stole $40 million in federal funds, wind up with the president of the country as their can opener. Indications are that the wife did it all." Said Breslin, "Every time Hillary Clinton passes a bank, the burglar alarm goes off. Her name now and forevermore is Senator Shoplift."[17]

Hillary reminded *Hardball* host and syndicated columnist Chris Matthews of the drug dealer's wife in the film *Traffic*: "She makes it her business not to know her husband's....Four Hasidic men in New York get their sentences commuted after their leaders deliver the community's vote for Hillary. The first lady knows nothing of the reciprocity. All she did, she says, was go to the White House, meeting with the leaders....A top contributor wins a pardon for her ex-husband, a fugitive financier high on the government's Most-Wanted list. Again, Hillary knows nothing." The senator "admits what is provable, denies what is not."

Matthews summarized the Rich and Vignali deals, concluding, "The loser in this deal is the country. Before this, we laughed at poor little countries that drug dealers and international crooks could buy. We mocked the Third World capitals where a little money in the fingers of a certain family member would open doors or close eyes. Thanks to Bill and Hillary Clinton, we have now forfeited that small national vanity."[18]

Pulitzer Prize–winning *New York Times* columnist Maureen Dowd called the Clintons New York's hottest couple. They reminded her of modern Bonnies and Clydes. "He tore up the joint in the wee hours and then left the scene. How she was terrified that the scandal would hurt her new stardom. How she distanced herself from him. How he is mired in a criminal investigation of bribes and secret deals that could vaporize his career." It was "Puff Billy and H. Rod. A gangsta love story."

Bill and Hillary, wrote Dowd, "are in a bizarre conjugal competition this week to see who can elicit more pity. They have had their problems, but they share one strong bond: a sense of entitled victimization. Or victimized entitlement. They grab when they want to, and whine when they need to."[19]

What an amazing, varied, yet consistent, collection of labels: liars, grifters, low-lifes, brain dead, disgusting, psycho, thoroughly corrupt, terminally unethical, vulgar, unfit for office, "Slick Hillie," a deal with the devil, princess sleaze, Senator Shoplift, devastating, appalling, possibly criminal, Puff Billy and H. Rod, gangsta love story.

This barbed inventory was offered up by liberals and Democrats, anxious to escape what they saw was a sinking ship. And the Carvilles and Begalas were not up to responding, except for a few lame attempts to claim that the pardons showed that Bill Clinton was a "big-hearted guy." Indeed, in the aftermath, it was hard to find any coherent defender of the Clintons. As for the brawling assessments, which taxed the writers' powers of invective to the limit, they were worthy of careful reflection on several levels.

But it all comes down to one thing: Character. Here, the gauge rests firmly on empty. According to their friends and supporters, they are cheats, users, liars, and as greedy as their worst depictions of comic strip Republicans. They are without dignity, as R. Emmett Tyrrell, editor of the *American Spectator*, wrote in 1995. That view seemed immensely bland and quite moderate compared to what Bob Herbert, the *New York Observer*, Maureen Dowd, Chris Matthews, Andrew Sullivan, and many others were now saying. However, Tyrrell was regularly savaged for having the audacity to investigate and report on the Clintons' shortcomings. He was even the subject of a Clinton Justice Department–inspired criminal investigation for daring to write and publish the truth. But Tyrrell's reporting and language, in retrospect, seemed modest and barely to have scratched the surface.

Former Clinton aide Dick Morris believes history will judge Bill Clinton as "one of the most corrupt U.S. presidents." Meanwhile, "the reality of what they have been and done will continue to cry out for an honesty and radical candor not even most of their strongest critics have yet managed."

In the end, Morris wrote, "The reflections they give back of a nation's longtime heedlessness, surrender, and in many cases complicity, will be ugly. Refusing to face the Clintons is a national transgression from which there is, and should be, no pardon."[20]

The need Morris saw for honesty and "radical candor" in evaluating the Clintons' tenure and legacy suggested another reality of the Clintons' America. In *Spin Cycle*, Howard Kurtz of the *Washington Post* noted the Clintons' famous antipathy to the press, which they saw as part of a global conspiracy out to get them.

When Jeff Gerth of the *New York Times* wrote about Clinton weakening Arkansas ethics laws in order to exempt himself and his wife from disclosing conflicts of interest, Clinton exploded, "Look at this piece of shit. This story is a fucking piece of shit!"[21]

When they weren't attacking the writers, the Clintons sought to discredit some stories because they came from tabloids. Unfortunately, those stories often turned out to be true. The tabloids were regularly beating the so-called mainstream press to the punch. The Clintons, after all, are prime tabloid material.

The Clintons created a tabloid presidency that blurred the differences between the *National Enquirer* and the *New York Times*. It also blurred the lines between comedians and commentators. This was, on reflection, a predictable development. By the year 2000 it had been forgotten that at Bill Clinton's first inauguration they had played the theme music from *Monty Python's Flying Circus*. That had been one of Bill Clinton's favorite shows. His administration regularly descended to that level of comic absurdity.

For this reason, comics had never considered the Clintons off limits for political reasons. In some cases, in fact, they were better equipped to supply the honesty and radical candor that Roger Morris wanted to see but which even Clinton's staunchest critics had, in Morris's view, failed to provide.

A prime example was Dennis Miller, who surely spoke for many Americans in his March 2, 2001, monologue, one day after the Burton committee held its lengthy hearings into the Clinton pardons.

Miller was flabbergasted that the Clintons had apparently packed all their vices and shortcomings into one incredible grand finale. "We've all been watching in astonishment these last few weeks as the Clintons merrily parade their greed and corruption past us like a garish Mardi Gras float powered by the drivetrain of Bill Clinton's gargantuan sense of entitlement. Hillary steers, while Bill sits on the top tossing pardons out to the crowd like a drunken Bacchus with a perpetual hard-on for a scepter."

Said Miller, "You almost have to admire the sheer audacity of granting pardons to two tax-scamming billionaire fugitives named Rich and Green. If the symbolism were any more obvious, Andrew Lloyd Weber would be writing music for it."

Miller did not say so, but Bill and Hillary Clinton ended their eight years in the White House with a grand-finale pyrotechnic show of historic proportions. The Clintons never believed that normal standards of behavior applied to them. As Bill Clinton said, "You know, you can make too much of normalcy. A lot of normal people are assholes."[22] The Clintons, whatever else can be said about them, were not normal.

They reprised the lowlights of their two terms in office by taking public property, soliciting gifts and favors, selling the powers of the presidency to friends, cronies, family members, and supporters, and otherwise trashing the noble office to which they had been privileged to occupy. All the old familiar tacky memories were revived: girlfriends, sleazy relatives, political favors, tawdry second-rate acts of avarice, and disdain for their country and even their own party.

Americans, at least the majority of them, had forgiven many of these past actions. But now the Clintons seemed to want to rub their noses in those acts of forgiveness by showing everyone that they could and would repeat the acts that had brought about so much controversy and, indeed, take them to newer and more appalling levels. They were saying to the American public, "We are what we are, you accepted that, you have elected us to your highest national office, not once, but twice, and you have no right or place to complain now." To paraphrase an old folk song, the American public knew that the Clintons were snakes when they took them in. They cannot complain when the snakes turn out to bite.

A Bang, Not a Whimper | **14**

"**Bill Clinton should never** have won the 1992 presidential election."[1] That was the view of Martin Walker of the British *Guardian*, whose book on Bill Clinton, *The President We Deserve*, was praised by White House aide and attack dog Sidney Blumenthal. Walker's statement is another instance of the phenomenon that foreign observers often capture realities about our national life that escape American observers.

Bill Clinton was facing a popular incumbent in George H. W. Bush, a World War II veteran who assembled the massive international coalition that rescued Kuwait, with remarkably little loss of American life. Even in the spring of 1992, television comedy shows such as *Saturday Night Live* assumed that the presidential race in November would be no contest, whatever candidate the Democrats put forward, airing skits such as "The Race to See Who Loses to Bush."

Furthermore, what was known about Bill Clinton even then was troubling, both in terms of competence and character. "He was an arrogant, no-good son of a bitch…a dirty rotten scoundrel," said John Robert Starr, managing editor of the *Arkansas Democrat-Gazette*, long before Pardongate or Monica Lewinsky.[2]

But he was—and is—one helluva politician. Through shrewd exploitation of economic issues, an unspeakably inept campaign by his opponent, and the participation of Ross Perot, the Arkansan and his relentlessly ambitious wife were able to co-occupy the White House despite garnering fewer votes than Democratic candidate Michael Dukakis who lost to the senior George Bush in the 1988 election. Clinton's youth and new generation image and the unprecedented buy-one-get-one-free deal Bill Clinton offered the American public were also factors. Clinton held the center and kept his campaign focused on the flagging economy and on George Bush's seeming complacency. It was a remarkable story. And the rest, as they say, is history. The Clintons, like the Gregorys they pardoned, launched their carnival on an eight-year, national tour.

In 1988, Bill Clinton gave the keynote speech at the Democratic convention. A plum assignment that Clinton blew spectacularly. Clinton's seemingly interminable and tedious speech drew applause only when he said "in closing." His presidency ended in somewhat the same way, although not with applause, but certainly with a lot of noise. To paraphrase T. S. Eliot, a bang, not a whimper.

Clinton White House counsel Beth Nolan had it exactly right. The president is the president. It is a huge office. Political realities normally constrain the exercise of the powers of the presidency. But when those restraints are lifted, the Clintons showed us what can happen.

In the latter days of the Clintons' presidency, the flaws and faults of their early days would swell to grotesque proportions, as though on steroids. In the final days, it was as if the parents had left town and the teenagers took over.

Bill Clinton and Hillary Rodham Clinton revealed themselves as the ultimate members of the "me generation." First and foremost, they used the power of the presidency to assure the perpetuation of their own careers in the regal style to which they had become so accustomed and which they saw as theirs by entitlement. Royalty, once assumed, is hard to relinquish.

In classic displays of raw power, Bill Clinton used executive orders, regulations, monuments, appointments, and pardons to help and enrich his allies, harm his foes, and extend the visible hand of government. And, of course, to glorify himself. The Clinton motto had become "Nothing exceeds like excess."

The Clintons got what they wanted. Beyond the money and influence, what they wanted was to come out on top, to exult in victory. In private, the feeling was doubtless the same as when Clinton, about to embark on a campaign of lying about Monica Lewinsky, told his friend and aide Dick Morris, "We'll just have to win."

The Clintons are intelligent people, as has been repeatedly observed, but which requires qualification. They possess intellectual candlepower, but their use of their talents causes one to speculate about what is missing. A previous generation of very intelligent people—writers, scholars, clergy, politicians, and statesmen alike—were caught up in the adulation of the Soviet Union, Communist China, and other totalitarian regimes. Paul Hollander chronicled it in *Political Pilgrims*, and the record confirmed the view of Saul Bellow that "A great deal of intelligence can be invested in ignorance when the need for illusion is deep."[3]

In the case of the Clintons, they invested their intelligence not in ignorance but in evasion and illusion because the need for deception and secrecy was great. Nothing that issued in the final days from either of the co-presidents surprised any of us familiar with the scandals. Legally speaking, the Clintons may have successfully disguised the various quid pro quos in the pardons. And we witnessed how they had applied their considerable skills to survive a series of crises of their own making that would have sunk any ordinary politicians. But there is little evidence that their skills were used to benefit the American public.

"Ask yourself, what did [Bill Clinton] get done?" says University of Alabama historian Forrest McDonald, author of *The American Presidency: An Intellectual History* and a biography of Alexander Hamilton, among many other works.

"Was there any major legislation he was responsible for? Welfare reform came from the Republican Congress. Health care was a disaster. He simply didn't get much done. He was a comedy of errors. Everyone approves of what he's doing, but when you ask the question, no one can say anything he did."

McDonald believes Clinton was popular, not strong, and "I think the presidency suffered in terms of prestige, and in terms of popular respect for the office."[4]

As Robert George, who compared Bill Clinton to O. J. Simpson, observed, "Here we have two men who have each been exonerated in one adjudicated body, yet found their obvious misdeeds exposed in later action—official and otherwise."[5]

This, of course, should not be seen as trivializing what O. J. Simpson did or exaggerating Bill Clinton's vices. But both wound up with legal victories that, in many respects, are both hollow and illusory. Both Clinton and Simpson found friends deserting them. Both found themselves looking rather sinister on the covers of national magazines. *Newsweek*'s February 26, 2001, "Bill's Last Days" issue bears a black-and-white image of Clinton in his presidential limousine on January 15. His eyes and mouth are heavily shadowed, the face in a pool of light, as though being interrogated by detectives in a dark room. "You talkin' to me?" his look seems to say.

Clues are emerging on the shape and coloration of Bill Clinton's legacy.

Bartlett's Familiar Quotations selected three memorable statements from Bill Clinton:

"I experimented with marijuana a time or two. And I didn't like it, and didn't inhale, and never tried it again."

"I am going to say this again: I did not have sexual relations with that woman, Miss Lewinsky."

"It depends on what the meaning of the word 'is' is. If the—if he—if 'is' means is and never has been, that is not—that is one thing. If it means there is none, that was a completely true statement."

What a way to be remembered. Three of the most extravagant and laughable lies in political history.

In his book, the boasting of a $10-million deal that surpassed Hillary's $8-million advance, Bill Clinton will surely tender a version of his own. It is not likely to include a damage assessment. If past statements are any indication, Clinton will blame all his misfortunes and shortcomings on others. He will not, one can say with virtual certainty, face the facts and tell the truth.

At a time when the United States stood as the world's only superpower, the Clintons exercised presidential power as if they ruled an emerging third world dictatorship. Pardoning a brother and an ex-girlfriend, pardoning billionaire fugitives, allowing drug kingpins to buy influence, buying votes, and acting like an absolute monarch—these are the actions of tin-horn autocrats in less respected countries. As Chris Matthews put it, those days should be over. The Clintons showed how much it is possible to get away with and that says a lot about *fin de siècle* America. But maybe more about the Clintons than about America.

The Clintons are a strange dialectic. Liberal-left progressive politics meets traditional corruption resulting in a synthesis of boundless arrogance and entitlement. In the Clinton dialectic, the truth was all too often the victim of expediency, exalting the dictum of "never believe anything until it's been officially denied." This had the effect of turning the nation, not so much into partisans and nonpartisans, but believers and nonbelievers, enablers and perpetual skeptics.

Those who "believed" the president usually did so against both the weight of the evidence and their own better judgment. And they were regularly forced to retreat into explaining that what they had agreed to deny did not really matter even if it was true. How degrading and enervating.

The "critical" school of which Hillary Rodham Clinton is a part, uses the expression "late capitalism" as a way of explaining developments they don't like. The Clinton character has revealed what could be called "late liberalism," in which partisanship overrides the empirical. Since belief figures so much in late liberalism, the nonbelievers tend to be demonized, in the style of Hillary's vast right-wing conspiracy. This is different from the traditional understanding of a loyal opposition and a bipartisan spirit. It is hardly healthy for democracy.

In politically correct style, liberals are fond of maintaining that the personal is the political. Hillary Rodham Clinton believes this but changes direction and complains bitterly when people write about aspects of her personal life that directly affect her politics.

Liberals who believe the personal is the political showed an astonishing ability to defend the Clintons on the grounds that sexual liaisons with twenty-one-year-olds were personal matters, different from the "political" sphere. Thus, it is assumed that only the religious right would criticize a politician for private sexual matters. The fact is that conservatives and others who decried the Clintons' disrespect for morality, decency, and the institutions of the presidency, cared little about Bill Clinton's sex life and a great deal about lying, obstruction of justice, and undermining the rule of law. Unfortunately for both camps, Bill Clinton was not able to cheat on his wife and misuse his presidency without also lying about it.

If the slippery slope of the Clinton years shows anything, it is that the personal and the political cannot be kept in separate compartments if the officeholder uses his office to further his personal agenda.

The false distinction between the personal and the political, when the personal is allowed to take over and intrude into the political, also affected the media. It might have been considered a mark of sophistication to regard the president's sexual life as distinct from his presidential duties. But it became a dereliction of duty when first as governor and then as president, Clinton risked his marriage, his office, his bond with the voters, and the credibility of his party to gratify his personal needs.

The prestige press can avoid these embarrassments by dropping the false distinction whenever the office seekers themselves cannot keep the political separate from the personal. We now know that President Kennedy took some dreadful risks to gratify his personal impulses. The press kept these adventures from the public. At some point, as Clinton has shown, that cannot be tolerated.

Politicians, of course, should be allowed their privacy, and their sexual appetites should be out-of-bounds. But not if they allow that part of their lives to intrude into public responsibilities, choices, and decisions.

In his book on Hillary's Senate victory, Michael Tomasky astutely noted that while Hillary had followed *Rules for Radicals* author and left-wing consiglieri Saul Alinsky, she ultimately expected not to fight the power but to *be* the power.[6]

Few can doubt that the former first lady, now a senator, wants to be president. Her forthcoming book will undoubtedly be written with that objective in mind, just as *It Takes a Village* was promotional material for her Senate campaign.

No serious observer can believe that Hillary's self-image or fundamental beliefs have undergone the slightest revision. Hillary Rodham Clinton remains, in her own mind, one of the anointed, and her quest remains how best to impose her ideas, especially concerning socialized health care, on the public. She is quite willing to act outrageously, stonewall and obfuscate, then proclaim that it is time to "move on." As her presidential campaign unfolds, the public will be wise to examine her conduct and motives in light of her past, consistent history. She will never really change.

Bill Clinton said that he reread Arthur Koestler's *Darkness at Noon* during the Lewinsky affair. That was a strange selection, given the nature of the book. But Koestler's words in another book, *Arrow in the Blue*, are certainly apropos. Koestler watched in horror as the "old out-worn concepts" of the Left were again taken up, twenty years after he had abandoned them. "The storm is still on," he wrote, and it was "as if under the spell of a destructive compulsion, they must repeat every single error of the past, draw the same faulty conclusions a second time, relive the same situations. One can only watch in horror and despair, for this time, there will be no pardon."[7]

To avoid repeating the errors of the past and reliving the same situations of the Clinton years, the American people should ponder the Clintons' lifelong goals in light of decades of hard and provable history. The Clinton anthem in 1992 was "Don't Stop Thinking About Tomorrow." When Americans think about the Clintons, they had better not forget about our yesterdays.

Notes

Chapter 1

1 George Stephanopoulos, *All Too Human: A Political Education* (Boston: Little, Brown, 1999), 278.

2 Weston Kosova, "Backstage at the Finale," *Newsweek*, February 26, 2001, p. 30.

3 Ibid.

4 Don Van Natta Jr. and Marc Lacy, "Access Proved Vital in Last-Minute Race for Clinton Pardons," *New York Times*, February 25, 2001, p. A1.

5 Jerry Oppenheimer, *State of a Union: Inside the Complex Marriage of Bill and Hillary Clinton* (New York: HarperCollins, 2000), 12.

6 Deb Riechmann, "America's Rich, Famous Asked Clinton to Grant Pardons," Associated Press, March 9, 2001.

7 Interview with Denise Rich, from her website www.richsong.com.

8 Gail Collins, "Public Interests; Everything's Relative," *New York Times*, February 23, 2001, p. A19.

9 John McLaughlin, *John McLaughlin's One on One*, January 26, 2001.

Chapter 2

1 Stephanopoulos, *All Too Human*, 198.

2 Roger Morris, "Don't Pardon Corruption," *Toronto Globe and Mail*, March 7, 2001.

3 Michael Isikoff, *Uncovering Clinton: A Reporter's Story* (New York: Crown, 1999), 350.

4 Roger Clinton with Jim Moore, *Growing Up Clinton* (Arlington, TX: Summit, 1996), 135.

5 R. Emmett Tyrrell Jr., *Boy Clinton: The Political Biography* (Washington, DC: Regnery, 1996), 65.

6 "Judge Regrets He Could Not Impose Death Penalty on FALN Terrorists," United Press International, February 19, 1981.

7 Gary Marx, "Terrorism on Trial: Justice and the FALN," *Chicago Tribune Sunday Magazine*, October 22, 1995, p. 22.

8 Katharine Q. Seelye, "Director of FBI Opposed Clemency for Puerto Ricans," *New York Times*, September 22, 1999, p. A1.

9 Michael Tomasky, *Hillary's Turn: Inside Her Improbable, Victorious Senate Campaign* (New York: Free Press, 2001), 78.

10 McLaughlin, *John McLaughlin's One on One*, January 26, 2001.

11 Ibid.

12 Peter Slevin and George Lardner Jr., "Rush of Pardons Unusual in Scope, Lack of Scrutiny," *Washington Post*, March 10, 2001, p. A3.

13 John Castellucci, *The Big Dance: The Untold Story of Kathy Boudin and the Terrorist Family That Committed the Brink's Robbery Murders* (New York: Dodd Mead, 1986), 35.

14 Lee Hockstader, "7 Indicted in 1983 Capitol Bombing; Members of Communist Group Face Charges in 7 Other Explosions," *Washington Post*, May 12, 1988, p. A1.

Chapter 3

1 Stephanopoulos, *All Too Human*, 317.

2 George Lardner Jr., "Study Names Clinton Most Frequent Flier: Taxpayer Group Faults Foreign Trips' Cost and Use as 'a Venue to Escape,'" *Washington Post*, March 16, 2001, p. A2; Jim Wolf, "Clinton's Frequent Flying Draws Watchdog Ire," Reuters, March 16, 2001.

3 Stephanopoulos, *All Too Human*, 132.

4 Clay Chandler, "Clinton Urges Vietnam to Open Its Markets," *Washington Post*, November 20, 2000, p. A18.

5 Jeff Jacoby, "Clinton Lets Down Vietnamese Once Again," *Boston Globe*, November 30, 2000, p. A23.

6 Bill Hutchinson, "Hillary's Visit Is Huge Hit in Hanoi," *New York Daily News*, November 17, 2000, p. 17; "Clinton Arrives from Israel," CNN, November 17, 2000.

Chapter 4

1 *Arkansas Democrat-Gazette*, November 27, 1997.

2 Tomasky, *Hillary's Turn*, 19.

3 Oppenheimer, *State of a Union*, 153, 141, 135.

4 Tomasky, *Hillary's Turn*, 207.

5 David D. Kirkpatrick, "The Kingpin of Washington Book Deals," *New York Times*, December 11, 2000, p. C1.

6 "$8 Million Worth of Memories," *Indianapolis Star*, December 26, 2000, p. A22.

7 Paul Singer, "Groups Seek Ethics Review of Hillary Clinton Book Deal," United Press International, December 18, 2000.

8 *The O'Reilly Factor*, Fox News, December 21, 2000.

9 Shannon McCaffrey, "Republican Reaction to Hillary Clinton Book Deal Muted," Associated Press, December 19, 2000.

10 *Inside Politics*, CNN, December 20, 2000.

11 Ibid.

12 Singer, "Groups Seek Ethics Review of Hillary Clinton Book Deal."

13 Roger Morris, *Partners in Power: The Clintons and Their America* (New York: Henry Holt, 1996), 225.

14 Tyrrell, *Boy Clinton*, 278.

15 Stephanopoulos, *All Too Human*, 92.

Chapter 5

1 OpinionJournal.com, March 20, 2001.

2 Susan Edelman and Lois Weiss, "Hillary's Got the Lease with the Most," *New York Post*, March 19, 2001, p. 2.

3 Ibid.

4 Kenneth R. Bazinet and Eric Herman, "Rent for Bill's Midtown Office Soars by 150G," *New York Daily News*, February 7, 2001, p. 6.

5 Ibid.

6 Kenneth R. Bazinet and Eric Herman, "Clinton May Go to Harlem," *New York Daily News*, February 13, 2001, p. 5.

7 Howard Fineman, "The Longest Goodbye," *Newsweek*, February 26, 2001. pp. 26, 28.

8 Karen Tumulty, "How Can We Miss You If You Never Go Away?" *Time*, February 26, 2001, p. 22.

9 Tom Carson, "Secrets and Lies," *Village Voice*, October 20, 1998, p. 65.

10 Jabari Asim, "Bill Clinton Isn't Black," Salon.com, February 26, 2001.

11 Anthony Breznican, "NAACP Honors Clinton with Image Award," Associated Press, March 4, 2001.

12 Tumulty, "How Can We Miss You If You Never Go Away?"

Chapter 6

1 Oppenheimer, *State of a Union*, 90.

2 Martin Walker, *The President We Deserve: Bill Clinton: His Rise, Falls, and Comebacks* (New York: Crown, 1996), 114.

3 Dick Morris, "How Bill Fell," *New York Post*, March 6, 2001.

4 Stephanopoulos, *All Too Human*, 132.

5 Maureen Dowd, "Hillary's Stocking Stuffer," *New York Times*, December 24, 2000, p. 9.

6 Maureen Dowd, "Your Fault. No, Yours. No, Yours," *New York Times*, February 21, 2001, p. A19.

7 Walter Scott, "Personality Parade," *Parade*, March 11, 2001.

8 Bill Burke, "Into the Storm: How Former Beach Resident Beth Dozoretz Came to Know the Clintons and End Up in the Midst of the Pardon Scandal," *Virginian-Pilot*, February 20, 2001, p. A1.

9 Ibid.

10 Lloyd Grove, "The Reliable Source," *Washington Post*, April 27, 2001, p. C3.

11 Cheryl Lavin, "Magazine Writer Tells How Hillary Became a New York Senator," *Chicago Tribune*, February 28, 2001, p. C4.

12 Margaret Carlson, "A Shower of Gifts for Hillary and Bill," CNN.com, January 29, 2001.

13 Dick Morris, "Cat's Out of the Bag on Hill's Gifts," *New York Post*, February 11, 2001.

14 "Hillary Clinton Blasts Article on White House Gifts," CNN.com, February 12, 2001.

15 Dick Morris, "Bill and Hillary a 'Crafty' Duo," NYPost.com, February 20, 2001.

16 George Lardner Jr., "Clinton Shipped Furniture Year Ago," *Washington Post*, February 10, 2001, p. A1.

17 "Hey, Wait a Minute," *The Hotline*, February 12, 2001.

18 Bazinet and Herman, "Clinton Opts Out of Pricey Manhattan Office Suite for Harlem."

19 Scott Shifrel, "Hillary Defends Self on Gift Raps," *New York Daily News*, February 12, 2001, p. 4.

20 *This Week*, ABC, February 11, 2001.

21 Shannon McCaffrey, "Hillary Clinton to Depart White House with President," Associated Press, January 19, 2001.

22 Jim McTague, "A Clinton Staffer Issues an Invitation to Rumble," *Barron's*, March 5, 2001.

Chapter 7

1 *In re Neagle*, 135 U.S. 1 (1890).

2 Michael Nelson, ed., *Congressional Quarterly's Guide to the Presidency*, Second Edition (Washington, DC: Congressional Quarterly, 1996), 507.

3 Ibid.

4 Ibid.

5 Elizabeth Drew, *On the Edge: The Clinton Presidency* (New York: Simon and Schuster, 1994), 42.

6 James Bennet, "True to Form, Clinton Shifts Energies Back to U.S. Focus," *New York Times*, July 5, 1998, p. 10.

7 Richard Johnson, Paula Froelich, and Chris Wilson, "Chelsea's Spa-tacular Ski Spree," *New York Post*, March 29, 2001.

8 Beth Miller, "Clinton Postpones Action on Pardons," *Washington Post*, January 20, 2001, p. A19.

9 Michael Valdez Moses, "A Rendezvous with Destiny: The FDR Memorial and the Clinton Era," *Reason*, April 2001, p. 53.

10 See Brett D. Schaefer, "Overturning Clinton's Midnight Action on the International Criminal Court," Heritage Foundation, Executive Memorandum No. 708, January 9, 2001.

11 Susan Bradford, "Treaty on Trial: International Criminal Court Deserves a Hearing," *Washington Times*, February 2, 2001, p. A17.

12 "Remarks on Signing the Second Taxpayer Bill of Rights and an Exchange with Reporters," *Public Papers of the Presidents*, July 30, 1996, p. 1375.

13 James Bovard, *Feeling Your Pain: The Explosion and Abuse of Government Power in the Clinton-Gore Years* (New York: St. Martin's, 2000), 344.

14 Ellen Nakashima, "Clinton Contractor Rule Is Suspended," *Washington Post*, March 31, 2001, p. A1.

15 Matthew L. Wald, "Clinton Energy Saving Rules Getting a Second Look," *New York Times*, March 30, 2001, p. A11.

16 Cindy Skrzycki, "Critics Assail Review of Final Rules," *Washington Post*, April 3, 2001, p. E1.

17 Richard Johnson, Paula Froelich, and Chris Wilson, "Bill Heaves Gift-Horse Treadmill," *New York Post*, March 28, 2001, p. 8.

18 Richard Cohen, "Blemishes on the Holocaust Museum," *Washington Post*, March 1, 2001, p. A19.

19 Bovard, *Feeling Your Pain*, 344.

Chapter 8

1 Howard Kurtz, *Spin Cycle: Inside the Clinton Propaganda Machine* (New York: Free Press, 1998), xxv.

2 Michael Weisskopf, "Inside Clinton's Last Deal," *Time*, January 29, 2001, p. 33.

3 Nat Hentoff, "The Liar's Legacy and America's Delusions," Jewish WorldReview.com, June 6, 2000.

4 Nat Hentoff, "Clinton's Deal: Justice Denied," *Village Voice*, February 20, 2001, p. 41.

5 Maraniss, *First in His Class*, 218.

6 Alan C. Miller, "Hillary Clinton Explains Why She Stayed," *Los Angeles Times*, August 2, 1999, p. A1.

7 Clinton, *Growing Up Clinton*, 34.

8 Isikoff, *Uncovering Clinton*, 63.

9 "Clinton Recalls Pickup Trucks and Dating," Reuters, February 8, 1994.

10 Art Harris, Gennifer Flowers, *Penthouse*, December 1992, p. 68.

11 Isikoff, *Uncovering Clinton*, 61.

12 Kurtz, *Spin Cycle*, 278.

13 Ibid., 48.

14 Ibid., 294.

15 Stephanopoulos, *All Too Human*, 436.

16 Oppenheimer, *State of a Union*, 267.

Chapter 9

1 Stephen Braun and Richard A. Serrano, "Clinton Pardons: Ego Fed a Numbers Game: A Desire to Add to His Legacy, Coupled with a Flood of Last-Minute Pleas from Every Corner, Overwhelmed the System," *Los Angeles Times*, February 25, 2001, p. A1.

2 Jerry Seper, "Clinton Broke Vow in Pardon of Rich; Violated His Pledge of Justice Review," *Washington Times*, February 2, 2001, p. A1.

3 Vernon Loeb, "Shelby: Spy's Sentence Should Stand," *Washington Post*, December 23, 2000, p. A12.

4 Braun and Serrano, "Clinton Pardons."

5 Michael Kranish, "Carter, Ford Urged Pardons, Pleas for Patty Hearst, Dan Rostenkowski," *Boston Globe*, March 3, 2001, p. A1.

Chapter 10

1 A. Craig Copetas, *Metal Men: Marc Rich and the 10-billion-dollar Scam* (New York: Putnam's, 1985), 26.

2 Ibid.

3 Ibid.

4 Ibid.

5 Ibid.

6 Ibid.

7 Ibid.

8 Aaron Luccheti, "While Marc Rich Was a Fugitive, His Firm Dealt with Pariah Nations," *Wall Street Journal*, February 23, 2001.

9 Ibid.

10 Ibid.

11 Copetas, *Metal Men*, 178.

12 *The Strange Case of Marc Rich: Contracting with Tax Fugitives and at Large in the Alps*, Hearings before the Government Information, Justice, and Agriculture Subcommittee of the Committee on Government Operations, House of Representatives, 102nd Congress, First and Second Sessions, December 4, 1991, February 18 and March 5, 1992, 8.

13 Copetas, *Metal Men*, 218.

14 "Busy Fugitive," *Forbes*, February 18, 1991, p. 10.

15 *The Strange Case of Marc Rich*, 7.

16 *They Went Thataway: The Strange Case of Marc Rich and Pincus Green*, Nineteenth Report by the Committee on Government Operations, House Report 102-537, May 27, 1992, 34.

17 *The Strange Case of Marc Rich*, 196.

18 Beth J. Harpaz, "Jewish Group Says Rich Reps Sought Pardon Help for Money," Associated Press, March 29, 2001.

19 Michael Isikoff, "Pardon Mess Thickens: New E-Mails Reveal Campaign to Pardon Rich More Elaborate Than Previously Known," *Newsweek* web exclusive, March 1, 2001.

20 James Ridgeway, "Documents Show Denise as Player in Hubby's Empire," *Village Voice*, March 20, 2001, p. 34.

21 James V. Grimaldi, "E-Mail Trail Shows Rich's Associates Brainstorming for Ways to Influence President Clinton," *Washington Post*, February 19, 2001, p. E7.

22 Michael Isikoff, "A Pardon's Path," *Newsweek*, February 19, 2001, p. 28.

23 For a full account of the e-mail machinations see Jake Tapper, "Anatomy of a Pardon," Salon.com, February 13, 2001.

24 Isikoff, "A Pardon's Path."

25 Ibid.

Chapter 11

1 Charles Krauthammer, "The Presidential Corruption Index," *Washington Post*, February 2, 2001, p. A23.

2 Pat Milton, "Source: U.S. Attorney Investigating Commutations," Associated Press, February 23, 2001.

3 *This Week*, ABC, February 25, 2001.

4 *Meet the Press*, NBC, February 25, 2001.

5 Krauthammer, "The Presidential Corruption Index," p. A23.

6 Clinton, *Growing Up Clinton*, 3.

7 Ibid., 28, 35.

8 Michael Isikoff and Daniel Klaidman, "His Brother's Keeper," *Newsweek*, February 26, 2001, p. 33.

9 Richard A. Serrano and Stephen Braun, "Roger Clinton Says He Promised Friends Pardons," *Los Angeles Times*, February 25, 2001, p. A1.

10 Ibid.

11 Isikoff and Klaidman, "His Brother's Keeper," p. 33.

12 Serrano and Braun, "Roger Clinton Says He Promised Friends Pardons," p. A1.

13 Ibid.

14 Rene Sanchez, "Drug Felon's Powerful Supporters Retreat on Pardon," *Washington Post*, February 24, 2001, p. A6.

15 John Daniszewski, "Prosecutor Quits Over Boss' Role in Pardon," *Los Angeles Times*, March 5, 2001, p. B1.

16 David Tell, "Unpardonable," *Weekly Standard*, February 26, 2001, p. 9.

17 Christopher Marquis with Michael Moss, "A Clinton In-Law Received $400,000 in 2 Pardon Cases," *New York Times*, February 22, 2001, p. A1.

18 Larry Bivins, "Pardoned Carnival Owners Made Political Gifts to Hillary Clinton, Others," Gannett News Service, March 1, 2001.

19 Kevin Sack, "Pardoned Couple Say Access Has Served Them Well," *New York Times*, March 10, 2001, p. A9.

20 David Johnston, "Hollywood Friend Had Clinton's Ear for 2 Late Pardons," *New York Times*, February 24, 2001, p. A8.

21 Van Natta Jr. and Lacey, "Access Proved Vital...," p. A1.

22 "Former Colombian Drug Agent Blasts Clinton's Pardon of Trafficker," Agence France Press, March 4, 2001.

23 "Mississippi Man Surprised Making Clinton's Pardon List," *Advocate* (Baton Rouge, LA), February 9, 2001, p. 6B.

24 M. E. Sprengelmeyer, "Clinton Pardons Anteater Smuggler," Scripps Howard News Service, March 4, 2001.

25 Michael Dobbs, "Pardon Smoothed by Ties to Israel; Barak, Others Aided Rich's Pardon," *Washington Post*, February 25, 2001, p. A1.

Chapter 12

1 Donald Lambro, "Carter Calls Clinton's Rich Pardon 'Disgraceful,'" *Washington Times*, February 22, 2001, p. A1.

2 Paul Goldman, "Democrats Must Censure Clinton," *Wall Street Journal*, February 15, 2001.

3 Bill Clinton, "My Reasons for the Pardons," *New York Times*, February 18, 2001, section 4, p. 13.

4 Michael Kelly, "The Pardoner's False Brief," *Washington Post*, February 21, 2001, p. A23.

5 Christopher Buckley, "Hillary: The Op-ed," *Wall Street Journal*, February 27, 2001.

6 Tomasky, *Hillary's Turn*, 76.

7 Morris, "Don't Pardon Clinton Corruption."

8 Michael Weisskopf, "Beth & Denise & Bill," *Time*, February 19, 2001, p. 33.

9 Lloyd Grove, "The Reliable Source," *Washington Post*, March 6, 2001, p. C3.

Chapter 13

1 Hamilton Jordan, "The First Grifters," *Wall Street Journal*, February 20, 2001.

2 Donald Lambro, "Carter Calls Clinton's Rich Pardon 'Disgraceful.'"

3 *Inside Politics*, CNN, February 15, 2001.

4 Richard L. Berke, "This Time, Clintons Find Their Support Buckling from Weight of New Woes," *New York Times*, February 23, 2001, p. A16.

5 Lambro, "Carter Calls Clinton's Rich Pardon 'Disgraceful.'"

6 Shannon McCaffrey, "Mrs. Clinton Spurs Ethics Reform," Associated Press, March 30, 2001.

7 Lambro, "Carter Calls Clinton's Rich Pardon 'Disgraceful.'"

8 Bob Herbert, "Cut Him Loose," *New York Times*, February 26, 2001, p. A15.

9 Andrew Sullivan, "Psycho," *New Republic*, March 12, 2001, p. 6.

10 "The Fugitive President," *Economist*, February 24, 2001.

11 *Larry King*, CNN, March 2, 2001.

12 Cynthia Tucker, "Our Opinion: War on Drugs' Victims Still Jailed, While Rich Go Free," *Atlanta Journal-Constitution*, March 4, 2001, p. 10D.

13 Walter Reich, "Pardons Jeopardize Good Name of Jewish People," *Houston Chronicle*, March 1, 2001, p. A27.

14 Charles Krauthammer, "The Unpardonable Offense," *Washington Post*, March 2, 2001, p. A25.

15 Ginger Munninger-Berlin, "Pardons Raise Doubts about Hillary Clinton," *Times Union* (Albany, NY), March 13, 2001, p. A10.

16 "Clinton Corruption Plays Us for Fools—We Won't Forget," *New York Observer*, March 19, 2001, p. 4.

17 Jimmy Breslin, "Begging Their Pardon: Bill, Hillary Deliver," *Newsday*, January 31, 2001, p. A6.

18 Chris Matthews, "'Traffic II'?" *San Francisco Chronicle*, March 3, 2001, p. WB1.

19 Dowd, "Your Fault. No, Yours. No, Yours."

20 Morris, "Don't Pardon Corruption."

21 Kurtz, *Spin Cycle*, 71.

22 Stephanopoulos, *All Too Human*, 219.

Chapter 14

1 Walker, *The President We Deserve*, 10.

2 Kurtz, *Spin Cycle*, 70.

3 Saul Bellow, *To Jerusalem and Back* (New York: Viking, 1976), 127.

4 Michael W. Lynch, "18th Century Man," *Reason*, April 2000, p. 17.

5 Robert George, "Bill Forever?—Clinton Comes to Harlem," *New York Post*, February 14, 2001, p. 49.

6 Tomasky, *Hillary's Turn*, 9.

7 Arthur Koestler, *Arrow in the Blue* (New York: Macmillan, 1952), 235–36.

Index

ABM Treaty, 84
abortion, 79, 91
Adams, John, 77
Adams, Roger, 184, 188
Adarand v. Pena, 79
AFL-CIO, 90
Africa, 2, 25, 49
African-Americans, 56–59, 201
Agriculture Department, 79
Aguinaldo, Emilio, 3
Air Conditioning and Refrigeration
    Institute, 91
Air Force One, 1–2, 3, 25, 26
AJC. *See* American Jewish Congress
Alaska, 82
Albania, 26, 144
Albright, Madeleine, 27, 167
Alinsky, Saul, 215
Allen, Barbara, 66
Allen, Woody, 73
America. *See* United States
American Jewish Congress (AJC), 135

*The American Presidency: An Intellectual
    History* (McDonald), 212
American Spectator, 98, 107, 111, 206
Anderson, William Sterling, 163
Angelou, Maya, 94
Anti-Defamation League, 135, 202
Antiquities Act of 1906, 82
Arafat, Suha, 38, 49
Arafat, Yasir, 38, 144
Arkansas, 62
Arkansas Bar Association, 99
Arkansas Democrat-Gazette, 210
Arkansas Industrial Development
    Commission, 107
Arkin, Mitch, 53
Armed Forces of National Liberation.
    See FALN
Arrow in the Blue (Koestler), 216
arsenic rule, 89–90
Ashcroft, John, 190
Asim, Jabari, 57
Athis, Arthur, 67

Atlanta Journal-Constitution, 201
Atlantic Monthly, 174
Auto Clock and Speedometer Shop, 164
Azulay, Abner, 135, 136–37, 139

Baca, Lee, 152
Badarch, Dendez, 67
Baker, Howard, 194
Baker, Jim, 194
Balkans, 2
Bank of America, 118
Barak, Ehud, 135, 202
Barnard College, 21
Barnett, Robert, 42
Barron's, 74
Barrymore, John, 106
Bartlett's Familiar Quotations, 212
Baum, Phil, 135
Becerra, Xavier, 151
Begala, Paul, 79
Bellow, Saul, 211
Bennett, Robert, 108
Berger, Benjamin, 143, 145
Berger, Diana, 16
Berger, Sandy, 154
Berks, Robert, 67
Bernson, Bruce, 67
Berra, Yogi, 37
Biden, Joe, 195
"Big Brother." *See* Clinton, William Jefferson
"Big Creep." *See* Clinton, William Jefferson
"the Big Guy." *See* Clinton, William Jefferson
"the Big He." *See* Clinton, William Jefferson
"bimbo eruptions," 48
Bin Laden, Osama, 20
Biodiversity Treaty (1992), 84
Birthright Israel, 134
Blackley, Ronald Henderson, 161
Black Liberation Army, 21
Black Panthers, 14, 21

Blockbuster video stores, 40
Bloodworth-Thomason, Linda, 38
Blumenthal, Sidney, 209
Bonior, David, 42
Borderes, William Arthur, 164
Borel, Art and Doug, 164–65
Boudin, Kathy, 23–24
Bovard, James, 95
Boxer, Barbara, 154
Boxer, Nicole, 154
Bradford, Susan, 86
Brandt, Bill, 67
Braswell, Almon Glenn, 153–54
Breedspun, Myra, 67
Breslin, Jimmy, 204
Browder, Leonard, 164
Brown, Jerry, 197
Brown, Phyllis George, 71
Brown, Waverly, 22
Buck Island Reef, 82
Buckley, Christopher, 182
Buddy, 70
Budget Committee, 39
Buena Vista Social Club, 166
Burton, Dan, 184
Burton, Donny, 191
Burton committee, pardons investigation of, 184–91
Bush, Barbara, 12
Bush, George H. W., 12, 209; Clinton's executive orders and, 79, 80; executive orders of, 78; foreign trips of, 26; McCarthyism and, 14; pardons of, 4, 171
Bush, George W., 29, 74, 103; arsenic rule and, 90; Clinton appointments and, 93
Bush, Laura, 74
Bustamante, John H., 158
Byrd, Robert C., 22

Cabe, Meredith, 73
California Coastal Commission, 82
Callaway, Ely, 66
Camargo, Gloria Libia, 162

Campbell, Bonnie, 93
Cantor, Iris, 66
Capital Gang, 191, 197
Capshaw, Kate, 64
Carlson, Margaret, 44–45, 66, 70
Carlson, Tucker, 44
Carnahan, Robin, 66
Carnegie Towers, 53–55
Carrizo Plain, 82
Carson, Tom, 57
Carter, Billy, 146
Carter, Jimmy, 7, 146; Clinton pardons and, 169; FALN and, 16; Hearst pardon and, 124; Iran trade ban and, 130; "misery index" and, 2; pardons of, 3–4, 171, 193–94
Carville, James, 101, 134, 195, 196
Castro, Fidel, 88, 130
cattle futures, 46
CBS Television, 40
Central Intelligence Agency (CIA), 161
Cheney, Dick, 172, 194
Chesimard, Joanne, 22
Chicago Mental Health Foundation, 157
Chihuly, Dale, 66
Children's Defense Fund, 84
China, 25, 84
Chomsky, Noam, 23
CIA. *See* Central Intelligence Agency
Cisneros, Henry, 160–61
Citadel Federal Savings Bank, 163
Clarendon, Ltd., 132, 184
Clark, Donald R., 162
Clark, Ramsey, 117
clemency. *See* pardons
Clinton, Chelsea, 71, 81, 109
Clinton, Hillary Rodham: as Arkansas first lady, 45–46; Black Panthers and, 21; book deal of, 39–49; character of, 12–13, 210–11; Clinton's sexual behavior and, 105, 106–7, 109; Clinton's Vietnam trip and, 32–33; as co-president, 11–15; gifts given to, 64–71; health care and, 5, 11–12, 39; leftist radicals and,

13–14; lifestyle of, 61–64; looting of White House by, 71–74; marriage of, 37–38; media and, 206–7, 215; nicknames of, 12, 14; office space of, 51–54; Pardongate and, 16, 19–20, 138–39, 143–46, 154, 175–84, 203–5; Senate campaign of, 15, 16, 19, 35–39; Travelgate and, 145; Whitewater and, 98
Clinton, Roger: Clinton's sexual behavior and, 105; Hillary's character and, 13; Pardongate and, 120, 146–50, 156; presidential favors and, 9
Clinton, William Jefferson: African-Americans and, 56–59; Air Force One and, 1–2, 25; appointments of, 92–95; character of, 209–11; draft dodging of, 3–4, 24, 28–29; executive orders of, 6, 77–81; false testimony of, 9–10, 97–103, 110–11; farewell address of, 5–6; farewell party of, 74–75; federal regulations and, 7, 87–92, 95; Filegate and, 48; foreign trips of, 25–33; gifts given to, 64–71; Hillary as co-president and, 11–15; legacy of, 1–10, 95, 212–16; lifestyle of, 61–64; looting of White House by, 71–74; marriage of, 37–38; media and, 206–7, 215; national monuments and, 6, 81–84; nicknames of, 1, 3, 110, 136, 146; office space of, 53, 54–60; popularity of, 3; Roger Clinton and, 146–50; sexual behavior of, 103–12; treaties of, 84–87; Vietnam trip of, 27–33. *See also* Pardongate
Clinton Library, 55, 139, 186, 188
CNN, 44, 107, 191
Cochran, Johnnie, 111
Cohen, Richard, 94–95
Cohn, Stuart Harris, 164
Coler, Jack, 117
Collazo, Oscar, 18–19

Colnes, Alan, 184
Commerce Department, 79
Commercial Alert, 41
Communication Workers v. Beck, 78
Communist China, 2, 26
Comprehensive Test Ban Treaty, 84
Condit, Gary, 111–12
Congressional Accountability Project, 41
Congressional Black Caucus, 201
Connor, Joseph and Thomas, 17
Constitution: executive powers and, 77; pardons and, 115; presidential appointments and, 92
Cooder, Ry, 166–67
Cooper, David Marc, 163
Copetas, Craig, 127–28, 129, 132
Craighead, Kelly, 9
Crossfire, 107
Cuba, 21, 88, 130
Cummings, Elijah, 201
Cunningham, William, III, 156
Curry, Derrick, 162
Cushman and Wakefield, 53

D'Etremont, Colette, 66
Dalai Lama, 117
Daley, William M., 94, 197
Danson, Ted, 64
Darkness at Noon (Koestler), 216
Davis, Gray, 195
Davis, Marvin, 129
Davis, Thomas M., 91
Debs, Eugene, 171
Defense Department, 79
Democratic Congressional Campaign Committee, 155
Democratic National Committee (DNC), 59, 95; Gregorys' contributions to, 155; Rich pardon and, 138, 186, 188
Democratic Senate Campaign Committee, 35
Department of Health and Human Services (HHS), 81

Desalus, Velinda, 162
Desco Inc., 128
Deutch, John, 161
DeVille, Duncan, 152
DiGenova, Joseph, 18, 19
DNC. *See* Democratic National Committee
Dohrn, Bernadine, 23–24
Dole, Bob, 159
"The Donald." *See* Trump, Donald
Doucette, Dennis, 66
Dowd, Maureen, 63, 205, 206
Downe, Edward, Jr., 159
Dozoretz, Beth: Clinton Library and, 189; gifts to Clintons of, 64–65; Rich pardon and, 8, 139, 174, 186–87; visits to White House of, 8
Dozoretz, Ronald, 64–65, 93
DuBois, W. E. B., 57
Duffy, James, 93
Duggins, George C., 30
Dukakis, Michael, 210
Duncan, Larry Lee, 165, 166
Dunlop, Cyd, 105
DV8 Records, 8

Eakley, Douglas, 159
Economist, 201
Edelman, Marian Wright, 84
Eisenberg, Denise Joy. *See* Rich, Denise
Eisenberg, Emil, 128
Eisenhower, Dwight, 25, 31
Elbaum, Jacob, 143, 145
Eliot, T. S., 210
"Elizabeth." *See* Rosenberg, Susan
Energy Department, 79, 172
Enlargement of the Craters of the Moon, 82
Environmental Protection Agency (EPA), 79, 87, 89
Environment and Public Works Committee, 39
EPA. *See* Environmental Protection Agency
"ergonomic" rules, 89

Espy, Mike, 118, 161
Europe, 2
Evans, Linda Sue, 23
Evans, Martin Patrick, 66
Evert, Daniel, 30
Evert, David, 30
Evert, Lawrence, 30
Every Secret Thing (Hearst), 124

Fain, Robert Clinton, 156
FALN (Armed Forces of National
    Liberation) pardons, 15–21
The Family, 21, 22
Farrakhan, Louis, 94
Federal Bureau of Investigation (FBI):
    FALN and, 16; pardons and, 115,
    149–50
The Federalist Papers, 115
Federalist Society, 14, 86
federal regulations, 87–92, 95
Feinstein, Dianne, 52, 183
feminists, 79
Fernandez, Marcos Arcenio, 162
Filegate, 13, 48, 98
Fink, Robert, 138
"The First Grifters," 193
First in His Class (Maraniss), 36
Flicks, Lee, 66
FLOTUS (first lady of the United
    States). *See* Clinton, Hillary
    Rodham
Flowers, Gennifer, 106, 111, 153;
    Clinton smear campaign and, 13
Forbes FYI, 182
Ford, Gerald, 7, 114; pardons of, 3,
    171
Forester, Lynn, 66
Foster, Vincent, 46–47, 72, 159
Fox television network, 184
Foxman, Abraham, 135, 202
Frank, Barney, 196
"Frankie" (Rich), 8
Fray, Paul, 37
Freeh, Louis, 18, 118, 150
"Free Yourself" (Rich), 8

"Friends of Bill," 153; Pardongate and,
    156–61
Frink, Antoinette M., 162
Fuchs, Esther, 74
*Fuerzas Armadas de Liberacion
    Nacional. See* FALN
Fugazy, William Dennis, 163

Gaddafi, Muammar, 130, 146
Gallagher, Neil, 18
Ganci, Nina, 66
Garment, Leonard, 172
G. B. Data Systems, 153
Gejdenson, Sam, 164
General Services Administration
    (GSA), 52, 54, 90
George, Lloyd Reid, 158
George, Robert, 212
Georgetown, 61, 67
Gerth, Jeff, 207
Gingrich, Newt, 42–43, 45
Giuliani, Rudolph, 23, 36–37, 118, 141
Glen Eden Carpets, 66
Glover, Danny, 117
Goldenberg, Paul, 66
Goldman, Paul, 170
Goldstein, David, 143, 145
Gonzalez, Elian, 88
Goode, Barry, 93
Gorbachev, Mikhail, 32
Gore, Al, 75, 88, 94, 95, 135; AFL-
    CIO and, 90; Gregorys' contribu-
    tions to, 155; Pardongate and, 196
Government Accountability Project, 53
Governor's Island, 82
Graham, Katharine, 39–40
Grand Canyon-Parashant National
    Monument, 82
Grand Sequoia Monument, 82
Grand Staircase-Escalante National
    Monument, 82
Green, Pincus "Pinky," 127; business
    exploits of, 130, 131; as fugitive,
    132, 133; pardon of, 135–36, 170,
    173, 174

Greenberg, Irving, 202

Greenfield, Gerard, 162

Greenspun, Brian, 160

Gregory, Roger, 92, 93

Gregory, Edward and Vonna Jo, 154–55

"Grodin, Barbara." *See* Rosenberg, Susan

GSA. *See* General Services Administration

Guardian, 209

Guevara, Che, 45

Guinier, Lani, 58

gun control, 87

Gupta, Vinod "Vin," 67, 94

Halprin, Lawrence, 82

Hamilton, Alexander, 115, 212

Hamilton, James, 159

Hammer, M. C., 59

Hannity and Colmes, 184, 197

Hanoi, 30

Hanoi University, 31

Hardball, 204

Harding, Warren G., 171

Harkin, Marc, 195

Harlem, 55, 57

Harlem Legal Services, 55

Harmon, Carrie, 124

Harper's, 127

HarperCollins, 42

Hart, Gary, 104–5

Hawaii Trial Lawyers Association, 93

Hawkins, Tramaine, 8

"Headache." *See* Clinton, Roger

health care, 5, 11–12, 39

Hearst, Patricia, 124

Hell to Pay (Olson), 13, 14

Helmsley, Leona, 70

Hemmingson, John, 161

Hendrick, Joseph R., 118

Henley, Don, 7

Hentoff, Nat, 103

Herbert, Bob, 198–99, 206

HHS. *See* Department of Health and Human Services

Hillary's Choice (Sheehy), 36

Hillary's Turn: Inside Her Improbable, Victorious Senate Campaign (Tomasky), 69, 183

Hitler, Adolf, 31

Ho Chi Minh, 21

Ho Chi Minh City, 29

Hockersmith, Kaki, 72

Hodges, Jim, 195

Hoffa, James, 171

Holder, Eric: Pardongate and, 18; Rich pardon and, 135, 140, 172, 184–85

Hollander, Paul, 211

homosexuals in military, 78–79

Honda Motor Company, 118

Hothem, Eric, 72

"Hot Pants." *See* McDougal, Susan

House Committee on Government Operations, 133

House Committee on Government Reform, 139, 184

House Judiciary Committee, 13, 47, 196

House of Representatives, book deals and, 41–43

House Ways and Means Committee, 118

Hoxha, Enver, 144

Hubbell, Webster, 118, 160

Huckabee, Mike, 195

Hughes, Howard, 146

Hughes, Langston, 57

Hunnicutt, Hal, 67

Hunt, Al, 191, 197

ICC. *See* International Criminal Court

Ickes, Harold, Jr., 35, 36, 156

Ickes, Harold, Sr., 35

"I Don't Wanna Be Misunderstood" (Rich), 8

Immigration and Naturalization Service (INS), 87–88, 115

Imus, Don, 106

Independent Counsel Act, 100

India, 59, 84
inflation, 2
InfoUSA, 94
Inouye, Daniel, 117
INS. *See* Immigration and
    Naturalization Service
Interagency Council for the
    Conservation of Migratory Birds,
    79
Interior Department, 79
Internal Revenue Service (IRS), 55, 87,
    115
International Criminal Court (ICC),
    85–87
International Law Committee, 86
Iran, 4, 130
Irani, Ghada, 67
Iraq, 2, 27, 130
IRS. *See* Internal Revenue Service
Iscol, Jill and Ken, 67
Israel, Jodie E., 162
Israel Philharmonic, 134
Istook, Ernest, 55
It Takes a Village (Clinton), 12, 38–39,
    40, 45, 215

Jackson, Jesse, 56, 79, 117, 153;
    Pardongate and, 7, 201
Jackson, Maynard, 59
Jefferson, Thomas, 77
Jobe, Stanley Pruet, 164
Johnson, Andrew, 3
Johnson, H. Alston, III, 92
Johnson, James Weldon, 57
Johnson, Lady Bird, 7
Johnson, Lyndon, 7, 25, 146
Johnson, Randel, 90–91
Johnson, Sam Houston, 146
Jones, Linda, 161
Jones, Paula, 9–10, 13, 48, 99,
    107–9
Jones, Todd, 151
Jordan, Ann, 189
Jordan, Hamilton, 193–94
Jordan, Vernon, 58, 189

Justice Department: Downe Jr. pardon
    and, 159; Elian Gonzalez and, 88;
    FALN pardons and, 18, 20–21;
    Hearst pardon and, 124;
    Pardongate and, 121, 149–50, 166,
    169–70, 175; pardon process and,
    113–16; Pollard and, 117; Rich
    pardon and, 136, 172, 186

Kasha-Katuwe Tent Rocks, 82
Katopodis, John, 148
Kaye, Walter, 67, 69, 70, 109
Kelly, Michael, 38, 174–75
Kendall, David, 97–98, 99, 101
Kennedy, Jim, 19
Kennedy, John F., 31, 47; foreign trips
    of, 25; personal life of, 215; sexual
    behavior of, 103
Kennedy, William H., 159
Kennedy Center for the Performing
    Arts, 93–94
Kerrey, Bob, 86, 98
Khomeini, Ayatollah, 130
Kilgarriff, David, 67
Kim Il Sung, 27
Kim Jong Il, 27
King, Martin Luther, 170
Kinsley, Michael, 107
Koestler, Arthur, 216
Krauthammer, Charles, 144, 146,
    202–3
Kroft, Steve, 106–7
Kunstler, William, 23
Kurtz, Howard, 98, 206
Kuwait, 130
Kyoto Protocol (1997), 84

Lafitte, Jean, 3
Langston, Billy Thornton, Jr., 162
Lasater, Dan, 46, 147
Laxalt, Paul, 40
Lazio, Rick, 37, 38, 44, 144
Lee, Bill Lann, 92
Legal Studies Corporation, 88

Le Kha Phieu, 30, 32
Levitt, Arthur, 140
Levy, Chandra, 111–12
Lewinsky, Monica, 10, 25, 48, 69, 99;
    Clinton's relationship with, 109–10;
    Clinton's testimony regarding, 100,
    109
Lewis, Ann, 196
Lewis, John, 42
Lewis, Salim B., 159
Libby, Lewis, 172
Libya, 2, 27, 130
Lieber, Judith, 71
Lieberman, Joe, 95
Limbaugh, Rush, 148
Lincoln, Abraham, 79
Lindsey, Bruce, 163, 187
Livingston, Craig, 48
Los Angeles Times, 28, 107, 149
Lott, Trent, 43
Louis XV, 121
Love, Margaret: FALN pardons and,
    20–21; Pardongate and, 113–16

Macheteros, 19
Madison, James: executive orders of,
    77; pardons of, 3
Malcolm X, 21
Mandela, Nelson, 17, 117
The Man from Hope, 156
Mann, Kellie Ann, 162
Manning, James Lowell, 156
Mantell, Edmund, 129
Mantle, Mickey, 37
Maraniss, David, 36, 48
Marc Rich & Co. AG, 129
Marc Rich International, 129, 132
Margolis, Jeremy D., 17
Martinous, David, 67
Marxism-Leninism, 26
Matos, Adolfo, 17
Matthews, Chris, 204–5, 206, 213
May 19th Communist Organization,
    21
Mayorkas, Alejandro N., 152

McAuliffe, Terry: Clinton Library and,
    189; DNC and, 52, 59–60, 95;
    investigation of, 190; Pardongate
    and, 196
McCain, John, 41
McCarthyism, 14
McColl, Hugh L., 118
McConnell, Mitch, 196
McCree-Lewis, Kathleen, 93
McCurry, Mike, 109
McDonald, Forrest, 212
McDougal, James, 116, 118
McDougal, Susan, 9, 116, 118, 160
McMillen, Thomas R., 17
McTague, Jim, 74–75
McVeigh, Timothy, 16, 20
media: Clintons and, 206–7, 215;
    Hillary's book deal and, 43;
    Pardongate and, 123
Meet the Press, 35, 36, 64, 101, 195
Menchu, Rigoberta, 117
Merck, Mandy, 104
Mfume, Kweisi, 59
Mickey Mouse, 37
Middle East, 2, 23
midnight appointments, 92–95
Milken, Michael, 118, 141
Miller, Dennis, 207–8
Miller, Marie-Bernarde, 99
Miller, Zell, 195
Mills, Cheryl, 188
Minidoka Internment, 82
Minnesota, 15
"misery index," 2
Mitford, Jessica, 14, 45
Mittman, Steve, 68
Miura, Katsushiro, 68
Mixner, David, 78–79
Moismann, Rudolf, 132
Molina, Gloria, 152
Monkey Business, 105
Monkman, Betty, 72
Monroe, James, 77
Moreno, Enrique, 92
Morgan, Charles W., III, 159
Morison, Samuel Loring, 161

Morris, Dick, 48, 62, 153, 206, 211
Morris, Roger, 12, 48, 189, 207
Morrison, Toni, 56–57, 58
Moynihan, Daniel Patrick, 15, 35, 53
"Mrs. President." *See* Clinton, Hillary
    Rodham
MTV, 40
Mullen, Erik, 9
Munninger-Berlin, Ginger, 203
Munro, Jan, 68
Murdoch, Rupert, 42
Murky Bottoms, 188

NAACP Image Awards, 59
Nadler, Jerrold, 23
National Archives, 71, 72
National Enquirer, 153, 166, 207
National Medal of the Arts, 94
national monuments, 81–84
National Park Service, 73
National Security Agency, 47
National Security Council, 12
Nation of Islam, 94
NBC, 195
Nelmstetter, Richard C., 67
Netanyahu, Benjamin, 117
Netherlands Antilles, 129
New Jersey Port Authority, 74
New Republic, 107, 199
Newsday, 204
New Square, 143–45
Newsweek, 6, 141, 148, 150, 212
New York: Hillary's political affiliation
    with, 15; Hillary as senator of,
    35–39
New York Daily News, 38
New York Magazine, 69
New York Observer, 203–4, 206
New York Post, 19
New York Times, 63, 98, 170, 198,
    205, 207; FALN pardons and, 17;
    Hillary's book deal and, 42, 43, 48;
    Pardongate and, 158, 173, 174
Nicaragua, 4
Nicholson, Jack, 64

Nickles, Don, 43
Nigeria, 129
Nike, 27
Ninemire, Peter, 162
Nixon, Donald, 146
Nixon, Richard, 12, 73, 146; foreign
    trips of, 25, 26, 29; impeachment
    of, 13, 47; pardoning of, 3, 114;
    pardons of, 171; resignation of,
    190; rule of law and, 97; Watergate
    and, 26
"No. 1." *See* Clinton, William Jefferson
Noe, Brad, 68
Nolan, Beth, 140, 150, 163; Clinton
    and, 210; Rich pardon and, 185,
    187–88
North Korea, 2, 9, 26–27, 31
*Not Guilty: Twelve Black Men on Life,
    Law, and Justice* (Asim), 57
Nussbaum, Bernie, 47

O'Connor, John Cardinal, 19
O'Grady, Edward, 22
O'Leary, Margaret, 68
O'Reilly, Bill, 43
The O'Reilly Factor, 43
Obermaier, Otto, 136
Office of the Pardon Attorney. *See*
    Justice Department
Oklahoma City, 2
Oppenheimer, Jerry, 37
Oro, Jose, 130
Owen, David C., 159

Paige, Peter, 22
Palestine Liberation Army, 38
Palmer, Robert W., 160
Panetta, Leon, 194
Panko, Joe, 68
Papini, Paolo, 68
Paramount Pictures, 40
Pardongate: Borels and, 164–65;
    Braswell and, 154; bribery convic-
    tions and, 164; Brink's attack and,

Pardongate (*cont.*)
    21–24; Burton committee and,
    184–91; Christmas pardons and,
    116–20; communist bombings and,
    21–24; commutations list from,
    121; criticism of, 193–203; Denise
    Rich and, 7–8; drug convictions
    and, 162–63; explanation of,
    169–91, 205–6; FALN terrorists
    and, 15–21, 116; fraud convictions
    and, 163–64; "Friends of Bill" and,
    156–61; Gregorys and, 154–55;
    Hearst and, 124; Hillary and,
    143–46, 175–84, 194, 200, 203–5;
    Holder and, 18; Hugh Rodham
    and, 120, 150–54, 156, 177,
    179–81; investigation of, 183–84,
    184–91; Justice Department and,
    117, 121, 149–50, 159, 166,
    169–70, 175; McDougal and, 9,
    118, 160; media and, 123; money
    and, 166–67; New Square Four
    and, 143–46; pardon process and,
    113–16; pardons list from, 121–23;
    Pollard and, 116–18; Rich pardon
    and, 127–41; Roger Clinton and,
    120, 146–50, 156; Rosenberg and,
    21–23; Tony Rodham and, 155,
    156; Vignali and, 150–52;
    Whitewater and, 160. *See also*
    Clinton, William Jefferson; pardons
pardons: absoluteness of, 7, 115; FBI
    and, 149–50; Justice Department
    and, 113–16; politics and, 20;
    process of, 113–16. *See also*
    Pardongate
Pastorella, Frank, 19
Patterson, Larry, 37
Payne, Julia, 75
PBS, 116
peace, 2–3
Peltier, Leonard, 117
Penthouse, 106
Peres, Shimon, 135
Perot, Ross, 210
Pezzopane, Richard, 164

Philip Brothers, 128–29
Piercy, Jan, 36
Podesta, John, 40, 163, 190; gifts to
    Clintons and, 63–64; Rich pardon
    and, 187; White House looting
    and, 73
Podesta, Tony, 40
Polanco, Richard, 152
Political Pilgrims (Hollander), 211
Pollard, Jonathan Jay, 116–18, 166
Pompadour, Madame de, 121
Pompey's Pillar, 82
Posner, Richard, 103
POTUS (president of the United
    States). *See* Clinton, William
    Jefferson
Powell, Colin, 57
presidency: appointments and, 92;
    benefits of, 1; executive powers and,
    77; pardons and, 7, 113–16; power
    of, 11
The President We Deserve (Walker), 209
press. *See* media
Project Pursestrings, 36
Puerto Rican Nationalist Party, 18–19
Puerto Rican terrorists. *See* FALN par-
    dons
Puerto Rico, 16
Pynoos, Morris, 68
Pyongyang, 27

Quinn, Jack: Rich pardon and,
    135–36, 138–40, 172, 174, 185,
    187, 188

Rabin, Leah, 32
Racketeer Influenced and Corrupt
    Organization (RICO), 131
Rainbow/PUSH Coalition, 157
Rangel, Charles, 42, 55
Ravenel, Charles D., 163–64
Ray, Robert: Clinton's plea bargain
    and, 9–10, 97–99; Travelgate and,
    47

Ready, Brian, 68
Reagan, Nancy, 12
Reagan, Ronald, 12, 31, 32, 40;
    Clinton's executive orders and, 79;
    executive orders of, 78; office space
    of, 54
Redford, Robert, 117
Red Guerrilla Resistance, 21
Reich, David, 128
Reich, Walter, 202
Reno, Janet, 18, 111
Republicans: Clinton's legacy and, 6;
    Federalist Society and, 14; Hillary's
    book deal and, 43–44
"Republic of New Afrika," 21
Reynolds, Mel, 157
Reynolds, William Bradford, 172
Rezai, Ali, 130
Rice, Condoleezza, 57
Rice, Donna, 105
Rich, Denise: Clinton farewell party
    and, 75; Clinton Library and, 189;
    gifts to Clintons of, 66, 70; Pardon-
    gate and, 7–8; Rich pardon and,
    134, 136–38, 141, 173, 185, 187,
    188; visits to White House of, 7–8
Rich, Marc, 66; background of, 128;
    business exploits of, 129–31; con-
    tributions of, 134–35; as fugitive, 8,
    132–34; pardon of, 134–41,
    169–74, 183–86
Rich Foundation, 134
Richardson, Bill, 91
Richardson, Margaret, 87
Richco Holdings, 129
RICO. See Racketeer Influenced and
    Corrupt Organization
Riddle, Howard Winfield, 165
Riley, Richard Wilson, Jr., 161
Rivers, Dorothy, 157
Robeson, Paul, 57
Robinson, Tommy, 45–46
Rodham, Hugh: Pardongate and, 120,
    150–54, 156, 177, 179–81; presi-
    dential favors and, 8; trouble of,
    154

Rodham, Tony: Pardongate and, 155,
    156; presidential favors and, 8;
    trouble of, 154
Rogers, Jimmy, 164
Romero-Barcelo, Carlos, 17
Roosevelt, Eleanor, 35, 36
Roosevelt, Franklin D., 31, 35, 98;
    executive orders of, 78; memorial
    to, 81–82
Roosevelt, Theodore, 3
Rose Law Firm, 62
Rosenberg, Emanuel, 21
Rosenberg, Susan, 21–23
Rostenkowski, Dan, 118–19
Rowland, David, 68
Rules for Radicals (Alinksy), 215
"Run, Hillary, Run!" (Herbert), 197
Ruskin, Gary, 41, 53
Russert, Tim, 35–36, 64

Safir, Howard, 133
Safire, William, 98
Saigon, 29
"Saint Hillary." See Clinton, Hillary
    Rodham
Samper, Ernesto, 163
Sarandon, Susan, 117
Saturday Night Live, 209
Schaeffer, Archie, III, 118
Schlesinger, Arthur, 7
Schumer, Charles, 23, 52, 183–84
Schwimmer, Adolph, 159–60
Securities and Exchange Commission
    (SEC), 140, 159
Senate: gift rules of, 69; Hillary's book
    deal and, 40–43; presidential
    appointments and, 92
Senate Health, Education, Labor, and
    Pensions Committee, 39
Senate Judiciary Committee, 183
Senate Rules Committee, 196
Serrano, Jose, 17
Serrano, Rosso, 163
Sharpton, Al, 182
Shays, Chris, 146, 186

Sheehy, Gail, 36
Shields, Mark, 197
Shiller, Stuart, 68
Siewert, Jake, 41–42, 45, 55, 95
Simon and Schuster, 40, 41
Simpson, O. J., 103, 196, 212
Sister Sledge, 8
Sister Souljah, 94
60 Minutes, 23, 106, 107
SLA. *See* Symbionese Liberation Army
Slater, Rodney, 148
Sleeper, 73
Small Business Administration, 89
Smaltz, Donald, 118
Smith, Jean Kennedy, 94
Smith, Stephen A., 160
Smithsonian Institution, 108
Sonoran Desert, 82
South Africa, 23, 129
South Korea, 2, 26
Sowell, Thomas, 57, 58
Spain, 129
Specter, Arlen, 196
Spielberg, Steven, 64
Spin Cycle (Kurtz), 206
Stakhanov, Alexei, 5
Stalin, Joseph, 26
Stallone, Sylvester, 64
Star, 106
Starr, John Robert, 36, 210
Starr, Kenneth, 10, 47, 97, 111
State Department, 79
*State of a Union: Inside the Complex
    Marriage of Bill and Hillary Clinton*
    (Oppenheimer), 37
Steenburgen, Mary, 64
Stephanopoulos, George: Clinton's false
    testimony and, 110–11; Clintons'
    marriage and, 48; Clinton's travel-
    ing and, 25, 29; Clinton lifestyle
    and, 2, 63; Hillary and, 12, 145
Stern, Kalmen, 143, 145
stock market, 2
The Strange Case of Marc Rich, 133
Streisand, Barbra, 138
Stringfellow, Cory, 162

Sullivan, Andrew, 199–200, 206
Supreme Court: executive powers and,
    77; racial preferences and quotas
    and, 79; unions and, 78
Symbionese Liberation Army (SLA),
    124
Synar, Mike, 133

Taiwan, 2
Talbott, Strobe, 45
"Tania." *See* Hearst, Patricia
Teachers Insurance Annuity
    Association of America, 52
Tel Aviv Museum of Art, 134
Thailand, 130
They Went Thataway, 133
Thomas, Clarence, 57, 58
Thomas, Harry, 156
Thomas, Mike, 30
Thomases, Susan, 36, 47
Thomasson, Patsy, 46, 47, 147–48
Tien Chau, 30
Tigar, Michael, 132
Time, 44, 56, 59, 66
Times Union, 203
Tomasky, Michael, 38, 69–70, 183,
    215
To Renew America (Gingrich), 43
Torme, Mel, 37
Torre, Joe, 37
Torres, Esteban, 152
Torresola, Griselio, 18–19
Torricelli, Robert, 35
*To Wong Foo, Thanks for Everything!
    Julie Newmar*, 8
Traffic, 204
Tramontano, Karen, 55
Tran Duc Luong, 30
Tran Hien Lan, 32
Transportation Department, 79
Travelgate, 13, 47, 98, 99, 145, 190
Treasury Department, 133, 166, 184
treaties, 84–87
Treuhaft, Robert, 14, 45
Tribe, Laurence, 88

Troopergate, 107–8

Truman, Harry, 18–19, 31, 68

Trump, Donald, 51, 53

Tucker, Cynthia, 201–2

Tumpson, Joan, 68

Tumulty, Karen, 56, 59

Tutu, Desmond, 117

TWA, 74

Twentieth Century Fox, 129

Twersky, David, 144

Tyrrell, R. Emmett, 48, 206

Tyson Corporation, 118

UN Convention on the Rights of the Child, 84

unemployment, 2

United Nations, 52, 84

United States: Puerto Rico and, 16; as superpower, 2–3; Vietnam and, 28

United States Holocaust Memorial Museum, 94–95

United States Mint, 132

UPN television network, 40

Upper Missouri Breaks, 82

U.S. Chamber of Commerce, 90

Vanity Fair, 66

"vast right-wing conspiracy," 14, 48, 111

"Venceremos." *See* Rosenberg, Susan

Ventura, Jesse, 15

Viacom, 40, 41

Vieques, 16, 20

Vietnam, 12; Clinton's trip to, 27–33

Vietnam Memorial, 30

Vietnam Veterans of America, 30

Vignali, Carlos Anibal, 150–52, 166

Vignali, Horace, 152

Village Voice, 57, 103

Villaraigosa, Antonio, 152

Virgin Islands Coral Reef, 82

Vo Viet Thanh, 68

Wade, Christopher V., 163–64

Walden School, 21

Waldorf-Astoria Hotel, 52

Walker, Martin, 209

Wallace, Larry, 148

Wall Street Journal, 182, 197

Walters, Gary, 72–73

Wang, Paula, 128

Warmath, Billy Wayne, 165

Washington, George, 6; Clinton's farewell address and, 5; executive orders of, 77; pardons of, 3, 171

Washington Post, 39, 94, 98, 144, 201, 206; Clinton's explanation of pardons and, 175; Hillary's book deal and, 42

Washington Post Book World, 57

Wasserman, Edith, 68

Watergate, 26, 190

Watkins, David, 145

Waxman, Henry, 189–90

Weather Underground, 21, 23

Weekly Standard, 44

Weinberg, Morris "Sandy," 131–32

Weinberger, Caspar, 4, 171

Weinig, Harvey, 162–63

Weisberg, Jacob, 200

welfare, 88

Wellesley, 21, 61

Wellstone, Paul, 117

Whiskey Rebellion, 3

White, Helene, 92–93

White, Mary Jo, 23, 146, 190

White House Americans Craft Collection, 72

Whitewater, 62, 98, 160, 190

Whiting, Allen, 68

Wiesel, Elie, 135

Will, George, 73–74

Williams, Edward Bennett, 132

Williams, Maggie, 47

Williams, Robert Michael, 164

Williams, Ron, 117

Williams, Walter, 57

Willis, Kim Allen, 162

Wilson, Ed, 133

Wise, Bob, 133, 184
Witt, James Lee, 68
Wood, Mitchell Couey, 162
Woodward, Bob, 201
World Bank, 36
Wright, Susan Webber, 100, 109, 112
Wynn, James A., 92

Yale, 21, 61
Yasak, Joseph A., 164
Yedioth Aharonoth, 166
Yogi Bear, 37
Yorkin, Bud, 68
Young Lords, 21